Brown

Today's student faces entirely
than students of a few decades ago. The university provides an environment where, according to a 2007 survey, 53% of professors have unfavorable views of evangelical Christians. Christian high school students who wish to begin preparing themselves for this environment would do well to start with *Contend*.

Dr. Michael R. Licona, Apologetics Coordinator, North American Mission Board, Southern Baptist Convention

This book provides Christians with a valuable tool in the ongoing attacks against the Christian faith by opposing worldviews. Best of all, it provides clear-minded teaching that can be understood and articulated by youth and adults alike.

Laird Crump, Headmaster, Shades Mountain Christian School, Hoover, Alabama

Dollar and Pinkerton's book is solidly biblical and written in a way that makes apologetics interesting and accessible to high school students. Christian educators, including home school parents, should consider making this a primary text to help ground their students in the faith.

Glenn Waddell, President, Birmingham Theological Seminary

With urgency in their writing and a heart for the Truth, Jason Dollar and Bradley Pinkerton loudly communicate the need for sound doctrine by equipping the reader to defend the truth. While some authors are merely noting a falling away from truth, Jason and Bradley take action by offering an answer to the doubtful and a hope to the curious. What a great book for any generation who is remotely interested in fulfilling Scripture by preparing a defense, a reason for this hope that lies within us.

Chris Altman, Minister of Youth, Roopville Road Baptist Church, Carrolton, Georgia

CONTEND

*A Survey of Christian Apologetics
on a High School Level*

CONTEND

A Survey of Christian Apologetics on a High School Level

Jason Dollar
Bradley Pinkerton

Aventine Press

Cover photograph by Brandon Robbins

Contend:
A Survey of Christian Apologetics on a High School Level

Copyright © 2009 by Jason Dollar and Bradley Pinkerton

ISBN: 1-59330-583-4

Printed in the USA
By
Aventine Press
750 State Street #319
San Diego, CA 92101

I found it necessary to write appealing to you to contend for the faith that was once for all delivered to the saints.
- Jude 3

Contents

Acknowledgments

I (Jason) would first like to express my heartfelt gratitude to Dr. Steve Cowan, my teacher and mentor. We spent many hours together discussing the great truths of God and the Christian worldview. You challenged me to think deeply, carefully, and critically, and to follow where the evidence leads. You made me read books that powerfully shaped my thinking – books that I would not have otherwise encountered were it not for your honest red pen. I feel sure your instruction, and hopefully a bit of your wisdom, is evident in the words of this volume.

I also want to express deep gratitude to all my students at Shades Mountain Christian School, who evaluated these arguments in class and offered insightful feedback. When I think of you, I smile and my heart senses great hope at what Christ is doing in the world through his people. At the end of the day, I learned much more from you than you did from me. Bradley Pinkerton, my coauthor, is one of these former students for whom I have a great amount of respect and admiration. I'm grateful to God for your mind and heart, and am challenged by your passion and zeal. Plus, you always make me laugh!

I must also give a word of thanksgiving to the two most influential pastors in my life, John Piper and Brian Branam. These men have given themselves to spreading the gospel of Christ in powerful ways. They continue to be instrumental in breeding within my soul a deep love for the word of God and a desire to live in the steady hope of God's glory. Keith Watson and David Donovan, you are my friends and mentors, and the two of you belong in this group as well.

It is with great delight that I present a very special thank you to my dearest friend and wife, Page, and our four children. This book is the product of your sacrifice. Your dedication and support have meant more to me than any words can accurately express. The ties that bind us together as a family are deeply rooted in the worldview we share that Christ is Lord. Mary, much of this book was written while I held you in my arms.

Finally, I lift my praise up to you, Christ Jesus, the Savior and the Lord of glory. This book is yours to use as you see fit. Your sovereign love and immeasurable beauty was the sustaining motivation that kept us writing. My deepest prayer, Lord, is that readers will be drawn to your throne of mercy to worship you, the one and only infinite, holy God.

It is with indebted gratitude that I (Bradley) acknowledge David Platt and Ravi Zacharias, who in their indisputably vast knowledge have epitomized the humility that the Lord so earnestly seeks, by which he has graciously crafted you into extraordinary vessels of his glorious message.

A heartfelt thanks also to the teachers in my life – Trace Donahoo, who exemplifies obedience mandated by the cross and challenges me to do the same, Paul Trinh, who was faithful to sow the seed of the word even in my youth, Brian Benscoter, who displayed a precedent for the stewardship of his gifts and abilities, and Jason Dollar, who has faithfully and patiently fostered my love for apologetics unto God's glory and not my own merit.

I am also privileged to acknowledge the family that invested so much into me. This book is a testimony to your enduring love, faith-

2

fulness, and patience through my childhood, without which none of this would have been possible.

I also want to express my gratitude to several mentors: Mateo Melendez, Kyle Kelley, Matt Grimes, Eddy McBroom, Josh Jacobs, my Grandfather, and so many others. The Lord used you in more ways than you know. I also gladly acknowledge Matthew Makar, who taught me that the joy of knowing the Lord far surpasses that of knowing about him.

And most of all, eternal thanks to the one who lavished out his grace and pursued with his love this wretched sinner that I may rejoice in the singing of your praises and the establishment of your Kingdom both now and forevermore. I am the clay in your hands, servant to your Lordship, citizen of your Kingdom, child rescued by my Father, and bride awaiting my Groom. "Not to us, O Lord, not to us, but to your name give glory, for the sake of your steadfast love and your faithfulness!"

Last but not least, we both give thanks to Ms. Marge Wolfe who, at the young age of 78, and in a great act of service, proofread each word and made it a much better work.

Though both authors have been deeply influenced by the people listed above, and many others, we alone take responsibility for the shortcomings contained in these pages.

Foreword

Almost three decades as a student, a teacher, and a pastor have taught me one inescapable lesson: Most Christian young people are ill-prepared to meet the attacks on their faith that they will encounter as adults in the world, and especially in college. The reasons for this are varied and complex, but among them is the fact that in the last century Christians have built for themselves a cultural ghetto in which they have largely insulated themselves and their children from the tough questions that unbelievers ask about the Christian faith.

Couple this with a view of spirituality that focuses almost entirely on experience and neglects the importance of the intellect, and you have a younger generation of Christians who are not only unprepared to answer the tough questions but are often unsettled, perplexed, and even shattered when their secular college professors raise them. Their faith is ridiculed as foolish and inconsistent with what we all really "know" to be true as revealed to us by science and history. Christianity, they are told, is an outmoded superstition held on a faith that is blind and contrary to the evidence.

My years of experience have taught me another lesson, too. When young Christians discover that there are actually good answers to these challenges, that faith need not be blind, that Christianity is not outmoded, superstitious, or foolish, but can in fact be rationally believed and even known to be true—most young Christians find this discovery to be emotionally refreshing, spiritually invigorating, and intellectually rewarding. I have seen weak and timid faith become vibrant and courageous when bolstered by good evidence that demolishes "arguments and every pretension that sets itself up against the knowledge of God" (2 Corinthians 10:5).

Jason Dollar and Bradley Pinkerton have made this discovery themselves and they desire to help others make it as well. Their book *Contend* is the product of this desire. In these pages, the authors present the evidence for the Christian worldview in a way that is clear and winsome to high school students. They address all of the major challenges to the faith that young Christians are likely to encounter when they transition to college and the workplace. And they point out the weaknesses of the non-Christian worldviews that vie for our allegiance in this fallen world. Here both parents and students will find a much-needed resource for defending and advancing the Christian faith in our time. It is my hope that this book helps to equip a new generation of Christians to "be prepared make a defense to everyone who asks you to give an account for the hope that is in you" (1 Peter 3:15).

Steven B. Cowan
Southeastern Bible College
Apologetics Resource Center

Introduction

What a person believes about God, the world, the human soul, and the afterlife are the most important beliefs he holds. These foundational convictions create his viewpoint of the world and therefore affect every other belief he has, eventually giving rise to his choices and behavior. This is the reality that birthed the pages you are now reading.

This book was written on a high school level, with the desire that young adults would be challenged to think deeply about their beliefs and the direction of their souls. Aggressive atheists and postmodern relativists are among those watering at the mouth to get hold of the minds and hearts of today's teens, and lead them down destructives paths. Their goal is to convert them to a way of life that is opposite the way of Christ, and to shred their faith into a thousand pieces.

Both authors have experienced the transition from high school to college. We know what it is like to have our views challenged by respected people in academic positions. Recent surveys have revealed that a large number of young people who hold Christian beliefs in high school end up abandoning those beliefs as archaic and irrelevant, often as a direct response to the pressure applied by non-believing professors and peers in college.[1]

Why is this happening? The simple answer: Christianity is misperceived as an opinion-based religion with no foundation in reality. *Contend* was written to challenge this faulty view of the Christian faith and mind. The reason we contend for the precious truth given by Jesus Christ is precisely because it is *the only truth.* We recognize that a mere opinion is not worthy of vigorous defense. But the call of God is clear: "I found it necessary to write appealing to you to contend for the faith that was once for all delivered to the saints" (Jude 3).

What is Christian apologetics? It means to "contend for the faith." It means to demonstrate to others that the historical man, Jesus Christ, *actually is* the way, the truth, and the life, and that this is not a mere opinion. Though this is not a book about boxing, you will find a battle for truth on every page you read. Though we strive for a gracious and humble spirit in our presentation, we do want to show as clearly and aggressively as possible that Jesus Christ is actually the Lord of glory and there are no exceptions to this reality. The following is a brief synopsis of each chapter to give you a broad perspective on the direction of the book.

In the first chapter we provide a basic overview of the apologetic process itself with a focus on the attitude a Christian should bring to the practice. Special attention is given to the limitations of apologetics. Christians can't expect to convince every unbeliever to bow their knee to Christ, even using the best apologetics arguments. Why? Because it is Jesus Christ who saves the guilty sinner, not our arguments. Thus, our dependence is on him as we share his truth with others, not on our own ability to articulate a persuasive case.

In Chapter 2 we bring the personal nature of apologetics to the spotlight. I (Jason) have utilized these particular pages to share my own personal testimony as a way of showing how apologetics starts with the human heart. Attention is given especially to the dilemma that every person faces, that of a guilty conscience. Jesus Christ deals with this dilemma in ways that no other religion or philosophy can.

Chapters 3 and 4 showcase Jesus Christ as the historical man who claimed to be God and proved it by rising from the dead. The mounting evidence for Jesus' resurrection is carefully examined and alternative theories to the resurrection are considered. If Jesus Christ did indeed rise from the dead, then his claims to be God should most certainly be taken seriously.

The next two chapters bring the Bible into focus as a historical and theological work. Here we explain why the Bible is reliable and should be trusted as the authentic word of God. Archeology and history are also discussed, since both confirm the cultural and geographic details given in the Bible.

Chapter 7 is unique from other chapters in the book. It examines how the biblical teaching that God does all things for his own glory provides an amazing explanation for all of reality. God's glory is the *eternal center* that holds all other things together and assures that all things make sense. This may be the most important chapter, since it explains the coherence of the Christian worldview, a key reason to believe it is actually true.

The next section, chapters 8-10, covers the three most significant arguments for the existence of God. The Cosmological Argument states that there must be a first cause for the universe and that the best explanation for this first cause is God. The Design Argument examines natural phenomena utilizing the scientific method, and shows that the best explanation for certain complexities is a supernatural designer. And the Moral Argument maintains that objective moral values, seen in the conscience of every person and every society, can only be explained by a supernatural lawgiver. These three arguments, though limited in some ways, bring strong confirmation to the teachings of Christianity.

Chapters 11-13 are comparison chapters. They compare and contrast the Christian worldview with its alternatives. Naturalism, pantheism, and alternative forms of theism are all showed to be inferior to Christianity. Agnosticism and pragmatism are also examined and demonstrated to be dangerous positions for people to hold.

In the final chapter we work through several objections often brought against the Christian worldview. All of these objections fail, however, and it is shown with decisiveness that Christianity is actually true and that Jesus Christ should be trusted by all.

At the conclusion of each chapter, there are a series of questions, glossary terms, and a memory verse that will help readers respond to the material, and better retain it. We suggest working through these exercises with a small group or class, if possible, in order to facilitate discussion.

We certainly hope that all who make their way through these chapters are blessed as a result. We further hope that this book will lead you to live for the glory of God, knowing beyond all doubt that this is his world, and that truth is certainly worth contending for.

CHAPTER 1:
The Task of Apologetics

What do you see when you look at a tree? You might be thinking that this is a weird question and you'd be exactly right; it does seem weird. Plus the answer seems so clear and obvious. When you look at a tree you see a tree! Don't you? Well, yes and no.

Sure, on the surface level of bark and leaves you see a tree there, tall, towering, shady, and sturdy. But the question goes much deeper than surface level. When you see the tree what do you believe to be true *about* the tree? How did it get there? Did it come about through accidental causes or did some intelligent being have a part in placing it there? Did the procedure involve God or just mindless natural processes?

For Christians there is a fundamental assumption about the tree: God put it there. He might have used someone to plant it and he might have used someone to water it, but he is *ultimately* responsible for putting it there, after all he created trees (Genesis 1:11).

For an atheist (a person who does not believe that any god or gods exist) there is also a fundamental assumption about the tree: unguided accidental force blindly "caused" it to be there. God could not have done it since, according to the atheist, God does not exist.[2]

When a Christian observes a tree he should be moved to worship the God who created the tree. When an atheist sees the same tree he detects nothing greater than un-designed cosmic chaos that happens to look orderly and designed. But why do the Christian and atheist see the same tree in two totally different ways?

SALLY'S AND RONNY'S SUNGLASSES

If Sally puts on a pair of sunglasses with red lenses then everything she sees will have a red tint to it. If Ronny puts on a pair of sunglasses with blue lenses then (you guessed it) he'll see everything in blue. Sally will see red and Ronny will see blue even though they are looking at the exact same things.

If these two go to the zoo and examine a zebra with black and white stripes, Sally will see the zebra in a red tint and Ronny will see him in a blue tint even though they are both observing a black and white zebra. Their sunglasses shade and influence how each one sees the zebra.

The same is true when people look at lions, tigers, bears, and monkeys. The same is also true when we look at other people. Our worldview – our sunglasses – dictate how we interpret the things we see around us.[3]

But we are not talking merely about sunglasses; we are talking about beliefs which are far more important. All people have several foundation beliefs that "tint" the way we see the world. These most basic beliefs, like a map of reality, form our individual worldview and shape the way we see everything including trees, other people, government, religion, the media, and everything else.

But sadly, even though our worldview structure molds the way we see everything, most people are not even aware they have one. The vast majority of people cannot give detailed rational explanations for why they believe the things they believe. Most people believe that Mercury is the closest planet to the sun, but they could not tell you why they believe this. They simply learned this fact at some point in school, but have no supporting data for the belief itself. They are content to take the word of others and not do the hard research for themselves. Christians often do the same thing, adopting beliefs from their parents or grandparents. Many atheists follow suit and settle on their atheism simply because they are angry at Christians or because they revolted against their upbringing. But we need more reasons than this to hold our beliefs! Beliefs about God are far too important and affect us in far too many ways for us to simply assume the unsupported beliefs of others or believe in what is convenient or agreeable.

For the Christian there is an entire body of knowledge called *apologetics* that is designed to support our faith in Christ and to defend it from the onslaught of attacks that confront it.

What Is Apologetics?

Amazingly, very few Christians realize the valuable resource available to them in apologetics. Even mentioning the word *apologetics* invariably provokes puzzled looks and questions like, "Who are you apologizing to?"

We cannot be too critical of the puzzled looks and questions since, when we first heard the word, we had no idea what it meant either. But we quickly learned that it does not mean *to be sorry*, as the word is most often used today. Christians after all have nothing to be sorry about! The word *apologetics* actually comes from a Greek word *(apologeomai)* which means "to make a defense."

A Christian who provides a rational defense of his beliefs about God, Christ, the Bible, and other Christian beliefs, is engaging in the practice of apologetics.

13

You might be thinking that apologetics is just for preachers or the "super-spiritual," but this is not so. Learning to defend the Christian faith is for all believers, regardless of their level of maturity. In fact, learning the reasons why we believe Christianity to be reality leads to greater conviction of the truth, and opens the door for Christians to speak of their faith with greater boldness. Likewise, apologetics can help those who are skeptical learn why Christianity is a rational worldview option.

I (Jason) remember as a sixth grader, while spending the night with a friend, trying to figure out where God came from and who made him. "He made everything else," Paul Langham, my friend, and I said to each other, "but who made him?" We just couldn't figure out an answer to that question even though we thought about it for a long, long time. I wish someone who was familiar with apologetics could have helped us out back then.

As I lay there that night and pondered, I knew I believed in God but I could not *defend* what I believed about him. It didn't make sense to me that God was just *always there.* Even the mind of a sixth grader struggled with these thoughts. I just couldn't accept that God was always there (no beginning!) without *some* explanation as to how that could be.

This is where apologetics is so vital in the Christian life. It helps us grapple with the tough questions of our faith and come away with reasonable and defendable answers. These answers stoke the flames of our faith in God and lead to greater passion to live for his glory. Here are some of the tough questions apologetics deals with:

Is there a God?
Is the Bible true?
Was Jesus born of a virgin and did he really rise from the dead?
What is a human being?
What is the purpose of my existence?

14

Is history going anywhere or are human events meaningless?

Don't all religions lead to the same "god"?

If God is so good why is there so much suffering in the world?

This is just a sample list of the questions that apologetics answers. It is a lifelong journey to seek those answers, absorb them, and be able to communicate them to others.

BUT SHOULDN'T WE JUST BELIEVE THE BIBLE?

Some people object to the practice of apologetics, stating that it might lead Christians to doubting their faith. They say that we should just believe in God without ever asking any questions. "God said it, I believe it, and that settles it" is a popular slogan used by these well-meaning Christians, and to some degree we are inclined to agree with them. After all, who are we to ever question the authority of God?

But there is a major problem with that point of view. When we read the Bible it commands us to defend our faith! So if we do what this slogan suggests, which is just believe the Bible without attempting to know why we believe it or how to defend it, then we would have to *disobey the Bible*. That would be crazy! The Bible tells us to be ardent and active defenders of the Christian faith in a world that is hostile against it.

Let's be careful here. It isn't as though *God* needs to be defended! That is emphatically not the purpose of apologetics. Who are we to presume to defend the one who is *our* Defender (Isaiah 19:20)? But nevertheless God has a purpose in apologetics. Christians are to defend their faith in order to bring about a greater knowledge and understanding of God in the world, which ultimately brings greater and

15

maximized glory to him. Consider a few passages from the Bible that teach this.

> But in your hearts regard Christ the Lord as holy, always being prepared to make a defense to anyone who asks you for a reason for the hope that is in you; yet do it with gentleness and respect. (1 Peter 3:15-16)[4]

These verses provide a power-packed punch of instruction. Christians are first of all to set Christ apart in our hearts, so that we consider him to be "Lord" and to be "holy." We are to be in awe of him and declare our allegiance to him. We are to recognize that this is God's world and we are part of *his* universe, not the other way around.

Next, we are to be prepared to set up a defense (an apologetic argument) to people when they see the hope we have in our lives and ask us about it. We are instructed to personally regard him as Lord *and then show others why he is Lord*. Can there be clearer instructions to defend our faith than this? The Apostle Paul is just as direct about how apologetics should be done:

> Though we walk in the flesh, we are not waging war according to the flesh. For the weapons of our warfare are not of the flesh but have divine power to destroy strongholds. We destroy arguments and every lofty opinion raised against the knowledge of God, and take every thought captive to obey Christ. (2 Corinthians 10:3-5)

Paul was extremely serious about engaging in apologetics. There is nothing silly about destroying arguments, which was his goal. Surely you have destroyed things before. Maybe it was a letter from someone you broke up with. After a break-up we often clean out our dresser drawers and trash those things that remind us of what might have been. This is sad but true.

On a more serious note I (Bradley) recently journeyed to New York City and visited the site where the World Trade Centers once stood. On September 11, 2001 those massive skyscrapers were toppled in total destruction by the cruel ploys of Islamic terrorists. As I examined the barren site I was struck with the amount and intensity of the devastation that had taken place there. I can say with confidence, not a single fragment of those buildings is left. They were brought to nothing, utterly destroyed. This is a picture of what Christians are obligated to do with false arguments.

When Paul says "argument," he is not talking about bickering in a mad, furious way. He is saying that an argument is the careful observation of evidence in order to know truth and/or prove a point. Some arguments are obviously better than others. Some come to true conclusions while others come to false conclusions. To destroy an argument, therefore, we must come up with a better argument that leads people closer to the truth.

For example, if someone states that Jesus was not the Son of God but merely a good teacher of right and wrong, could you destroy that argument? How would you go about doing it, and what evidence would you reveal to show that this person is wrong?[5]

CONTENDING FOR THE FAITH

Christians must take Paul's instructions to defend the Christian faith seriously. We cannot cross our arms and pretend that it doesn't matter. It does. Whether Jesus is just an ethical teacher or the living Son of God matters a great deal. It matters eternally!

We hope this book will help you think deeply about how to build good arguments and destroy bad ones. Christianity is true, God is real, Jesus is the Savior who was born of a virgin and rose from the dead, and the Bible is God's perfect word. Since all of these statements are actual fact, then we should be able to tear down false arguments that stand against them.

Don't be afraid of arguing for what you believe. The most basic form of human communication is argumentation. Again this is not necessarily being mad and venting your frustrations, but simply giving reasons for what we say and do and believe. Whether it is something as insignificant as deciding what to wear or where to eat, or something as important as our choice for marriage or what career we will pursue, we should always back up what we are doing with good reasoning. Should we neglect such a basic function of human communication when it comes to eternal issues? Read Jude's words to see the answer:

> Beloved, although I was very eager to write to you about our common salvation, I found it necessary to write appealing to you to *contend for the faith* that was once for all delivered to the saints. For certain people have crept in unnoticed who long ago were designated for this condemnation, ungodly people, who pervert the grace of our God into sensuality and deny our only Master and Lord, Jesus Christ. (Jude 3-4, italics ours)

The word *contend* means to strive and fight for the faith. It contains the idea of agonizing over something. Christians are to be so convinced of the truthfulness of our faith, that when people oppose it we agonize to defend it.

Our high school in Hoover, Alabama, is important to both of us. Jason teaches there and Bradley is a 2008 graduate. The school has a cross country team that is always fun to watch, especially after the athletes have run several miles. All of them, almost without exception, have a look of agony on their faces. Sometimes the pain level can get so intense that tears of anguish run down their cheeks. That is a picture of what the word *contend* conveys to us. Christians should labor to the point of tears in contention for the truth.

18

Notice the problem that Jude reveals. People who are in opposition to the truth have "crept in unnoticed." They are interested in perverting the truth and leading people to believe lies. This is one of the problems orthodox Christianity continues to face today. Our task is to contend against false teachers by proving them to be phony. We face challenges not only from people outside the church who are openly hostile to Christianity, but also from the wolves in sheep's clothing inside the church, who pervert the truth for personal gain.[6]

Obviously, if we are to obey the Bible we must engage in the vital task of defending our faith. Our culture embodies a huge need that only Christ can satisfy and laziness is no excuse for not exploring and proclaiming the riches of his majesty through apologetics.

FOOTBALL AND APOLOGETICS

The rest of this chapter will focus on some of the fundamentals of the apologetic discipline. To begin, apologetics has many uses that are easy to remember when you compare them to a football game.

Positive apologetics resembles a football team's offense, whose ambition is to put points on the board. They want to move the ball down the field, score touchdowns, and kick field goals. In order to do this they must have a solid offensive line, strong running backs and receivers, and a quarterback who can pass with accuracy.

Christians must have a strong offense as well, making every attempt to "score points" for Christianity – that is build the case for its accuracy and *show* that it is true. A person engaging in positive apologetics would share with an unbeliever arguments that God exists and that the Bible is trustworthy. He would further show why it is reasonable to believe that Jesus *actually* was born of a virgin and rose from the dead.

19

Positive apologetics also fends off assaults against the Christian faith, like a football team's offense line. It blocks their attack and protects the ball, so to speak. For example, here is a common attack: "Christianity cannot be true since the Bible is full of contradictions." The Christian would respond to this assault showing that there are no contradictions in the Bible.

So positive apologetics builds up the Christian position, and deals with objections brought against it, without necessarily dealing with what the unbeliever believes.

Negative apologetics can be compared to a football team's defense, which desires to protect the field behind it from the onslaught of the opposition. The goal of the defense is not to score (unless there is a turnover) but rather to keep the other team from scoring.

When a person engages in negative apologetics, he is not simply building a protective wall around Christianity, but is tearing down the walls of false belief systems. This is like sacking the quarterback. Not only do you protect the field behind you but you push the opposition backward. If you are talking to a Buddhist, for example, you would show the many weaknesses of Buddhist beliefs and how Buddhism is, therefore, false.

Both uses of apologetics work together just as both the offense and defense is necessary to win football games. In order to be a faithful defender you must be able to build the case that Christianity is true, fight off attacks against it, and dismantle false worldviews and religions that compete with it.

PRESENTING APOLOGETICS EFFECTIVELY

The football illustration is good for understanding the various ways apologetics can function, but not so good when it comes to presentation. When we argue for the truth of Christianity with real people, our hope is not to sledgehammer the opponent, as in football, but rather to persuade people to come to Christ and be free from sin.

To get a grasp of what an effective defense of the faith includes, Ravi Zacharias discusses three necessary realms of apologetic presentation designed to effectively move people closer to the gospel.[7] Certainly these three can be combined and a particular audience may require an emphasis of one above the other, but if one is left out altogether a healthy apologetic is not possible.

Logic

The logical realm is probably the most familiar and basically involves using our reasoning to conclude that Christianity is correct. This includes formal debates and well-developed arguments, as well as relaxed conversations. Put simply, whenever you ask someone to think about what they believe and why they believe it, you are employing logic.

Expression

The realm of expression involves taking the logic that has been reasoned through and communicating it to a specific audience. When Paul stood before the skeptical Athenians, he spoke these words:

> Men of Athens, I perceive that in every way you are very religious. For as I passed along and observed the objects of your worship, I found also an altar with this inscription, "To the unknown god." What therefore you worship as unknown, this I proclaim to you. (Acts 17:22-23)

Paul was preparing to use logic to show the Athenians that there is only one God, and that he raised Jesus Christ from the dead (Acts 17:24-31). Before he did, however, he would first use expression to his

21

specific audience in ways that captured their imagination. His listeners were familiar with the altar inscribed to the unknown god. It was a safety net for them. Just in case they accidentally missed a god in their public worship, this altar was designed to appease any deity they might have overlooked. Paul focused their attention on this familiar site and sought to inform them of the God they had missed, the *only living God* who created them. This creative and expressive act led to many people understanding Paul's logic more clearly (see v.34).

We too must take the truths we proclaim and present them in ways that actually communicate to people where they are. Our use of logic can certainly reach the mind, but we must never neglect to reach the imagination, for the gospel which we proclaim using logic, can never be fully understood without the imagination.

For example, it's one thing to say that God works all things out for a greater good (Romans 8:28). This is a logical and joyful truth, valuable not only for the comfort of Christians but also for the defense of the Christian worldview. But what if you were to teach that truth through the capturing of the imagination?

There was once a man named Joseph, who endured persecution from his brothers, having been tossed into a pit and sold into slavery at their hands. Afterward, he was unfairly accused of a crime he didn't commit and spent years in prison. Eventually, he was released and raised to be second in command of the greatest empire on earth, and was able in that position to save thousands of lives, including the lives of the brothers who persecuted him.

This riveting story is dramatic and captivating as anyone knows who has read it. At the climax of the story, Joseph revealed to his brothers that throughout his great ordeal, God was behind the scenes working a greater good. He informed them, "As for you, you meant evil against me, but God meant it for good, to bring it about that many people should be kept alive, as they are today" (Genesis 50:20). This is the value of expressive illustration – the same message presented through real life situations.

22

Another example comes from a situation at my (Jason) home church. It is one thing to come to the logical conclusion that God answers prayer, as James 4:2-3 and many other passages teach us, but it is another thing to *see this reality* happening before your very eyes. Josiah, the one-year-old son of our associate pastor, was severely injured when a large television fell squarely on his head. His skull was seriously fractured and his brain began to swell at a fatal rate. He was airlifted to the local hospital where doctors and nurses did not give him much chance of survival.

Our church came together that evening specifically to pray for this family. People poured their hearts out to God, begging him to work and heal Josiah for his own glory. Meanwhile at the hospital, Josiah was going into surgery to remove part of his skull in order to release the pressure building up on his brain. His death seemed imminent to the medical staff involved. And even if he did survive, the chances of his living a normal life were astronomically low from a medical standpoint.

But God had other plans in mind. Josiah survived the surgery. Later that evening, when his parents came into his intensive care unit, he did the unexpected and unthinkable. His eyes popped opened and he began to reach out for his dad and mom. The doctors were astounded to say the least. A few days later, as a direct result of specific prayers, he was talking and smiling, and soon he was walking up and down the halls of the hospital, a living testimony of the power of God. God proves himself as powerful and loving by answering prayer in real life. Answered prayers are not merely a hypothetical, logical argument.

This is the realm of expression. Though defending the faith requires intellectual labor, it is not a cold academic discipline, but rather real life revealing the presence and power of the Lord. God is an actual God, not a mere science experiment that we are attempting to "prove exists." Expression helps us relate our arguments to the actual lives of actual people.

Don't misunderstand the point here. Our message is certainly not *relative;* that is, it does not change to meet our audience. But we still must work in order to ensure that the words and methods we use for our presentation are *relevant*; that is, that they relate to our audience. Children love to amuse themselves with play-doh. They mold it into whatever they desire only to change it into something entirely different five minutes later. But this cannot be the case with Christianity. The gospel is a diamond. When we present it we must not seek to mold it to our audience, but rather to illuminate it for our audience through expressive illustrations.

Application

What has been reasonably understood and expressively imagined must now be practically lived. We can read our books and tell our stories but it will mean nothing if it does not reach the dinner table. We must be faithful in actively, intentionally, and regularly spreading the truth which we have, and conducting ourselves according to it. Application is the extension of apologetics to our personal lives. The beliefs we claim to hold intellectually must dictate the lifestyles we lead. Christians must strive to be consistent. We cannot tout Christ as our all-satisfying King, but live as if the world is the only happiness we know.

The story is told of a group of missionaries in an Asian country tenaciously witnessing to those around them and organizing church gatherings. Though their message was wisely and relevantly communicated, they were hated by the community. A group of Muslim extremists eventually had enough of them and attacked a gathering of the believers and burned their church, slaughtering many of those who were present including women and children.

But following this attack, the love of the local believers for those around them was shown all the more as they forgave their assailants and continued to witness Christ to them. It was only after such a remarkable exhibition of love that the vast majority of those who had

24

once hated the Christians in that village received salvation and joined them. This is a living apologetic. It is the demonstrable application of the Christian worldview to life, and it affects others in major ways. Yet not all stories have such a happy ending. When a group on a mission trip checked into their hotel, one man had the opportunity to present and illustrate Christianity to an interested receptionist. The receptionist soon had to end their conversation but promised to resume it the next morning. However, the next morning the receptionist displayed no interest in the man's message. When asked why, the receptionist stated that a member of the group had viewed pornographic material the previous night. Because the group did not live the message they taught, their witness was lost. Application of truth to our lives is a major realm of apologetics and must never be neglected.

The Attitude of Apologetics

Logic, expression, and application are the three realms of presenting apologetics. But what type of attitude should the Christian have when making his presentation to others? Here again the football illustration fails. In football the goal is to crush the opposition; in apologetics the goal is to save the opposition.

We are not free to gain great amounts of knowledge about divine matters only to go around and smack people on the head with it! The following is a list of several attitudes that are gleaned from the Bible which set parameters around how we bring apologetic arguments to bear upon the lives of others.

With Joy and Excitement

Gaining knowledge, especially knowledge about God, is an incredible process. Nothing is better and nothing fills our hearts with happiness sooner.

But let him who boasts boast in this, that he understands and knows me, that I am the LORD who practices steadfast love, justice, and righteousness in the earth. For in these things I delight, declares the LORD. (Jeremiah 9:24)

Far from being a cold, academic discipline, apologetics invigorates our hearts with hope, exhilaration, and pleasure. The study of apologetics can strengthen the faith of a believer and lift his heart to heaven. It can take a cold rule-laden religion and turn it into a daily experience of the presence and power of the living God.

With Prayer and Humility

One of the major problems in the engagement of apologetics is the big-head syndrome. Once people begin learning these arguments there is a tendency to feel a measure of superiority over "lesser beings." Tearing down opposing arguments can cause a swelling with pride, and it is easy to forget the point of it all, sharing the gospel of Christ with the lost so that they become believers.

During my (Jason) college years I worked at a coffee shop for a while. One of my coworkers was a lesbian. She informed me once that another of our coworkers, who was a Christian, had deeply offended her. She said of this co-worker, "He just came out and told me if I died right now I would go to Hell." She was angered at his high and mighty attitude which came across to her as arrogant.

I knew the other Christian pretty well, and I knew his heart. He wasn't trying to be mean-spirited. He really cared about this girl's soul and was attempting to scare her into the Kingdom. After all, what he told her was true. But the *manner* in which he spoke was arrogant and brash, and it turned a girl away from the gospel. Truth must be spoken, but it must be spoken in love, and in dependence upon the Holy Spirit. We must see that people operating alone cannot convince anyone to come to the Lord.

26

This is a humbling reality. It doesn't matter how well we construct our arguments for God's existence or the deity of Christ, there are thousands of atheists who will still laugh at us. We may be thinking and saying to them, "Why don't you see it? It is so clear!" but they will ignore us and present the same, tired, atheistic arguments again and again.

Christians must realize that we are not the primary agents of salvation. The Holy Spirit is. We must be dependent upon him before, during, and after we engage in the apologetic task. That means prayer is a must since this is how we show our reliance upon him. If you love apologetics just so you can load your argument rifles, taking aim on the first unbeliever you encounter, but you have not been praying through the process, then you are in a dangerous position of self-reliance. Apologetics exists not to win arguments but to win souls.

With Heart and Mind

Apologetics takes both heart and mind. Neither one can be neglected. Don't be a smart but passionless Christian, engaging your mind but not your heart. But also don't be a non-thinking Christian who is filled with zeal for God. It takes both heart-felt desire and deep thinking.

Most Christians lean one way or the other. Some feel that apologetics is too hard and that people should just love God and quit thinking so much. If that is how you feel then you are in sin and disobeying God's word. "And he said to him, 'You shall love the Lord your God with all your heart and with all your soul and *with all your mind*'" (Matthew 22:37, italics ours).

But if you're a braniac who despises feeling and emotions, then you too are in the wrong, for the verse above also instructs Christians to love God "with all your heart." Strive for the balance between heart and mind. Learn the important apologetic arguments (mind work) but use them with grace and love (heart work).

With the Goal of Glorifying God

Glorifying God is what apologetics is all about. In fact, this is what God himself is all about! God is in the business of honoring himself and making himself famous.[8] God worships God, loves God, reveres God, is awestruck by God, and is intensely God-centered.

I (Bradley) recently went on a mission trip to Turkey. While there I visited the cities of Istanbul and Ephesus. Although there are countless differences between these two cities, perhaps the greatest is the economic difference. Istanbul is a city of production. The whole city either produced or consumed goods constantly, each individual business owner always striving to be better than the shop or restaurant right next to him. Ephesus, in stark contrast, produced very little besides necessities and tourist contraptions, because the whole city revolved around *showing off* the ruins of ancient Ephesus.

When it comes to apologetics, we as Christians are called not to be a part of Istanbul, but of Ephesus. Our lives must revolve not around producing God, but rather around showing him off. We are not to create God, but to display God. Baptist pastor Charles Spurgeon once quipped, "The gospel is like a caged lion; it need not be defended but only let out of its cage."

In chapter 7 we will unfold this fact in more detail, but for now let it be known that apologetics is fundamentally about the worship of God. The point is to show people just how wondrous, powerful, mighty, holy, and honorable our great King Jesus is!

With Gentleness and Love (1 Peter 3:16)

When Peter gave Christians the command to defend the hope within them, he reminded them to do it with a certain gracefulness. How often do Christians argue with unbelievers, and even sometimes fellow Christians, in a hateful way? Red-faced bickering is not allowed, for we are obligated as light-bearers for Jesus Christ to maintain a certain dignity and respect as we engage in the task of apologetics. Do not allow yourself to get angry, frustrated, or restless. Rather trust in God and speak with loving and graceful words (1 Timothy 4:12). Remember our lives are apologetic arguments too. *How* we argue for the existence of God will point people either toward him or away from him. Let us show his attractiveness by arguing in a winsome way for his glory. We don't want to beat people down but rather show them true life and see them saved.

LIMITATIONS OF APOLOGETICS

Despite its obvious value, apologetics certainly has limitations. To try to make apologetics do something it cannot is a disservice both to it and the theology it seeks to protect.

First, apologetics is limited since it is not an end in itself. Christians do not argue for the Christian faith for the entertainment it brings, or to gain the intellectual high ground. Its value lies in its ability to open a door for the gospel – the central message that Jesus Christ saves guilty sinners through his sacrifice on the cross and resurrection from the grave. Although basic, this principle is often neglected by many who try to replace the gospel itself with the gospel's defense. This is a grave blunder. Apologetics details our reasons "for the hope," but is not the hope itself.

This means that our focus within apologetics must be to establish a channel to present Christ as Savior and Lord, not to simply prove we are right. Our purpose is to confront and expose lies so that they can be replaced by the "word of truth" (Colossians 1:5). Apologetics must be done, as with all things, "looking to Jesus, the author and perfecter of our faith" (Hebrews 12:2).

Secondly, apologetics is limited because human reasoning is limited. When dealing with the divine being, the Creator of all things, people will naturally fall short of coming to exhaustive understanding of God's nature. We can, for example, defend the doctrine of the Trinity as logically possible, but to fully understand the nature of infinite and divine three-in-one-ness is humanly impossible. Apologists should never be so arrogant as to presume that all questions can be answered exhaustively. If this were the case, man would be God and not the other way around!

French apologist Blaise Pascal wrote the following: "If we submit everything to reason our religion will be left with nothing mysterious or supernatural."[9] It is the beauty of the divine to supersede man, not resemble him.

> "For my thoughts are not your thoughts, neither are your ways my ways," declares the LORD. "For as the heavens are higher than the earth, so are my ways higher than your ways and my thoughts than your thoughts." (Isaiah 55:8-9)

We do not engage in apologetics to show the world that we have made sense of God. Rather, we engage in apologetics to demonstrate that the world makes no sense without God. We must not assume we have all the answers, but we fall on our knees in humble submission to our Creator as we defend our faith in him.

When I (Bradley) was a kid, I loved reading the intriguing stories of Sherlock Holmes. From the day my sixth grade teacher assigned our first story I could not stop turning the pages. I even tried to write my own detective story (although I doubt my English teacher read more than half of it before dismissing it as the garbage that it was).

What always stood out to me was how absurd each Holmes story ended. There is no way I could have unraveled the mystery, until Holmes spelled it out to my ever-eager eyes. Yet I never set the book down upset about the outcome. Why? Because each story, by its nature, required an absurd explanation. There is simply no way that such plots could have been resolved within standard means, and it was the outrageous explanations, far more interesting than any standard explanation, that kept me excitedly turning the pages.

The universe where we live is the same way, only on a much larger scale. It is so delicate in design, so infused with order, so infinitely gigantic, and so tuned to maintain life. Such a universe requires a ridiculous explanation; ridiculous to our finite minds, anyway.

Yes, the idea of some God who has always been there and decided to create for his glory can seem preposterous, but the notion that something came from nothing, that order emerged from chaos, rationality from idiocy, is infinitely more preposterous. In fact, every worldview offers a preposterous solution, and the overwhelming task of apologetics is to demonstrate the preponderance of evidence for Christianity among these alternatives.

Conclusion

In this chapter we have provided a basic overview of the apologetics task, demonstrating from the Bible that all Christians should be engaged in defending the faith. We differentiated between positive and negative apologetics. We also showed that apologetics must be done by using the realms of logic, expression, and application with the attitude qualities commanded of believers. Finally, we presented some of the limitations of apologetics. In the next chapter we will move into an actual defense of the Christian faith, focusing initially on humanity and his greatest need.

Chapter 1 Review Exercise

1. Explain the concept of a worldview.
2. What is Christian apologetics?
3. How does a person destroy a false argument?

31

4. Explain what idea is contained in the word *contend*. How does this relate to apologetics?
5. Describe the three realms used to present apologetics (logic, expression, and application). Why is it important to include all three realms when engaged in defending the faith?
6. Discuss positive and negative apologetics using the football team analogy.
7. Why must apologetics be done with certain attitude qualities? Choose one of the attitude qualities discussed in this chapter and elaborate on why you think that quality is important when engaging in apologetics?

Key Terms

Christian
Atheism
Apologetics
Worldview
Argument
Evangelism
Positive apologetics
Negative apologetics

Scripture Memory

But in your hearts regard Christ the Lord as holy, always being prepared to make a defense to anyone who asks you for a reason for the hope that is in you; yet do it with gentleness and respect. (1 Peter 3:15-16)

CHAPTER 2:
Meeting Your Greatest Need

If someone asks me why I (Jason) am a Christian the first answer I feel obligated to give is a personal answer. Before I can give more brainy answers like the Cosmological Argument for the existence of God, or detailed arguments on why I trust the Bible, or why naturalism is bankrupt, I first have to show that all of this is very, very personal.

Francis Schaeffer once wisely wrote, "Christian apologetics do not start somewhere beyond the stars. They begin with man and what he knows about himself."[10] I couldn't agree more. What was it that first made me even consider God at all? What was it that initially drove me to him? Was it science and nature? Was it the words of a preacher? What was it?

The answer to these questions is indeed personal. I began seeking after God because of what I was personally feeling inside my own heart about the meaning and purpose of life. As I was growing up and contemplating my own existence, I sensed certain longings and desires within me that seemed to have no corresponding satisfaction anywhere on earth. It was somewhat like Adam must have felt as he yearned for a mate who was like him, but none could be found (Genesis 2:20).

These yearnings led me to seek God through a study of the Bible. There I found that God has made a promise to me as an individual to meet my greatest need. My greatest need (and yours too), is to be forgiven of sin and reconciled to God. Therefore, through his enablement I ran to him and threw myself at his feet, pleading for his sweet mercy. This is the primary reason I am a Christian. He has turned my personal "mourning into dancing."

You have turned for me my mourning into dancing; you have loosed my sackcloth and clothed me with gladness, that my glory may sing your praise and not be silent. O LORD my God, I will give thanks to you forever! (Psalm 30:11-12)

A DEEP DOWN KIND OF BAD

Perhaps sharing a bit more of my own biography will help explain the point we are attempting to make in this chapter.

It all started with a deep down knowledge of my own badness. Even as a child I knew that I was bad. I could sense my heart leaning toward the "dark side." I felt much like Anakin Skywalker, who desperately struggled with his true nature. Was Anakin good or bad? Most of us know the story. He started out as good, or at least as a "good guy." But eventually the man that was Anakin Skywalker became the dreaded killer Darth Vader, mostly machine and seared conscience. The pull towards evil was much too powerful for Skywalker to resist.[11]

I felt those same evil urges in my own life, but this was no movie – it was real. What is worse, I liked it. To me it was more fun lying, cussing, stealing, cheating and thinking dirty thoughts than it was to be good and obedient. I enjoyed evil, not because it benefited me in any way, but just because it was evil. There was a certain sport to it for me. An exhilarating adrenaline-rush thrill was produced in knowingly violating the rules.

As a pre-teen living in Hattiesburg, Mississippi, my "friends" and I were already smoking cigarettes, but that is not all. We obtained our cigarettes by going on what we called a "run." We would say, "Well, we're out of cigarettes, it's time to take a run." The "run" was actually a ride – on our bicycles down to Jitney Jungle, our local supermarket.

We would walk smoothly through the electric sliding doors, the same ones we used to open and close over and over again while waiting on our parents to bag the groceries. Then we would calmly walk up to the massive display of cigarettes, which at that time were not yet out of reach behind the counter as they are in most stores today. Instead, they were right in the open, and low enough that a three year old could crawl by and grab them.

I reached my hand out and took two or three packs or Marlboro Lights, usually three. My friends did the same. Then we would walk down an obscure and abandoned aisle and, while walking, we would stuff the cigarettes down our pants – not our best moments. Then we would walk out of the store as quickly as we came in. We never got caught. But God had caught my heart.

Oh, I knew I was bad. Even as we fled the scene of the crime, hearts racing faster than our bikes, ecstatic to have gotten away with it, my conscience was crying out with immeasurable guilt and shame. And it wasn't just the normal kind of wicked behavior that could be justified with words like, "Everybody does it." No, I sensed a deep depravity that went all the way down to my soul. This guilt also made me inescapably aware that I was most likely in serious trouble with God. Perhaps you know exactly what I'm talking about.

There were times when the sense of guilt was intense and sometimes overwhelming. I remember when my parents caught me sneaking out of our apartment in the middle of the night. I felt so awful. I really had let them down and they let me know about it as only parents can do. Something was terribly wrong in my heart and soul and I knew it and even as a young teenager I desperately wanted that problem repaired. I could not stand living with it.

Plus, I knew that it wasn't *just* the Bible that called me bad. I really didn't care at all about church or the Bible or anything related to those things. So it wasn't as though I was conditioned to *think I was bad*, but I knew that I was *really and actually bad*. And that scared me.

UNIVERSAL BADNESS

All of us deep down face this same dilemma. We may not know what we have done to make ourselves wicked, or the level of badness that we possess, but we all do know that we play a role in the evil that overrides this planet.

Often we try to deny it. We rate our own faults and compare them to others, saying "At least I haven't murdered anybody," or "Surely Hitler deserves worse than I do." We speak as if somehow possessing a lesser degree of depravity excuses the immorality that so clearly marks our own lives. We like to think of ourselves as pretty good people overall.

The denial of the evil that dominates our hearts can be clearly seen in the words of Superman's father, Jor-El, who believes that people are innately good, at least for the most part. In the most recent movie manifestation of the caped hero, Kal-El (Clark Kent's Kryptonian identity) is remembering his father's advice to him about living on planet earth among the humans. Using eerie, messianic terminology, Jor-El makes the following recommendations to his son:

> Live as one of them, Kal-El, to discover where your strength and your power are needed. Always hold in your heart the pride of your special heritage. They can be a great people, Kal-El, they wish to be. They only lack the light to show the

way. For this reason above all, their capacity for good, I have sent them you... my only son.[12]

This description of humanity as basically good, perhaps needing a little "light to show the way," is well received by the majority. We justify this positive assessment of our own ethical condition by comparing ourselves with the worst sinners on the planet. When we do this, we look in the mirror and deceive ourselves into believing that we are decent folks, since we are not the Lex Luther's of the world. But we fail to realize that the very action of passing the blame to others, in itself reveals our insecurity about our condition. We are the same as our first parents who, when they fell into sin, attempted to improve their outward image by passing the blame to someone else. Adam blamed Eve and Eve blamed the serpent:

> [God] said, "Who told you that you were naked? Have you eaten of the tree of which I commanded you not to eat?" The man said, "The woman whom you gave to be with me, she gave me fruit of the tree, and I ate." Then the LORD God said to the woman, "What is this that you have done?" The woman said, "The serpent deceived me, and I ate." (Genesis 3:11-13)

At other times we attempt to compensate for our badness, as if we could make up for it by balancing it with our good deeds. In a neighborhood in the Bible Belt of Mississippi, I (Bradley) once talked with a woman who was engrained in the moral standard of the area, citing how her attendance to church and contributions to charity qualified her for salvation. She was working with the underlying assumption that she could repair her wicked heart by overriding it with goodness.

The prophet Isaiah stunningly debunks this type of thinking when he states, "We have all become like one who is unclean, and all our righteous deeds are like a polluted garment" (Isaiah 64:6). Our badness consumes our very being and pollutes our every action. There is a devastating brokenness that infiltrates every area of our lives. This is why, when we carefully analyze the condition of the world in which we live, we find hate, violence, malice, greed, and every conceivable vice at every turn. Badness is a universal and undeniable reality that each of us must face.

This sin, deeply imbedded within us, reveals its grotesque face clearly as we abandon God and turn to worship idols. We worship primarily the idols of me-and-my-stuff. Rather than loving, obeying, and rejoicing in God, we attempt to please our own hearts by spending the majority of our days focused on ourselves and the stuff we can get our hands on. This is why in the first of the Ten Commandments, God clearly directs us to "have no other gods before me" (Exodus 20:3). But for the wicked heart, that is easier said than done.

GOD SENT ME A NOTE

Yet God is a God of grace and mercy beyond our wildest imaginations, and he works in astonishing ways. As I (Jason) struggled through my own badness and how I planned to deal with it, God sent me a little note. The note was a tract, which is a small booklet that has the message of Jesus Christ printed on it. I was only eleven or twelve years old when I stumbled across it on a sidewalk that ran next to my family's apartment. It was, ironically, the same sidewalk I was walking on the night I was caught sneaking out. I'm not sure how the note got there. Perhaps someone tossed it out of the window of their car. Such is the grace of God.

I read the tract while standing there on the curb. I had always believed in the existence of God, but had never really understood what a relationship with him really meant. As I read, I was being exposed to truth I hadn't really considered seriously before. But with my heart freshly guilty with the stains of thievery and underage smoking, I was deeply interested in and intrigued by what this little note from God said.

If you are familiar with the gospel, or gospel tracts at least, you might be able to guess the first thing I read. It said that all people are "sinners and fall short of the glory of God" (Romans 3:23). Wow! This little booklet was identifying my heart! The Bible confirmed the truth that I already knew – I am bad and desperately needing help, and so is everyone else.

I kept reading the tract. I saw that a great Day of Judgment was coming; a Day on which God would take his seat upon his throne and books would be opened. The Lamb's Book of Life would be among them. The little note from God made it clear to me that anyone who did not have his or her name recorded in the Lamb's Book of Life would be cast into a lake of fire and be forever punished for sin.

> And I saw the dead, great and small, standing before the throne, and books were opened. Then another book was opened, which is the book of life. And the dead were judged by what was written in the books, according to what they had done...And if anyone's name was not found written in the book of life, he was thrown into the lake of fire. (Revelation 20:12; 15)

My heart was gripped and it was melting. I did not desire to face this holy Judge in my condition and I was afraid. Perhaps you are reading these words right now and you understand the fear I felt, because you are feeling it, too. If this is you, our prayer is that as you read the next section, you will be moved from fear to joy.

CHRISTIANITY PROVIDES A DEFINITIVE AND PERMANENT ANSWER

As I continued analyzing the note from God I began to sense the wonder of the gospel message. Jesus Christ had come to earth, not as a mere ethical teacher to show us how to be good, but rather to pay a high and permanent price to redeem us from our badness. It was becoming clear to me that Jesus had come to repair my heart problem. He could take my evil and wicked heart and trade it for a heart of love, peace, and joy. He could take my empty and bankrupt moral account and replace it with his own righteousness.[13] I could not rid myself of the guilt and sin that polluted my being, but his atoning life, death, and resurrection was sufficient to get the job done! Through his loving work of cleansing my sin and repairing my heart, I found true peace with God. "Therefore, since we have been justified by faith, we have peace with God through our Lord Jesus Christ" (Romans 5:1).

Christ provided for me a personal answer to my biggest problem. As I prayed for his forgiveness that night in my bed, I was overtaken by his embrace. This is why Jesus is so enticing. He is a glorious, ever-existing, all powerful being who concerned himself with my problem and provided a definitive and permanent solution. The Maker of an uncountable billion-plus stars, in all their majestic brilliance, saw fit to reach his mighty hand into my wicked life and adopt me, wretch that I am, into his own family. Truly the great psalmist, David, has captured in words my thoughts about the Lord's mercy:

> When I look at your heavens, the work of your fingers, the moon and the stars, which you have set in place, what is man that you are mindful of him, and the son of man that you care for him? (Psalm 8:3-4)

Even if there were no other defenses of the Christian faith, I would still be convinced that Jesus Christ is the Savior because I can sing with personal confidence that "I once was lost, but now I'm found." I also can sing, "I need no other argument; I need no other plea. It is enough that Jesus died and that he died for me!"

Even further (as if this could get any better), I cannot be re-lost again. The Bible makes it clear that Christ holds me, along with all his children, in his powerful hand. It is not up to me to hold myself in his hand any more than it is up to a two-month-old to hold herself in her mother's arms. He is the Father who eternally embraces his bought and beloved children.

> I give them eternal life, and they will never perish, and no one will snatch them out of my hand. My Father, who has given them to me, is greater than all, and no one is able to snatch them out of the Father's hand. (John 10:28-29)

This is really good news! It means my cleansing and salvation is definitive. It is a life-change from now throughout eternity. In other words, my badness can no longer be grounds for my punishment in Hell, because I am securely hidden in Christ. He is my newfound goodness and righteousness.

What a unique idea this is, that Christ would end our suffering by entering it himself. He would remove our guilt by taking our blame. He would restore our fellowship with the Father by severing his own. He would solve the problem of humanity by the gift of divinity. "For our sake he made him to be sin who knew no sin, so that in him we might become the righteousness of God" (2 Corinthians 5:21).

A GREAT SALVATION

In the movie *I Am Legend*, an alleged "cure for cancer" has turned nearly every human on earth into zombie-like creatures, with Will Smith playing one of the few surviving humans left. The climactic scene presents Smith's character as finally discovering an antidote for the disease, but also being vehemently attacked by the very zombies that he had worked so hard to save. He is inside a protective barrier that the zombies are attempting to break, the entire time he is screaming to them, "I have your cure! I have what you need!" But the zombies keep coming, unaware and unconcerned that a cure is available. When they are about to break the barrier and kill everyone, Smith hands the cure off to two other humans and detonates a hand grenade, blowing himself up along with all of the assailant zombies. As a result of his sacrificial act, the cure eventually was applied to the remaining zombies, restoring them to normal life. Smith's character died to reinstate life to those who had so despairingly hated his.

This film offers a powerful picture of our great salvation. The earth was infiltrated by the serpent in the Garden of Eden, claiming to have a so-called "cure" for ignorance that left the world utterly depraved and hopeless.[14] Jesus himself came to these very people proclaiming, "I am the cure! I am what you need!"[15] But in our badness we hated him to the utmost. And he would die at the hands of humanity, in order to bring salvation to the people so violently opposed to him.

But the film fails to capture the full picture of our salvation. No story or work of art can truly encapsulate as an illustration what Christ has done in reality. A salvation from our Creator himself is no fiction. Just as our Savior cannot be "an image formed by the art and imagination of man" (Acts 17:29), so his salvation cannot be of our own imagination.

The work of Jesus is far greater than that of the Smith character. The disease of sin has not infected most of us, but *all of us*, requiring someone outside of humanity, someone much greater than us, to save us from ourselves. He died to cleanse our sin and guilt, but was resurrected to restore our fellowship with himself providing for our ultimate satisfaction and his maximized glory. The cure is not something created by Jesus, but is Jesus himself. He did not pass on a created cure but instilled a personal cure – himself – through his Holy Spirit. Such a great salvation is so infinitely beyond what we as humans could ever dream up, and for that very reason so incomparably better.

Other Worldviews Are Insufficient

After my conversion to Christ I began to notice over a period of years that other religions could not have done for me what Christ did. If I had remained in the more-or-less agnostic state I was in, I would have continued to suffer under my own shame and guilt.[16] I don't know how long I could have held out that way. My conscience bothered me so much that, honestly, without some form of relief, suicide would probably have been a serious option for me. But suppose I had attempted to find peace with God through some other religious framework. Think about what would have happened in the following hypothetical scenarios.

If I had joined the Jehovah's Witnesses seeking relief for my guilty soul, I would have been taught that salvation was not an act of pure grace, but also involved my own righteous works. Former JW member Lorri MacGregor wrote about their version of salvation:

> I was told [that "working out your salvation"] consisted of "publishing the good news of God's Kingdom" by selling their publications door-to-door, attending five meetings a week, and meeting numerous other quotas.[17]

I would have been extremely frustrated trying to please God by knocking on a certain number of doors in order to earn his favor. After all, I am bad to the core of my being. How terribly irritating it would have been for me trying to produce righteous fruits from a dead and unholy heart! There just aren't enough doors to knock on or meetings to attend to wash away the guilty stains that tarnish the soul.

If I had joined the Mormon Church I would also have been required to perform a certain amount of good deeds in order to maintain my right standing before God.[18] If I had joined Islam I would have been required to keep Islamic Law faithfully. These two options would have been similar to the Jehovah's Witnesses option. Frustration, frustration, frustration!

If I had fled to eastern religions, such as Hinduism or Buddhism, I would have been told that, contrary to what I feel and know I am not *actually bad*. In fact, many Eastern sects teach that all of reality is an illusion. My guru would have taught me that I need to work diligently to escape the brutal cycles of reincarnation that entrap me and then the illusion that I am bad would go away forever.

I think this type of belief system would have driven me insane! In spite of denying that evil is in my heart, I would still have felt the evil there. A person can deny they have cancer, but if they really have it, the denial is ridiculous and dangerous. Eastern religions do not fix the problem that resides in every human heart. They just simply deny that a problem exists.[19]

Only biblical Christianity deals with my problem. During the course of this book we want to show you the reasonableness involved in believing Christianity to be true, but we also want to show you that it alone provides a solution to man's deepest need and solves our biggest problem. Christ alone can reconcile God to man. "We also rejoice in God through our Lord Jesus Christ, through whom we have now received reconciliation" (Romans 5:11).

No Other Than What We Are

This chapter is meant to demonstrate that the discipline of apologetics is a very personal enterprise. We are Christians first and foremost because Jesus saved us. Our personal experiences of God's grace motivate us to share Christ with others and tear down every lofty argument that is lifted up against the truth. We have experienced God personally and know his grace directly. We are convinced that there is a God, and that Jesus is the Son of God, and that Christianity is true because of his act of grace upon our souls. Nothing could convince us otherwise. He made us his and we can be no other than what we are.

Even though this is a fact, the incredible reality about Christianity is that, since it is totally true, everything in creation backs it up. A person's faith in Christ can be further strengthened when he examines creation and sees God's holy fingerprints on everything. From the stars above to the moral code written on the heart of every human, everything points to the authenticity of the Christian faith as detailed in the Bible. The remaining chapters of this book unfold this reality, beginning with a focus on the God-man, Jesus Christ.

Chapter 2 Review Exercise

1. Why is apologetics such a personal enterprise?
2. Do you think every human being knows that he or she is bad? Why or why not?
3. Why do religions other than Christianity fail when attempting to solve the problem of guilt?
4. Consider your own life for a moment. Do you think you are a sinner who needs to be forgiven? Why or why not?

Key Terms

Guilt
Sin
Grace
Gospel

Scripture Memory

We also rejoice in God through our Lord Jesus Christ, through whom we have now received reconciliation. (Romans 5:11)

CHAPTER 3:
The Man Who Said He Was God

The greatest moment in baseball folklore was sealed in history by the greatest player of the game: Babe Ruth. The fate of his team's entire season depended on how he performed against one of the league's best pitchers. At a time as important as this, he still had the audacity to point to the spot in the stands where he claimed he would hit his home run.

How he would have been mocked and ridiculed by everyone, and how cocky and incompetent he would have seemed, had he failed. But we all know how the story turned out. He has been the undying idol of the baseball world, because he did exactly what he claimed he would do. He backed up his claim with action that supported it.[20]

How do Christians back up their claim that Christianity is reasonable and true? In particular, how do we show it is true to those who do not believe that it is? It is one thing for us to be personally convinced that Christianity is true because of our own experiences with God, but it is another thing for us to faithfully demonstrate this to others. It is one thing to point at the fence and make a claim, but it is another thing to hit the homerun.

To be sure, we are justified in sharing our experience with unbelievers. We love telling others about how God made his way into our hearts and changed us. The Apostle Paul also shared his testimony as a way of showing others the love of Christ.[21] He let others know what kind of man he was before Christ saved him – a ruthless murderer – and how his life was totally changed on the road to Damascus. Our personal testimonies are powerful witnesses of the existence of God and salvation through Christ.

But the unbeliever might want more. He might say, "I'm glad you had an experience with God, but I have not. Can you give me other reasons that I should believe Christianity is true?"

It is our desire to show you that not only can we *know* that Christianity is true, but that there are also many ways we can reasonably *show* it to be true.[22] Before we get there, here's a little story.

LeBron James and Reasonable Faith

Suppose LeBron James and I (Bradley) are both on the basketball court shooting hoops together. Suppose he says that he is about to jump and rotate three hundred and sixty degrees in the air, and then slam-dunk. I would reply, "Okay, I believe you can do it."

This is an example of faith. I used the word *believe* which means faith. It is faith because it has not happened yet. If it had already happened and I saw LeBron do it, then it would be sight, not faith. When things are in the future, we must have faith if we believe they are going to happen.

But in this case my faith is a *reasonable faith*. Why? Because, hello, this is LeBron James! He is 6'8" tall! He is arguably the best basketball player who has ever lived! For crying out loud, they call him The Chosen One! So even though I must exercise faith in order to believe that he will do a three-sixty, it is obviously a reasonable faith, based on good and valid grounds.

But let's suppose that LeBron successfully performs his dunk and walks back over to me. There I am, standing on the court with a confident swagger, bouncing a basketball. I look up at him (way up) and say, "Nice dunk, Chosen One, now it is my turn!"

Well, anybody who knows me knows that I can't play basketball at all. I repeat – I have no skills on the court. When I jump as high as I can, I can barely touch the rim. So when I say I am about to do a three-sixty, it is *not reasonable* to believe that it will ever actually happen. I have never shown that I can dunk before and I am not tall enough to dunk if I wanted to.

Sure, I can have faith! Yes, I can believe that somehow a strong wind will blow through the gym at the precise moment I leap for the hoop and carry me up to the basket, twisting me in a full circle as I go. Sure, I can believe that. But that is NOT a reasonable faith. That is called blind faith. There is a major difference between reasonable faith and blind faith!

Our faith that Jesus Christ is the Son of God and that he rose from the dead is *not* blind faith. It is reasonable faith. It is reasonable because he has proven himself. His life, his words, and his deeds are the most convincing apologetic arguments that the world has seen. When it comes to showing that Christianity is true and reasonable, the first place to look is the heart of Christianity – Christ Jesus himself. He is the most amazing and incredible person who has ever lived.

BUT SOME SAY JESUS NEVER EXISTED

There is a small group of extreme radicals who have proposed the Jesus-myth hypothesis. This is the view that Jesus of Nazareth never actually existed, but was a created legend, invented by the apostle Paul and other early church leaders, apparently to manipulate their followers. Earl Doherty, author of *The Jesus Puzzle*[23] and Robert M. Price, a member of the Jesus Seminar,[24] are two of the most prominent individuals holding this extreme view. Additionally, a recent independent documentary called *The God Who Wasn't There*, written and directed by Brian Flemming, takes this unsupportable position.

It should first be noted that the vast majority of historians and other experts of the life of Jesus strongly disagree with these radicals. Even those who are not Christians are convinced, at the very least, that Jesus of Nazareth was a *real person*. They just do not believe he was the Messiah, the Son of the living God. But to deny that he ever existed is to go against a mountain of evidence that speaks clearly to the contrary. To say that Jesus was merely a myth is like claiming that George Washington was a myth.[25]

But how do we know Jesus really existed? There are numerous historical writings that speak of Jesus as a real person, both inside and outside the Bible. Some of these are from his friends and some of these are from his enemies. Many of these sources were written very close to the time of Jesus' life. This fact argues heavily against the Jesus-myth hypothesis, since there were many people still alive at the time of the writings who would have known about Jesus first-hand, and some who would have known him personally. These people provide historical checks and balances. The following is a list of many of the historical sources that prove that Jesus actually existed.

Christian sources

The New Testament is a collection of books written by Christians to convince people to become Christians. No doubt, it is Jesus-friendly. But even still, the books of the Bible do recount history, and a telling of history can be either verified or falsified. In the case of the gospels and epistles of the New Testament, the best evidence shows that the apostles were not making up stories, but were writing actual accounts of the life of Jesus.

The Bible is not one book written by one person. It is a collection of books written by many different people. Therefore, the individual books of the Bible constitute independent witnesses of the history recorded inside the Bible. Matthew, Mark, Luke, John, Paul, Peter, James, Jude, and the writer of Hebrews are all in agreement that Jesus Christ was an actual person. His life is described in detail in these sources. Plus, it is clear that several passages in the New Testament are based on sources that are dated even earlier than the New Testament documents themselves.

For example, biblical scholars speak of a mysterious Q document, that explains the origin of the material shared by Matthew and Luke, but that does not appear in Mark. Though we do not possess a copy of the Q document itself, its theoretical existence indicates another ancient source for the life of Jesus.

In addition, several ancient creeds are recorded in the Bible. These creeds predate the books we find them in, providing more early and independent sources for the life of Jesus. A clear case of this can be found in Paul's first letter to the Corinthian church:

> For I delivered to you as of first importance what I also received: that Christ died for our sins in accordance with the Scriptures, that he was buried, that he was raised on the third day in accordance with the Scriptures. (1 Corinthians 15:3-4)

Many scholars indicate that this was a creed recited by the early church and Paul is simply quoting it. If this is so, then the creed itself is older than the first letter to the Corinthians, and probably much older, since creeds take time to be circulated and accepted. Other similar creedal formulas are found in 1 John 4:2, 1 Timothy 3:16, 2 Timothy 2:8, and Romans 1:3-4. Since these are sources quoted by the Bible, then they give us evidence that people other than the biblical authors believed that Jesus was real, prior to the writing of the New Testament. This evidence alone shows that it is hardly possible that the apostles could have invented Jesus.[26]

51

In addition, there are hundreds of other ancient Christian sources that provide evidence for the existence of Jesus. These include the Didache, a collection of teachings practiced by the early church,[27] as well as the writings of the early church fathers who confirmed the writings of the apostles. The Apostles' Creed could also be included in this list, since it was probably written prior to 100 AD.

But someone might object by saying that all of these documents were written by Jesus' friends and followers. Perhaps they somehow made a pact together that they would all lie about Jesus and fabricate a story about his life. Of course this is historically impossible, since most of these sources were written by people who did not know each other. But beyond this, there are other sources proving the life of Jesus written by those outside the circle of his friends, who would have no reason whatsoever to promote a Jesus myth.

A Jewish Historian

The most prominent Jewish source for the life of Jesus was a man named Josephus, a historian most famous for his detailed accounts of the Jewish war with Rome, which included the famous Siege of Jerusalem in 70 AD. Josephus was not a Christian, so he was not interested in promoting Christian beliefs. He simply wrote down what was happening in the world at the time. Here is a famous passage from his *Antiquities*:

> At this time there was a wise man who was called Jesus, and his conduct was good, and he was known to be virtuous. And many people from among the Jews and the other nations became his disciples. Pilate condemned him to be crucified and to die. And those who had become his disciples did not abandon their loyalty to him. They reported that he had appeared to them three days after his crucifixion, and that he was alive. Accordingly they believed that he was the Messiah, concern-

ing whom the Prophets have recounted wonders. (18.3.3 Arabic 10th C. version)

Not only did Josephus identify Jesus as a historical figure, but he also indicated that Jesus had many followers, that he was crucified by Pilate, the Roman governor, and that some people believed he rose from the dead. All of this from a careful historian who was not interested in promoting Christian belief! No wonder the majority of scholars dismiss the Jesus-myth hypothesis so quickly. But the words of Josephus are only the tip of the iceberg of evidence for the existence of Jesus.

Roman sources

The life of Jesus and the history of the early church occurred during a time when the Roman government controlled a major part of the civilized world. Archeologists have uncovered several letters and other works written by Roman historians and officials that indicate some of the empire's difficulties in dealing with the growth of the early church. For example, the Roman senator Tacitus (c.55-117 AD), in recounting the history of the reign of the emperor Nero, wrote:

> Consequently, to get rid of the report, Nero fastened the guilt and inflicted the most exquisite tortures on a class hated for their abominations, called Christians by the populace. Christus, from whom the name had its origin, suffered the extreme penalty during the reign of Tiberius at the hands of one of our procurators, Pontius Pilatus, and a most mischievous superstition, thus checked for the moment, again broke out not only in Judaea, the first source of the evil, but even in Rome, where all things hideous and shameful from every part of the world find their centre and become popular. (*Annuals* 15:44)

Here is solid evidence from a man who was not a Christian, nor even a Jew, that Jesus of Nazareth was an actual historical figure, and that he was put to death by crucifixion under the authority of Pontus Pilate.

Other Roman sources include Seutonius and Pliny the Younger. Seutonius was a historian who in his *Life of Claudius* mentions the expelling of the Jews from Rome because they had been stirred up by a leader called "Chrestus," a probable reference to Jesus, who was called the Christ. This event finds a strong parallel in the book of Acts:

> Then Paul left Athens and went to Corinth. There he became acquainted with a Jew named Aquila, born in Pontus, who had recently arrived from Italy with his wife, Priscilla. They had been expelled from Italy as a result of Claudius Caesar's order to deport all Jews from Rome. (Acts 18:1-2)

Pliny the Younger was the Roman governor of Bithynia who wrote a letter to Emperor Trajan asking him how to deal with the growing Christian population in his territory. In this letter, written very close to the actual life of Christ, Pliny indicates that Christians worshiped Jesus as though he was God.[28] Pliny's letter is solid proof that the worship of Jesus as deity did not develop over centuries after his life, but that Jesus was a real man who was thought to be God himself by his earliest followers.

Greek sources

In addition to the Christians, Jews, and Romans, several writers of Greek origin also join the chorus and confirm the existence of Jesus. Celsus was a 2nd Century Greek philosopher, famous for poking fun at Christianity. But in so doing, he actually confirms many of the beliefs and practices of the early Church, and he never denies that Jesus was an actual person.

Thallus was another Greek historian who apparently mentions Jesus. We do not possess any of his original writings, but a 3ʳᵈ Century Christian historian named Julius Africanus, in writing about the darkness that came when Jesus was crucified states, "In the third book of his history, Thallus calls this darkness an eclipse of the sun--wrongly in my opinion."[29] This quote indicates that people were aware of the mysterious darkness that occurred at the crucifixion of Jesus, and debated what might have caused it.

Assyrian sources

One last category of sources for the life of Jesus needs to be mentioned. Two prominent Assyrian sources also testify that Jesus was an actual person. The first was a famous playwright named Lucian of Samosata (c.125-180 AD). In one of his plays, Lucian writes:

> The Christians, you know, worship a man to this day—the distinguished personage who introduced their novel rites, and was crucified on that account...
>
> You see, these misguided creatures start with the general conviction that they are immortal for all time, which explains the contempt of death and voluntary self-devotion which are so common among them; and then it was impressed on them by their original lawgiver that they are all brothers, from the moment that they are converted, and deny the gods of Greece, and worship the crucified sage, and live after his laws.
>
> All this they take quite on faith, with the result that they despise all worldly goods alike, regarding them merely as common property. (*The Death of Peregrine* 11-13)

Like the Roman sources, Lucian lived close enough to the actual events, and was a strong enough enemy of early Christianity, that if

Jesus had never existed, he would have certainly focused his attention on that reality. But Lucian never denies the actual existence of Jesus. He simply makes fun of him and his followers. In so doing, however, he unwittingly proves to us today without doubt, that Jesus of Nazareth was a real man.

The second Assyrian confirmation of Jesus comes from a letter that a man wrote to his son, encouraging him to pattern his life after the lives of wise people. In his list of wise people, he mentions a Jewish king who was executed at the hands of his own people. He writes, "What advantage did the Jews gain from executing their wise king? It was just after that that their kingdom was abolished."[30] Again, another confirmation that many people, not only Christians, knew many facts about the life of Jesus, and their writings confirm that Jesus was an actual person, and not just a myth.

Those who hold to the Jesus-myth hypothesis must do so by blind faith. The evidence argues solidly against their position. It is clear that their goal is not to find truth, but rather to discredit Christianity. We suggest a better course of action; follow the evidence where it leads.

NOT TO BE IGNORED

In spite of all this evidence, Jesus is often treated as the embarrassment of Christianity. We feel he is someone who should be helped out and pitied, or even set in a far off corner so that he doesn't ruin our reputations. There is a tendency to subject him to our sympathy and censorship rather than present him as the object of our worship.

I'm still not sure why, but I (Bradley) once enjoyed watching the infomercials that air at three in the morning. You never know what you'll find being advertised there. Perhaps there'll be an eighty-foot long garden hose, or finely tuned nose hair clippers, or knives sharp enough to cut straight through a solid kitchen counter! Funny, there is inevitably some drawback to every item they offer, something the

56

advertisers want to hide, something that keeps their product from being the perfect product they desire the public to think it is. Whether it's in unreadable print flashing on the screen for three seconds, or the speaker talking faster than anyone could hope to understand, there is something they are ashamed of.

Sometimes Christians present Jesus this way. He is a good "product," as far as it goes, but he comes with many disclaimers. For example, we have to believe he made postmortem visits to his followers (1 Corinthians 15:5-7). Well, that is just weird. We also have to believe that he commands believers to eat his flesh and drink his blood in an act of communal remembrance.

> So Jesus said to them, "Truly, truly, I say to you, unless you eat the flesh of the Son of Man and drink his blood, you have no life in you. Whoever feeds on my flesh and drinks my blood has eternal life, and I will raise him up on the last day. For my flesh is true food, and my blood is true drink. Whoever feeds on my flesh and drinks my blood abides in me, and I in him." (John 6:53-56)

In our modern culture, this can be downright embarrassing. Even in Jesus' day, after he taught this, "many of his disciples turned back and no longer walked with him" (v. 66). So Christians often elevate the ethical teachings of Christianity – like love your neighbor as yourself – and downplay Jesus the person, who has a tendency to come across as an oddity.

But if we are not presenting Jesus, what are we left with? Jesus is not only the destination of apologetics, but he is an absolutely essential part of the path. He is not only the supreme figure within Christianity, but also the greatest argument for it. He is the argument God himself uses (John 1:1-14).

Furthermore, he cannot be ignored. Jesus forces a conscious and intentional acceptance or rejection, and stands as a fork in the road of life. He asks that heart-wrenching question to all people, "Who do you say that I am?" (Mark 8:29). Every person is under obligation to answer. Is he merely a Jewish religious teacher? An ethical guide? A prophet from God? A manipulative deceiver? A myth who never existed? Or God himself?

Jesus Christ stands in the way of every man's routine life, and demands to be everything or nothing. He issues this warning to all who will hear:

> Whoever does not bear his own cross and come after me cannot be my disciple. For which of you, desiring to build a tower, does not first sit down and count the cost, whether he has enough to complete it? (Luke 14:27-28)

So let's examine this man and see if following him is worth the cost. If his claims prove to be false, so be it, leave him to the history books. However, if he is truly God in flesh, then abandon everything in relentless pursuit of his glory. But let none of us be guilty of simply ignoring him.

When Moses saw an unexplainable phenomenon in his normal pursuits of life – a burning bush – he made a decision. "I will *turn aside* to see this great sight, why the bush is not burned" (Exodus 3:3, emphasis ours). Let us follow his example and turn aside to see this great sight, the person of Jesus Christ.

THE GOD-MAN

Read the following passage from the Gospel of John carefully. Make the connection between Jesus proving his power by coming back to life from the dead, and the belief of the people: "When therefore he was raised from the dead, his disciples remembered that he had said this, and they believed the Scripture and the word that Jesus had spoken" (John 2:22).

The disciples saw Jesus alive after he had died, they remembered the Old Testament prophecies that he fulfilled, and *they believed*. The amazing evidence was set before them. Jesus Christ fulfilled hundreds of Old Testament prophecies in ways that could not have been faked. This proved to them that Jesus was not a liar, but was actually the Messiah. Having faith in Jesus was not a blind leap, but rather was the most reasonable thing to do!

Read the next verse: "Now when he was in Jerusalem at the Passover Feast, many believed in his name when they saw the signs that he was doing" (John 2:23). The same thing was true of the people in Jerusalem. When they saw Jesus working mighty miracles, they had *reason* to believe the words that Jesus spoke. It was not an irrational faith, but rather a reasonable faith based on clear evidence.

The same is true for us today. We have many good and rational reasons to believe that Jesus Christ is the only way of salvation. We will attempt to demonstrate this with the following simple argument:

1. Jesus claimed he was God.
2. Jesus proved that his claim was true.
3. Therefore, Jesus is God.

JESUS CLAIMED HE WAS GOD

What do you make of folks who say they are God? There have been a few people listed on the pages of history who have made this outrageous claim. Many others declared themselves to be a prophet of God. Most people, however, never make any claims like this. Personal declarations of deity can be a real turn-off.

Imagine if one of your longtime friends stood up one day in a public setting, cleared his throat, and asserted loudly, "May I have your attention please! It is time for me to reveal that I am actually the Lord God Almighty! I insist that everyone who hears my voice fall down and worship me immediately!" You probably would be slightly irritated by your friend's actions, and wouldn't want to be seen with that person anymore. After all, claiming to be God is a big deal.

So when people *do* claim to be God, what should we do with them? David Koresh was the guru of a cult group in Waco, Texas known as the Branch Davidians. Several years ago the group was in the news for stockpiling weapons and eventually the government removed them. Their compound was burned and most of the people in their group, including Koresh, perished in the flames.[31]

This story was in the news for several days and reporters continually pointed out that Koresh believed himself to be the Messiah. His followers were also apparently convinced of this. Most people outside the cult, however, thought the guy was out of his mind – missing a few cards, elevator not going all the way up, a wacko in Waco. People who say they are God or god-like usually have only a small following of deluded people.

But when Jesus Christ entered the public scene of history, he was much different. He openly and continually referred to himself as the Messiah, the anointed and prophesied One of the Old Testament. "The woman said to him, 'I know that Messiah is coming (he who is called Christ). When he comes, he will tell us all things.' Jesus said to her, 'I who speak to you am he'" (John 4:25-26).

Jesus never hid the reality that he was the One predicted by the prophets in the days of old. But that is not all! He even declared himself equal with God the Father, an action that got him into real trouble with the Jewish authorities: "'I and the Father are one.' The Jews picked up stones again to stone him" (John 10:30-31). They picked up the stones because they wanted to kill him. Why? Because he had just made himself out to be equal with God! That was total blasphemy as far as they were concerned, and a blasphemous man was a dead man.

60

This goes even further. People often worshipped Jesus, and when they did, he did not stop them. One time people tried to worship Paul and Barnabas because they had worked a miracle. But Paul immediately prohibited them and said, "Men, why are you doing these things? We also are men, of like nature with you" (Acts 14:15). In stark contrast look what happens when Jesus heals a blind man who shows his appreciation to Jesus by worshipping him:

> Jesus…having found him [the blind man]…said, "Do you believe in the Son of Man?" He answered, "And who is he, sir, that I may believe in him?" Jesus said to him, "You have seen him, and it is he who is speaking to you." He said, "Lord, I believe," and he worshiped him. (John 9:35-38)

As you continue reading the passage you will observe that Jesus did not correct the man. He did not say, "Stop worshiping me! I'm just a man like you." This is because Jesus was not a mere man. He was different and he knew it and he proved it.

He even had the audacity to forgive people of their sins. Suppose you and your mom got into a nasty argument. After shouting at her, you did the unthinkable and slapped her to the ground, leaving the house in a fury. Now imagine that while you were out, thinking about the horrors of your actions, you bumped into a man who said, "I forgive you of the sins you just committed against your mom." What? Who does this guy think he is? How can he forgive you for something you did to someone else? He wasn't even involved in the incident!

This illustration sounds strange, but this is exactly what Jesus did on many occasions. He forgave people of their sins which they committed against *other people*. The Jewish leaders knew that when he did this, he was essentially claiming to be God:

> And when he saw their faith, he said, "Man, your sins are forgiven you." And the scribes and the Pharisees began to ques-

tion, saying, "Who is this who speaks blasphemies? Who can forgive sins but God alone?" (Luke 5:20-21)

Good question! Who can forgive sins but God alone? There is no doubt that Jesus claimed and believed that he was God in the flesh.

He even acted like God. He multiplied (created) food out of nothing when he fed 5,000 men and their families.[32] He calmed furious storms.[33] He walked on the surface of water.[34] He miraculously transformed water into wine.[35] He raised people from the dead.[36] Who else can do these things but God?

At one point he infuriated the Jewish leaders by referring to himself as the I AM. If you know the Old Testament at all, you know that when Moses asked God for his name, God called himself "I AM" (Exodus 3:14). The Jewish leaders certainly knew that this was God's covenantal name. So when they heard Jesus say the following, it is clear they wanted him dead for claiming to be God himself: "'Truly, truly, I say to you, before Abraham was, I am.' So they picked up stones to throw at him, but Jesus hid himself and went out of the temple" (John 8:58-59).

To further support his deity, Jesus claimed to be able to do things that only God himself could do. He promised a group of his followers, "Where two or more are gathered in my name, there I am among them" (Matthew 18:20). But how could Jesus make this claim if he was only a human?

He also claimed to have power over everything. When he was about to ascend into heaven, Jesus said to his followers, "All authority in heaven and on earth has been given to me" (Matthew 28:18).

It is abundantly clear that Jesus claimed to be God. But there is a problem – all of these claims are found in the Bible. How do we know the Bible is true? Is it possible that the followers of Jesus who wrote the Gospels (Matthew, Mark, Luke, and John) just made all this stuff up about him? Is it possible that he never claimed to be God, but they just said he claimed to be God?

These are good questions, and in chapter 5 you will find answers. There, we will make a strong attempt to show that the Bible is true and can be reasonably trusted, but this raises a very important point. We must understand that all of these arguments for the Christian world-view work together. This argument you are reading now about Jesus is supported strongly by the argument that the Bible is true. All of the arguments for the Christian faith must be taken *together* as a group. When they are all taken together they support each other and comprise a powerful and persuasive set of truths.

LISTENING IS IMPORTANT

If someone says he is God or a spokesperson for God, what should we do with him? We think that, at the very least, people should listen to him and test his claims to see if he is telling the truth.

Think about it. Here we are – humanity – swirling about on this planet called Earth in the midst of a vast and mostly unknown universe. How did we get here? Why are we here? Most people would really like to know the answers to these questions, and a lot of answers have been offered. Some say that life is a sort of cosmic accident that arose in this far corner of the universe and that it has no real meaning. It just happened, so hey, we might as well enjoy it. This is the answer of the naturalist (whom we will talk more about later on).

But Christians are not at all happy with that answer and nobody should be. We feel life is significant and meaningful, an idea shared by many. The fact that people exist at all seems to be a pretty big deal, not just some sort of universal fluke. Our existence seems to be *on purpose*, as Sir John Templeton pondered, "Would it not be strange if a universe without purpose accidentally created humans who are so obsessed with purpose?"[37]

People want sufficient answers to our big questions of existence and purpose, but there is a major problem. Where do we find those answers? With the exception of the folks who landed on the moon and orbit around the earth on occasion, we're stuck on this planet. We can't just fly up into Heaven and ask God what is really going on. So what we need is someone to come down from God to us.

If someone says that he has been sent from God, then, as a minimal response, we should listen to what he has to say. We don't have to believe him, and we should certainly test his words to see if he speaks truth, but at the very least we should listen to him.

For example, Muhammad, the founder of Islam, declared himself to be a prophet of God. A seeker of truth named Whitney might listen to Muhammad but not believe him. Muhammad said that he was a prophet of Allah (the standard Arabic word for "God") and that he had the answers people were looking for, but as Whitney studies the Qur'an she is not convinced that Muhammad was telling the truth. In fact, it seems as though Muhammad was very confused. So she listens to him, but then refuses to believe him.[38]

Most people who claim to be God or a prophet of God are the same as Muhammad. They fail to follow through in proving their claim. But this is where Jesus Christ was so different and unique. Not only did he claim to be God, having all the answers that people needed about the meaning of life, but he also verified and substantiated his claim.

JESUS PROVED THAT HIS CLAIM WAS TRUE

Get ready, here comes another Superman story. Suppose someone walks up to you on the street and says, "My name is Clark Kent and whenever the need arises, I can turn into Superman." You would say, "Whatever!" Most folks are smart enough not to believe such an outrageous claim. But then suppose he rips off his coat and tie revealing his blue and red Superman suit, complete with majestic cape flapping heroically in the wind. He shouts, "Up! Up! And away!" Then with a bounce he flies up into the air and circles around the sky. When he lands you stare at him in amazement and say, "Wow! It is true, you really are Superman!"

It is one thing to claim to be Superman, but it's another thing altogether to prove it. It is one thing for Jesus to *say* he was God, but it is another thing altogether for him to *prove* it. As unlikely as it might seem, that is exactly what He did.

We've already mentioned some of the miracles that Jesus worked in demonstrating that he was God – healing the blind man, turning water into wine, feeding 5,000, walking on the water, and calming the storm. After each of these miracles, people became convinced that Jesus was really what he claimed to be. "Many of the people believed in him. They said, 'When the Christ appears, will he do more signs than this man has done?'" (John 7:31). These people believed Jesus was the Messiah because Jesus proved it to them by performing miracles. These signs and wonders were pointers to the reality that God had become flesh and was dwelling among them (John 1:14).

Of course, many people say that miracles are impossible. Therefore, Jesus could not have worked miracles. The flaw with that reasoning is that it starts from a premise of unbelief. It assumes that there is no God first, then states that miracles are impossible. Well, in a universe where there is *no god* or supernatural being of any kind, one would expect there to be *no miracles.*

But the Christian can use the same approach. If there *is* a God, as we have good reason to believe there is, then miracles are not only possible, but to be expected. It is the blatant denial of God that leads people to deny the possibility of miracles. To take it one step further, if miraculous events do occur, then they offer an incredible amount of proof that there actually is a God.[39]

It should also be noted that Jesus worked miracles mostly in front of many people, without the benefit of a stage, lights, and emotional music, as seen in the services of various self-proclaimed healers of our own day. Indeed, Jesus healed all types of diseases, many that were visible to the eye, so that the validity of the miracle could not be questioned.

> On another Sabbath, he entered the synagogue and was teach-ing, and a man was there whose right hand was withered... And after looking around at them all he said to him, "Stretch out your hand." And he did so, and his hand was restored. (Luke 6:6, 10)

Modern day "healers" who are interested in manipulating people for financial gain and in order to acquire personal prestige, do not do things like this! They prefer to "heal" people of invisible diseases like headaches or backaches or the like. But this man had a visibly deformed hand that was restored before the eyes of many witnesses, some of whom were the enemies of Jesus. Even these enemies did not deny that Jesus was actually performing miracles, since this was undeniable. Instead, they attributed his work to the power of demons (Matthew 9:34).

This fact lends a great deal of historical credibility to the reality that Jesus of Nazareth was known as a miracle worker. If a person's enemies admit that the miraculous is happening, even if they do not believe it is coming by the power of God, then the chances are much greater that the Bible is recounting factual history, and not just the thoughts and theology of Jesus' friends and followers.

THE PROOF OF THE RESURRECTION

But of all the miracles of Christ, one of them stands out above the rest – he returned from the dead. People don't usually come back from the dead. If they did, we would all freak out.

I (Jason) remember my brother renting the movie *Return of the Living Dead* when we were kids. I do not suggest you watch it, nor would I ever recommend it. It isn't exactly edifying art. It portrays zombies who return to life because of exposure to a particular gas. The zombies are not happy at all, nor do they make the "living" people very happy. Flicks like this do not paint resurrection in a good light.

Interestingly, the Jews during Jesus' day would have thought even less of the idea of resurrection. They considered dead bodies "unclean" (Numbers 9:7). The thought of a man back from the dead would not have been very appealing to them. Paul says that for this reason the resurrection is a "stumbling block to the Jews" (1 Corinthians 1:23).

In spite of this, Paul maintains that the resurrection of Jesus Christ was and is a reality. Of greater importance, the resurrection is the proof that Jesus is who he says he is. "[Jesus] was declared to be the Son of God...by his resurrection from the dead" (Romans 1:4). The fact that Jesus conquered death is the principal proof that he is the One who has the power over death. When the disciples saw that Jesus had returned from the dead, all of their doubts quickly disappeared.

This is why John the Apostle referred to Jesus as the "Word" and wrote, "In the beginning was the Word, and the Word was with God, and the Word was God" (John 1:1). By rising from the dead, Jesus proved beyond all question himself to be the Son of the living God.

This point is so important that we have devoted the entire next chapter to examining the evidence for the resurrection of Jesus Christ. There we hope to show just how incredible it is that Jesus rose from the dead and why it is reasonable to believe that he did.

JESUS IS GOD

The amazing conclusion of Christ's proofs for his divinity is the reality that he is actually God in the flesh. This is a worldview-altering fact. Since he is God, everything he said was true. He said the Bible was true and indeed it is.[40] He said salvation comes by grace alone through faith in him alone and indeed it does.[41]

If he is God then our lives have meaning and purpose. We were created to bring honor and glory to God forever by seeing him as the eternal treasure that he is, and enjoying what we see (Psalm 16:11; John 17:13). Christianity is not about having a checklist of spiritual duties like Bible study, prayer, and church attendance, and going through the motions of those religious activities. Yes, those disciplines of grace are vital to Christian life and growth, but the heart of the Christian faith is a Person who is God in the flesh (John 1:14).

He came down from Heaven to give us the answers that we so desperately need. He proved that he was indeed God and therefore has the right to speak with authority. When we worship, we do not worship an idea or a concept. We worship him, a real Person who supplies us with all we will ever need.

Why are we Christians? Because Jesus, the most amazing man who ever lived, who claimed and demonstrated his divinity, instructed us to be Christians. And though we may not be able to have all the answers we want here and now, we trust him. He is a lot smarter than we are.

Come to me, all who labor and are heavy laden, and I will give you rest. Take my yoke upon you, and learn from me, for I am gentle and lowly in heart, and you will find rest for your souls. (Matthew 11:28-30)

Chapter 3 Review Exercise

1. What is the difference between *knowing* Christianity is true and *showing* Christianity is true?
2. What is the difference between blind faith and reasonable faith?

3. Name at least four ancient sources outside the Bible that provide clear evidence for the existence of Jesus.
4. Why should people listen to those who claim to either be God or speak for God?
5. What were some of the ways Jesus openly claimed to be God?
6. List three ways Jesus proved that he is God?
7. If Jesus is God, what does this mean for other religions like Islam and Hinduism? Why?

Key Terms

Jesus-myth hypothesis
Prophecy
Messiah
Proof

Scripture Memory

Jesus said to them, "Truly, truly, I say to you, before Abraham was, I am." So they picked up stones to throw at him, but Jesus hid himself and went out of the temple. (John 8:58-59)

CHAPTER 4:
Back from the Dead

As Christians, everything we believe hinges on Jesus and what he did. Even more specifically, it all hinges on one climactic event – his resurrection from the dead. If Jesus did not rise again, we should tear down all the churches in the world because Christianity is not true. We should go skiing on Sundays or perhaps fishing or maybe just sleep in. But whatever we do, if the resurrection did not *actually* happen, we should NOT waste time by going to church or pretending to worship.

It is his resurrection that is the primary proof that he is God and that everything he said was true. The Apostle Paul understood this when he wrote the following: "If Christ is not risen, then our preaching is empty and your faith is also empty...And if Christ is not risen, your faith is futile; you are still in your sins!" (1 Corinthians 15:14; 17).

The words "empty" and "futile" in these verses show us just how important the resurrection of Jesus really is. Without it, Christian preaching is empty and Christian faith is futile. They are like soap bubbles, soon to pop and disappear altogether.

So there is a lot that depends on the resurrection. The entire Christian faith is on the line! To be a Christian means to believe what seems to be impossible: that Jesus *actually* died, was buried in a tomb, and after three days physically came back to life. In this chapter, we present several lines of evidence that demonstrate that the resurrection event actually happened.

OLD TESTAMENT PREDICTIONS

The Old Testament predicted that Jesus Christ would come, that he would be a great teacher, that he would die, and that he would rise again. That's a very big deal because the Old Testament is just that – old! It was written hundreds of years before Jesus was born and yet it predicts events in his life in precise detail.

For example, we read the words, "My God, my God, why have you forsaken me? Why are you so far from saving me, from the words of my groaning?" (Psalm 22:1). These are the very words Jesus uttered as he was dying upon the cross.[42] When Jesus spoke these words, he was not merely speaking random thoughts, but rather showing the world that Psalm 22 is an incredible, direct prophecy of his crucifixion. A few verses later we read this:

> But I am a worm and not a man, scorned by mankind and despised by the people. All who see me mock me; they make mouths at me; they wag their heads; "He trusts in the LORD; let him deliver him; let him rescue him, for he delights in him!" (Psalm 22:6-8)

This is Jesus talking, even though these words were written approximately one thousand years before he was born! This is how he felt upon the cross as he was being ridiculed by the Jewish leaders, as detailed by the Gospel of Mark:

So also the chief priests with the scribes mocked him to one another, saying, "He saved others; he cannot save himself. Let the Christ, the King of Israel, come down now from the cross that we may see and believe." (Mark 15:31-32)

The mockery and derision against Christ grows even more intense as the next section in the ancient Psalm reveals:

For dogs encompass me; a company of evildoers encircles me; they have pierced my hands and feet – I can count all my bones – they stare and gloat over me; they divide my garments among them, and for my clothing they cast lots. (Psalm 22:16-18)

The "dogs" of this passage refer to the Roman soldiers who tortured and crucified Jesus. Jewish people often referred to Gentiles as dogs, which they viewed as unclean animals.[43] Jesus felt these evildoers surrounding him and inflicting him with tremendous pain (Mark 15:15-20). These are things that Jesus could not have faked since it is impossible to plan one's own crucifixion in such detail that the soldiers who carry out the execution gamble ("cast lots") over your clothes (Luke 23:34)!

The prophecies of Psalm 22:16 also indicate that when the Messiah was killed, it would be through a piercing of his "hands and feet." Amazingly, King David made a prophecy about crucifixion, probably not even realizing what is involved in crucifixion. He predicted that the Messiah would be pierced, but surely David himself could not fully understand what that meant. Of course he did not have to fully understand it, since it was God who was superintending this entire process.

Psalm 22 also states that the Messiah would have no bones broken, another fact that the Gospel accounts confirm: "For these things took place that the Scripture might be fulfilled: 'Not one of his bones will be broken'" (John 19:36).

73

BEYOND THE GRAVE

As you read deeper into Psalm 22, you see that death is not the end of the story for this anointed One.

> But you, O LORD, do not be far off! O you my help, come quickly to my aid! Deliver my soul from the sword, my precious life from the power of the dog! Save me from the mouth of the lion! You have rescued me from the horns of the wild oxen! I will tell of your name to my brothers; in the midst of the congregation I will praise you. (Psalm 22:19-22)

These are not the words of a person who plans on staying in the grave. Notice the last statement, "In the midst of the congregation I will praise you." That is future tense! "After I am tortured and ridiculed and crucified, I will praise you!" Jesus plans on more than just death. He plans on a future *after* death.

In Psalm 16, Christ's resurrection is spoken of as well. In Peter's famous Pentecost sermon in Acts, he quotes directly from this ancient Psalm of David:

> For you will not abandon my soul to Hades, or let your Holy One see corruption. You have made known to me the paths of life; you will make me full of gladness with your presence. (Acts 2:27-28)

Peter later spells it out for his listeners, interpreting David's words as an incredible prophecy of the resurrection of Christ. "[David] foresaw and spoke about the resurrection of Christ, that he was not abandoned to Hades, nor did his flesh see corruption" (Acts 2:31).

Peter wanted to make it clear that this was no simple coincidence; that he was not just reading Christ's resurrection into an Old Testament passage. David really was talking about Jesus rising from the dead,

74

even though David lived around a thousand years before Jesus was born!

This point is made even clearer by the prophet who became a meal for a large marine creature. Jonah is more than a story about a guy who was swallowed and vomited by a big fish. Remember how long Jonah was in the fish's belly? "And the LORD appointed a great fish to swallow up Jonah. And Jonah was in the belly of the fish three days and three nights" (Jonah 1:17).

Okay, big deal. He was in the belly of the fish for three days and three nights. But look at what Jesus says about this.

> An evil and adulterous generation seeks for a sign, but no sign will be given to it except the sign of the prophet Jonah. For just as Jonah was three days and three nights in the belly of the great fish, so will the Son of Man be three days and three nights in the heart of the earth. (Matthew 12:39-40)

Amazingly, the story of Jonah is a prophecy of the resurrection of Jesus Christ! The Old Testament overflows with these types of prophecies. Check this one out:

> Yet it was the will of the LORD to crush him; he has put him to grief; when his soul makes an offering for sin, he shall see his offspring; he shall prolong his days; the will of the LORD shall prosper in his hand. (Isaiah 53:10)

It was the "will of the LORD," that is, God the Father, to "crush" Jesus Christ the Son. This is the only way God could be just and justify sinners at the same time (Romans 3:26). The Father crushed the Son in order to redeem guilty sinners for his glory.

But notice the rest of the verse: "He shall see his offspring." What offspring? The offspring is referring to God's children, adopted into his family and saved by his grace. If you are in Christ you are a child of God. He (Jesus) will *see* his offspring. But how will he see his off-spring if he is dead? How will his days be prolonged if he is crushed by the Father? Of course the answer is resurrection. He will be crushed but he will live!

One more verse to prove the point that the Old Testament thoroughly predicted the resurrection of Jesus.

> And I will pour out on the house of David and the inhabitants of Jerusalem a spirit of grace and pleas for mercy, so that, when they look on me, *on him whom they have pierced*, they shall mourn for him, as one mourns for an only child, and weep bitterly over him, as one weeps over a firstborn. (Zechariah 12:10, italics ours)

This is actually a prediction of the *second coming* of Christ. When he comes, people will mourn because of their refusal to trust him. But notice that they will look on the one "whom they have pierced." In other words, people will see the same Jesus who was crucified and killed. In order to see a person who was killed, that person has to rise again from the dead!

Jesus did not simply spring up from out of nowhere on the pages of history and say, "Hey everybody, I'm God." Rather, he personally fulfilled hundreds of ancient prophecies written about him, including his resurrection from the dead. This substantiated his claim to be God.

In order for the resurrection to have been a hoax or a fake, Jesus would have had to plan some things that he had no control over – like his death by crucifixion and the actions of the Roman soldiers and the Jewish leaders. This is impossible unless God was controlling all of the events, and fulfilled prophecy is mighty powerful evidence that he was.

EYEWITNESS TESTIMONY

I (Jason) once served an intriguing week of jury duty. I was elected as the jury foreman in the criminal trial of a man charged with multiple armed robberies. We listened carefully as the witnesses were brought into the courtroom one after the other. We were informed by the judge and attorneys that the witnesses were not allowed to speak with each other before they testified, assuring they could not share their stories.

One store owner angrily identified the defendant with a pointed finger, as the man who stole several hundred dollars from him. The security camera in his store provided an unclear, grainy picture of the gunman, but even though his face was obscured, the assailant in the photograph shared many similarities with the defendant sitting in the courtroom.

Next, the clerk of a check cashing business, wiping her tears as she spoke, recounted to the jury her story. She said that the defendant, whom she also pointed out in the courtroom, had held her at gun-point and sprayed a mace-like substance in her face as he fled with the money.

Other witnesses were also questioned, confirming to one degree or the other that the defendant was guilty. When the trial was over and the jury gathered to make our decision, it did not take long for us to agree upon the verdict. Because of the testimony of several independent, eyewitnesses, this guilty man will be sitting in jail for a long time. Such is the power of eyewitness testimony.

If a number of independent sources inform us that they saw Jesus alive after his death, then this provides solid evidence that he rose from the dead. Paul wrote about this reality to people who were skeptical regarding the resurrection:

> For I delivered to you as of first importance what I also re-
> ceived: that Christ died for our sins in accordance with the

Scriptures, that he was buried, that he was raised on the third
day in accordance with the Scriptures, and that he appeared to
Cephas, then to the twelve. (1 Corinthians 15:3-5)

Paul states that Jesus "appeared" to Cephas (Peter) and also "to the
twelve," meaning the twelve disciples. In other words, they saw him,
spoke with him, and ate with him *after* he had been put to death (John
21:1-14).

But these men were not the only ones to see him. He also appeared
to Mary Magdalene and other women who had come to the tomb on
the first Easter morning (Luke 24:10). Here are at least fifteen people
all making the same claim – that Jesus was alive. Imagine if Peter was
the *only person* who claimed to have seen Jesus alive. We would then
have reason to seriously doubt that Jesus actually rose from the dead.

If one person came and told you he saw a flying saucer land in
his backyard, you probably would not believe him. In fact, you might
think his chair had fallen clear off its rocker. You'd suspect he lives on
the outskirts of left field. But if fifteen different people came, one after
the other, and told you about the flying saucer, you would be more
prone to take seriously what they were saying. The greater amount
of independent eyewitness testimony, the more assurance we have to
believe that something is true.

At least fifteen people all claimed that they saw him alive after
he had died! But there is more. Paul recounts that Jesus "appeared
to more than five hundred brothers at one time, most of whom are
still alive, though some have fallen asleep" (1 Corinthians 15:6). What
an incredible verse! When Paul wrote this he knew that many people
would find it hard to believe that Jesus had actually come back from
the dead. So he points out that not only fifteen or so people had seen
Jesus, but on one occasion he appeared to over five hundred people,
all at the same time!

Paul challenges skeptics to ask those witnesses about the resurrected Christ. He says that many of them "are still alive" and this evi-

dence can be verified by interviewing them. Of course, in the present day, all of those five hundred witnesses are now dead. We cannot question them like people could in Paul's day. But here is the point: Paul would not have written those words in his day, challenging people to interview witnesses, unless he actually believed Jesus had risen from the dead. Put yourself in Paul's shoes and think about it. He was laying the Christian faith on the line with this challenge. He was opening the door for skeptics to prove him wrong if they could. That says a lot! And he goes even further: "Then he appeared to James, then to all the apostles. Last of all, as to one untimely born, he appeared also to me" (1 Corinthians 15:7-8).

Paul points out that he too had seen Jesus Christ face-to-face after Jesus had been crucified. Remember, Paul was not always a Christian. In fact, the book of Acts tells us that Paul hated Christians and sought to kill them. He was on his way to a town called Damascus in order to throw some of the Christians there into prison when something astounding happened. Jesus Christ showed up!

Now as he went on his way, he approached Damascus, and suddenly a light from heaven flashed around him. And falling to the ground he heard a voice saying to him, "Saul, Saul, why are you persecuting me?" And he said, "Who are you, Lord?" And he said, "I am Jesus, whom you are persecuting." (Acts 9:3-5)

So Paul also saw the resurrected Savior. We cannot see Jesus today (yet), but hundreds of people saw him back then. All of these people claimed the same thing – Jesus is alive. They verified it personally. Did they all lie? Where they all deceived? We don't think so. The number and diversity of independent eye-witnesses is overwhelming, especially considering that belief in the resurrection of Christ often led to severe persecution in their day. In that type of environment most people would not say they believed the resurrection, unless they actually did, since this belief often led to severe suffering or death.

THE ACTIONS OF THE GUARDS

Another line of evidence pointing to the actual resurrection of Jesus involves the Roman guards who sealed the tomb and were commanded to guard it. The seal involved a cord that would have been stretched across the outside of the tomb, and sealed with wax on both sides. The purpose of this sealing was to show that the tomb was under the official protection of the Roman government and to ward off vandals. The tomb was protected with maximum security. "Pilate said to them, 'You have a guard of soldiers. Go, make it as secure as you can.' So they went and made the tomb secure by sealing the stone and setting a guard" (Matthew 27:65-66).

It is very important to note that Matthew wrote his Gospel when there were people still alive who could have verified the setting of this guard and the Roman seal. When a Roman guard was given an assignment, these trained killers took their jobs seriously. If they failed in their tasks, they often were threatened with death! This becomes clear in the biblical text.

> While they were going, behold, some of the guard went into the city and told the chief priests all that had taken place. And when they had assembled with the elders and taken counsel, they gave a sufficient sum of money to the soldiers and said, "Tell people, 'His disciples came by night and stole him away while we were asleep.' And if this comes to the governor's ears, we will satisfy him and keep you out of trouble." So they took the money and did as they were directed. And this story has been spread among the Jews to this day. (Matthew 28:11-15)

The Pharisees made a bargain with the soldiers after the body came up missing, offering to protect the soldiers from Pilate. All they had to do was lie and say they fell asleep while guarding the tomb. The Pharisees and the soldiers both knew that if Pilate found out that the body of Jesus was missing, the poor soldiers would probably be put to death.

The Pharisees were trying to minimize the damage done by the missing body of Jesus. But they could not cover up the story even though they bribed the Roman guards to lie. If the tomb were sealed and guarded by the Romans, then it is clear the disciples did not take the body of Jesus. They could not have breached this type of protection. Something else had to happen – something extraordinary.

EMPTY TOMB

Another line of evidence supporting the actual and physical resurrection of Jesus Christ is the empty tomb. He was buried in a tomb, but after he was buried, that tomb was empty!

But how do we know the tomb actually was empty? None of us were alive back then. None of us went to the tomb to check and see if it was really empty. Today we do not know exactly where the tomb of Jesus was located, so we still have no way to know that the tomb was really empty. Right?

Not so fast. Actually, we can make some powerful, logical deductions showing that the tomb was actually empty. Think for a moment. What happened in Jerusalem fifty days after Jesus rose from the dead? It was the day of Pentecost. The Apostle Peter preached a powerful sermon then, the same one mentioned earlier in this chapter. Here is another part of it:

Men of Israel, hear these words: Jesus of Nazareth, a man attested to you by God with mighty works and wonders and

signs that God did through him in your midst, as you yourselves know – this Jesus, delivered up according to the definite plan and foreknowledge of God, you crucified and killed
by the hands of lawless men. God raised him up, loosing the
pangs of death, because it was not possible for him to be held
by it. (Acts 2:22-24)

What is it that Peter is preaching in front of thousands of people in
Jerusalem on Pentecost? It is the resurrection of Jesus Christ! "God
raised him up!" That is the central message of the sermon.

Now if I were in Jerusalem and heard Peter preach that message, but I was skeptical about the resurrection of Christ (after all,
I have never seen anybody come back from the dead), what could I
do to prove Peter wrong? How could I show the world that this crazy
preacher was saying things that are impossible?

Well, obviously, I would go to the tomb of Jesus and pull out the
body and show it to everyone. Peter's message would then be immediately dismissed. Remember, the tomb was located in Jerusalem, the
very place where Peter was preaching this message. Plus, the tomb belonged to a well known Jewish leader, Joseph of Arimathea (Matthew
27:57-58). In other words, the tomb was not obscure or hidden, but
rather it belonged to a familiar man, and people would have been
aware of its location. If Jesus' body was *in* the tomb, then his body no
doubt could have been produced. *But his body was not produced.* He
was not in the tomb.

So here we have strong evidence that the tomb was indeed empty.
The question still remains – how did it become empty? We know that
the disciples could not have stolen the body, because the Roman guard
was there and the tomb was sealed. We also know that the Jewish leaders would not have stolen the body. That would have worked against
them. They were trying to get rid of Jesus, not promote a resurrection
idea. If they had the body hidden (so that the disciples would not steal
it perhaps), then they could have produced the body when Peter was

preaching on Pentecost in order to squelch the growth of the early church. They did not do this, because they did not have the body.

So how did the tomb become empty? Are you starting to see how all the evidence points to the actual resurrection of Jesus Christ from the dead? When we take all the information together, the resurrection makes more sense than any other alternative.

Now an unbeliever will probably not be convinced by all of this evidence. This is because he has already decided that people *cannot* come back from the dead under any circumstances. So even though all the evidence points to the resurrection of Christ he will still not believe it, because in his mind it is impossible.

But think about it. Sure, people do not *normally* come back from the dead. We can all agree on that. But if we have good reason to believe that there is a God and that he is the God of the Bible (and we do), then the idea of resurrection is not so hard to conceive. If God is the giver and taker of life, then he can give and take life as he pleases. If there is a God, then the possibility of resurrection is not only likely, but highly probable. And there is even more evidence pointing toward the actual resurrection of Jesus Christ. Keep reading.

LARGE STONE MOVED

Historians and archeologists know quite a bit about Jewish burial practices in Jesus' day. Tombs were commonplace and large stones were rolled in front of them. These stones were designed to move back and forth so that others could be buried in the tomb, usually other family members. But it was not easy to move these enormous and heavy stones. Some suggest that the stone covering Jesus' tomb weighed one to two tons and would have required several men to move.

If this is true then it leads to several conclusions. First, the women who came to the tomb in order to anoint the body of Jesus could not have moved it by themselves. This was indeed a major concern for them, as Mark points out: "They were saying to one another, 'Who will roll away the stone for us from the entrance of the tomb?'" (Mark 16:3). Even if they could have moved the stone on their own, remember the Roman guard was stationed there to be sure there was no stealing of the body.

As it turns out, they did not have a problem with the stone at all. The Bible makes it clear that when the women arrived at the tomb, the stone was already moved away and the Roman guard had already left the scene. The Roman soldiers would never have fled the scene like this without good reason. In fact, as we have already seen, their lives depended upon them succeeding in their tasks. Something big must have happened! The Gospel of Matthew tells us what this "something big" was.

> And behold, there was a great earthquake, for an angel of the Lord descended from heaven and came and *rolled back the stone* and sat on it. His appearance was like lightning, and his clothing white as snow. And for fear of him the guards trembled and became like dead men. (Matthew 28:2-4, italics ours)

The movement of this large stone also shows that Jesus' disciples could not have taken the body. They might have been physically able to move the stone, but they could not have done it with the Roman guard there. Even if the guard had fallen asleep, the noise involved in moving the stone would have awakened them. Besides that, it is unlikely that all the guards would have fallen asleep since it was their job to be guarding the tomb!

Our knowledge of this giant stone in the mouth of the tomb is another powerful line of evidence that shows the resurrection of Christ makes more sense of the data than any other scenario.

WOMEN SAW HIM FIRST

Historians speak of the *criteria of embarrassment* which raises the credibility of historical documents. If a historical document includes embarrassing statements it is more likely to be true, since manufactured stories usually attempt to make the heroes look as good as possible. Scholars Gary Habermas and Mike Licona explain, "An indicator that an event or saying is authentic occurs when the source would not be expected to create the story, because it embarrasses his cause."[44]

As we read the Gospel accounts of the resurrection we find a major case of the criteria of embarrassment. In fact, considering that cultural context, it is startling to find that Jesus' male disciples did not find the tomb empty first. Nor did they see Jesus alive first. The first people to have this honor were women (Luke 23:55).

Now there is nothing at all wrong with being a woman, but we have to put ourselves into their first-century sandals. According to Jewish principles of legal evidence, "women were lowly esteemed and their testimony was regarded as questionable, certainly not as credible as man's."[45] In other words, in a court of law the words of a woman were considered unreliable and might even damage a case. So what?

If a deceitful person or group of people were making up the story of the resurrection, which many skeptics say this is exactly what the disciples did, then would they have included in their story women finding the empty tomb first? Of course not!

If a person is contriving a tall tale in order to create and promote a religion for personal gain, he would want to make the story seem as convincing as possible. He would not want the *first witnesses* to be people whose witness did not count! If the resurrection accounts were manufactured in order to convince others that Jesus had come back from the dead, women would never be included in the story as the *first witnesses*.

The fact that women found the empty tomb first does not prove the resurrection of Christ by itself, but it does lend a great deal of historical credibility to the Gospel accounts. And when you take this fact with all the other evidences we've seen so far, the resurrection makes a lot of sense. Here's another fact to add to our list of reasons to believe Jesus actually came back from the dead.

COURAGE OF THE DISCIPLES AFTER THEY SAW HIM

Scholars and historians inform us that after the life of Jesus, the church grew at an astounding rate. In fact, within four hundred years, Christianity was adopted as the official state religion of the Roman Empire. That was incredibly rapid growth in a hostile environment! This type of growth would be very surprising if there had been no resurrection. Jesus' followers were unremitting preachers of his resurrection, and they paid a high price for their belief and public bravery. The Romans and Jews wanted them either silenced or dead.

After the crucifixion, the disciples were basically hiding out for fear of their lives. The cruel death of their Master had shaken them up pretty badly and understandably so. Jesus was their leader, the One they expected to deliver them from the Roman oppressors and restore Israel. Now he was dead! He was not the Messiah after all.

But several weeks later we see Peter and the other apostles no longer afraid. In fact, we see them laying their lives down in order to boldly preach that Jesus had risen from the dead. According to tradition, all of the disciples of Christ, with the exception of John, were martyred for their faith that Jesus had actually risen from the dead. In John's case, he was exiled to the island of Patmos (Revelation 1:9) as punishment for his tenacious and faithful preaching. All of these men were willing to sacrifice everything, including their very lives, because they believed that Jesus had truly risen from the dead.

What happened to change the disciples from a frightened and confused group who were hiding out for fear of their lives, to being radical and bold preachers of the gospel? The answer is clear – they were convinced that Jesus had risen from the dead and that they had seen him personally! How do we know? It is a psychological reality that people will generally not die for what they know to be a lie. They will not give up everything in order to promote a message that they know is false.

Let's be careful here because, yes, some people will die for a lie so long as they *believe it is true*. For example, militant Muslims often become suicide bombers, because they actually believe Allah will reward them for their "bravery." But if those same Muslims knew that Allah was a false god and that there was no reward for suicide bombing, then they would not go through with blowing themselves up. People do not die for what they *know is a lie*.

What is the point? If the disciples knew that the resurrection did not actually happen, then they would not have been willing to die for it. But they were willing to die for it. *All of them* were willing to die for it (not just one or two crazy lunatics). This tells us at the very least, that the disciples actually believed Jesus rose from the dead or they would not have preached so boldly in such a hostile environment. This evidence, taken in conjunction with everything else we have seen, points clearly to the reality of the resurrection.

No Contradictions in the Resurrection Accounts

Some people who deny that Jesus rose from the dead say that we cannot trust the Bible because it is filled with contradictions. The accounts in the four biblical Gospels about Jesus coming back to life are often attacked as being inconsistent with each other. If the four Gospels are all telling different stories, should we trust them?

However, a close look at these four accounts of the resurrection of Christ, comparing them with each other, will show them to all be entirely consistent. There are no contradictions between what Matthew, Mark, Luke, and John says about the resurrection.

Sure they read a little bit differently. But any time you have multiple authors, they are going to write in different styles, and focus on different points. That is not a problem at all. In fact, this proves that the Gospel writers were *not* teaming up to manufacture a false religion. The relevant question is, do the contents of the resurrection accounts mesh with each other or do they contradict each other? A fair reading of the texts shows that they mesh perfectly.

For example, the objection is often raised that Matthew, Mark, Luke, and John all disagree on the number and identification of the women who found the tomb empty. Here are the texts in question.

Now after the Sabbath, toward the dawn of the first day of the week, Mary Magdalene and the other Mary went to see the tomb. (Matthew 28:1)

When the Sabbath was past, Mary Magdalene and Mary the mother of James and Salome bought spices, so that they might go and anoint him. (Mark 16:1)

Now it was Mary Magdalene and Joanna and Mary the mother of James and the other women with them who told these things to the apostles. (Luke 24:10)

Now on the first day of the week Mary Magdalene came to the tomb early, while it was still dark, and saw that the stone had been taken away from the tomb. (John 20:1)

Outspoken atheist, Michael Martin, says that these accounts are hopelessly irreconcilable.[46] That means no matter how hard you try, you cannot make them fit together. He says they contradict and there is no way to make them mesh.

If Martin is right, then clearly we cannot trust the Bible. If it contradicts itself at any point then there is error in it. If there is error in it, then we cannot truly trust any part of it. But is he right? Are these four passages contradictory? Is Martin giving the text a fair reading?

Notice first of all that Mary Magdalene is mentioned in all four of the accounts. In fact, it seems clear that she is the main character in all the resurrection narratives, other than Jesus of course. John *only* mentions her and none of the other women that Matthew, Mark, and Luke mention. Does that mean that John contradicts Matthew, Mark, and Luke?

Of course not! Just because he does not include the other women in his version of the story does not mean they were not there. John has a special interest in focusing on Mary Magdalene and so he only mentions her. This is not lying, but rather an example of selective history. A story will show how selective history works.

THE SUNDAY SCHOOL PARTY

Becca went to a Sunday School party last night. There were thirty people at the party. While there Becca spent some time talking to Nick and Gerard. They had a long and enjoyable conversation about their ministry project coming up at Children's Hospital. Becca soon walked over to Sarah, who seemed to be crying.

"What's wrong?" Becca asked. Sarah told her that her dad had been diagnosed with cancer and her family was really struggling right now. So Becca spent the rest of the time at the party right beside Sarah, being a friend in a time of need.

After the party Becca went home. Her mom asked her, "How was the party?" Becca told her it went well. Her mom then asked, "What did you do?" Becca recounted to her mom the conversation with Sarah about her dad's illness and then the conversation ended.

But wait a minute, what about Nick and Gerard? Was Becca lying or being deceitful when she told her mom she talked to Sarah? After all, she talked to more people than just Sarah. Of course she wasn't lying or being deceitful. She was giving her mom a selective history. She was not giving all the details of the party, but just the ones she thought were important and relevant.

It is the same in the Gospel accounts of the resurrection. John only mentions the presence of Mary Magdalene, but that does not mean the other women mentioned by the other Gospel writers were not there! John does not see the need to list them out in his account. There is *no contradiction* here at all. There is just a difference in emphasis among the Gospel writers. As you read the Gospel accounts you will see this type of selective history all the way through, just as you will when you read two different news articles of the same event. So the objection that the resurrection could not have happened since the Gospels contradict is faulty and should be abandoned.

JESUS IS ALIVE

As we study all of these evidences for the resurrection of Jesus Christ, and take them all together as a group, it becomes amazingly clear that Jesus actually came back from the dead. All the other theories that people have considered look silly in the face of the evidence.

For example, some have suggested that the women went to the wrong tomb. They say it was still dark and the women were very emotional, so they simply went to the wrong place. They saw an empty tomb, but it was not the tomb Jesus had been buried in. They only *thought* Jesus had risen, so they went and told the disciples that he was alive. The disciples then began to preach that Jesus was resurrected, merely taking the word of the disoriented women.

But we know this could not have happened! John informs us that Peter and he checked out the tomb very carefully (John 20:3-9) and verified that it was empty. Plus the tomb was identified clearly as the tomb of Joseph of Arimathea, a well-known person during that time. The women were not going to some random tomb, but to a specific tomb.

In addition to this, if the women went to the wrong tomb, then the body of Jesus was still in the actual one. So when the disciples were preaching the resurrection, the Jewish leaders could have produced the body from the "real" tomb to disprove the disciples. But we know they did not do that.

Some who deny the resurrection suspect that the disciples had mass hallucinations. They so much wanted to believe that Jesus was alive that they worked themselves up into a high-pitched hysteria. In this atmosphere of hysteria, they "saw" Jesus in their midst. The skeptics say this explains why the disciples would be willing to die for their faith that Jesus came back from the dead. They believed they saw him, when in fact they did not.

This kind of theory is ridiculous in the face of the evidence. The Bible tells us that Jesus appeared to different people in different places. It does not say there was just one appearance, but we read this in the book of Acts: "To them he presented himself alive after his suffering by many proofs, appearing to them during forty days and speaking about the kingdom of God" (Acts 1:3).

Luke (who wrote Acts) makes it clear that Jesus gave "many proofs" that he was alive. Plus, if the disciples simply had mass hallucinations, then (again) when Peter was preaching on Pentecost the body of Jesus could have been produced to disprove his claim that Jesus came back from the dead. These facts deny the possibility of the mass hallucination theory.

THE BEST EXPLANATION OF THE FACTS

Given these clear historical evidences and the trustworthy nature of the Bible, it is totally reasonable to believe that Jesus actually rose from the dead. Perhaps even more reasonable than the belief that LeBron James can do a three-sixty! In fact, it is by far the best explanation of the facts.

Though it seems strange to us that a resurrection might have actually happened (since we do not normally see people come out of their graves), the resurrection of Jesus nonetheless makes more sense of the data than any alternative explanation.

Of course, if Jesus did rise from the dead, then everything he said was true! His resurrection authenticates his words. The Bible is true, God exists, Heaven is real, Hell is real, and salvation is possible through Christ. If you have never come to this risen Savior to experience his life-giving grace, we encourage you to set aside your pride and rebellion and bow your knee to the living King.

The Spirit and the Bride say, "Come." And let the one who hears say, "Come." And let the one who is thirsty come; let the one who desires take the water of life without price. (Revelation 22:17)

Chapter 4 Review Exercise

1. Skeptics find it difficult to believe Jesus rose from the dead. Why?
2. If God exists, as we have good reasons to believe, is the resurrection of Christ difficult to believe? Why or why not?
3. List five evidences that Jesus actually rose from the dead.
4. Why is eye-witness testimony such a strong line of evidence for the resurrection of Christ?

5. What is significant about the fact that women found the empty tomb first?

6. History tells us that Jesus' disciples became very courageous about preaching the resurrection, even though they faced death for it. What are some possible explanations for this fact and what is the best explanation?

Key Terms

Pharisees
Crucifixion
Mass hallucination theory
Pentecost
Joseph of Arimathea

Scripture Memory

Men of Israel, hear these words: Jesus of Nazareth, a man attested to you by God with mighty works and wonders and signs that God did through him in your midst, as you yourselves know- this Jesus, delivered up according to the definite plan and foreknowledge of God, you crucified and killed by the hands of lawless men. God raised him up, loosing the pangs of death, because it was not possible for him to be held by it. (Acts 2:22-24)

Chapter 5:
A Book Sent from God

I (Jason) remember as a child spending lots of time thinking about the Bible. My family had one of those huge family Bibles with a black leather cover. It had a unique scent that my nose will never forget. I was not very interested in the words back then, especially since I couldn't understand King James English, but there were several collections of paintings in that Bible that caught my eye. I spent considerable time staring at them, trying to figure them out: Daniel in the lion's den, Jonah being swallowed by the giant fish, the Nativity scene, Herod slaughtering the babies in Bethlehem, Jesus on the cross, and then alive from the dead.

I did not realize at the time just how much of an impression those paintings would have on me. I can still visualize them in accurate detail. The stories of the Bible are captivating. They reveal the very heart of God and the things that he desires. They are a mirror for our souls, showing us who and what we really are. But not everyone thinks so.

An internet search on "errors in the Bible" tells a different story. Many people consider the Bible to be nothing more than a man-

manufactured collection of religious thoughts. Far from revealing the heart of God, it is alleged that the Bible is full of contradictions and errors and, therefore, cannot and should not be trusted. The Bible Babble website, for example, holds an extremely negative view of the Scriptures:

> There are a great many errors, contradictions, and misrepresentations as far as the scientific accuracy of the Bible. The stories are often jumbled and don't match the other books. Worst of all it justifies a great deal of negative things in society such as gay bashings and abusing women and children.[47]

Or for a more sophisticated – and smug – negative assessment of the Bible, consider the words of aggressive atheist, Sam Harris:

> The Bible, it seems certain, was the work of sand-strewn men and women who thought the earth was flat and for whom a wheelbarrow would have been a breathtaking example of emerging technology. To rely on such a document as the basis for our worldview…is to repudiate two thousand years of civilizing insights.[48]

Other people take a less severe approach. The Bible (or at least some of it) is from God, yet there are still errors in the text itself, they will say. Of course if these folks are right and the Bible cannot be trusted, then the Christian faith topples.

The Bible is our source of authority and truth. It is the foundation upon which Christians base all of their beliefs and practices. It is the lens through which we view the world for the glory of God. But why should *you* trust the Bible and believe that it is true? The goal of this chapter is to answer that question.

Hopefully, if you are a Christian, you will see that there are very good reasons for your belief that the Bible is truly breathed out by God himself, and that your faith in him will be strengthened as a result. If you are not a Christian, we hope you are challenged by the power of the life-changing Bible, to consider your eternal destiny in light of the revealed word of God.

So why should you trust the Bible and believe it is true?

The Biblical Authors Say the Bible Is from God

The first reason to believe that the Bible is from God is because the Bible *says* it is from God. "The sum of your word is truth, and every one of your righteous rules endures forever" (Psalm 119:16). This same teaching is repeated by Paul in the New Testament:

All Scripture is breathed out by God and profitable for teaching, for reproof, for correction, and for training in righteousness, that the man of God may be competent, equipped for every good work. (2 Timothy 3:16-17)

These are just two of many passages that say essentially the same thing: God's word is *from God*. The written declarations of God, through his prophets and apostles, are nothing short of divine and holy words from God himself.

Someone will object, however, and say that this is circular reasoning. "You cannot use the Bible in order to support the Bible!" This is like a person saying "I am the president of the United States and I can prove it by simply saying 'I am the president of the United States.'" Just because a person says it does not automatically make it true. Now he might be justified in believing he is the president if there is some external evidence that verifies his claim, like the fact that he lives in the White House or regularly meets with world leaders. But in the absence of such external evidence, his mere claim is not enough.

Likewise, just because the Bible says it is from God does not mean it *actually is* from God. There must be some evidence *outside* the Bible to show that it is trustworthy. And we will be looking at many outside evidences in this chapter and in the next that serve to validate the Bible. But first, is this really an example of circular reasoning? Or is it legitimate for the Bible to support the Bible?

One of the problems with the *circular-reasoning objection* is that it assumes the Bible is merely one book. Yes, it is one *volume,* but it is actually composed of many different books, written by different authors, over a long span of time.

For example, the writer of Psalm 119 did not write 2 Timothy 3. These verses come from the pens of two different people, both of them agreeing on the nature of God's word. It would be different if the Bible were written by only one person.[49] Then the objection that this is circular reasoning might stand. But the Bible was not written by one person and thus the objection fails.

Rather than saying the Bible tells us the Bible is trustworthy, it would be clearer to say that the various individual authors of the Bible tell us that all of God's words are trustworthy. Look at this incredible list.

Moses tells us the Bible is trustworthy:

If you say in your heart, 'How may we know the word that the LORD has not spoken?' – when a prophet speaks in the name of the LORD, if the word does not come to pass or come true, that is a word that the LORD has not spoken; the prophet has spoken it presumptuously. You need not be afraid of him. (Deuteronomy 18:21-22)

David tells us the Bible is trustworthy. "This God – his way is perfect; the word of the LORD proves true; he is a shield for all those who take refuge in him" (Psalm 18:30).

The author of Psalm 119 spends 176 verses telling us the Bible is trustworthy. Verse 160 was quoted above and here are further examples: "Forever, O LORD, your word is firmly fixed in the heavens...But you are near, O LORD, and all your commandments are true" (Psalm 119:89; 151).

Isaiah tells us the Bible is trustworthy: "The grass withers, the flower fades, but the word of our God will stand forever" (Isaiah 40:8; repeated in 1 Peter 1:24-25).

Paul tells us the Bible is trustworthy:

We also thank God constantly for this, that when you received the word of God, which you heard from us, you accepted it not as the word of men but as what it really is, the word of God, which is at work in you believers. (1 Thessalonians 2:13)

And yes, Jesus Christ the Lord also tells us the Bible is trustworthy:

Do not think that I have come to abolish the Law or the Prophets; I have not come to abolish them but to fulfill them. For truly, I say to you, until heaven and earth pass away, not an iota, not a dot, will pass from the Law until all is accomplished. (Matthew 5:17-18)

Sanctify them in the truth; your word is truth. (John 17:17)

All of these individuals and many others, whose words are collected in the Bible, testify that we can trust the Bible. Because these are *individual* authors writing at different times and places, the charge of circular reasoning is drastically weakened.

God wants us to see that these writings can be trusted, so he tells us through these various authors, time and time again, that we can have confidence that the Bible really is the word of God. But this is not the only reason to trust the Bible.

THE BIBLE IS INCREDIBLY UNIFIED

The content and flow of the Biblical narrative is stunning. As you read it, it presents an atmosphere of divine authority. It comes across as though it is from God himself.

Browsing through former president Ronald Reagan's letters give us a sense of how certain writings create an authoritative and majestic atmosphere. Reagan, who was considered a larger-than-life figure in American politics, was a prolific letter writer, and his correspondences are studied at length in an effort to understand the man and his policies. His words come off the page with a presidential quality and an innate sense of authority. They are not ordinary words because they are not coming from an ordinary person.[50]

Likewise, the Bible has a divine edge to it, an extraordinary sense of authority and power. If you have never read it, here's some important advice – drop this book and find your Bible! The book you are reading does not even begin to compare with the power and truth of the word of God.

But how is this divine edge seen? In what ways can we tell the Bible is from God? The most obvious way is seen in its incredible unity. In many respects the Bible reads like a good novel and follows the story-telling pattern of the best movies. It has an introduction (Genesis), rising action (Exodus-Malachi), climax (the Gospels), falling action (the Epistles), and a conclusion (Revelation). These sections are intertwined and connected by strands of themes that run throughout each of them. Respected Bible scholar F.F. Bruce confirmed this fact when he wrote, "The Bible is not simply an anthology; there is a unity which binds the whole together."[51]

As you read, it becomes clear that every book within it is telling *only* one story. Malachi and Mark, Exodus and Ephesians, Jonah and John are all telling the same story; the story of the Messiah. The Bible has one main character, Jesus Christ, who is the central focus. His work of redemption, to the glory and honor of God the Father, is the central theme. The Bible has a striking unity to it. But what is the big deal about that? How does this give the sense that the Bible is from God and speaks with divine authority?

Consider this reality. The Bible was written over a span of more than 1,500 years. That is a long, long time. Most of us only live into our seventies or eighties and a few of us make it to one hundred. So when we speak of 1,500 years, we are talking about many generations, spanning from the days of Job and Moses to the days of John and Paul.

A lot of things change over 1,500 years. Cultures and ideas change. Religions and languages change. In spite of these drastic transformations, the Bible still remains incredibly unified!

For example, even though Genesis is much older than Revelation, when you read them side by side, it is clear that they are telling the *same* story and they are united in their common theme. They both speak of the same God, Jesus Christ (the seed of the woman in Genesis 3:15), the Holy Spirit, Satan, the serpent and the dragon, and the Tree of Life. They both speak of the blessings of obedience and the way to life. They also both speak of the curse of disobedience and its detrimental result which is death. Both books speak of all these themes in exactly the same way. And every book between Genesis and Revelation demonstrates the same connections. This type of unity, over that period of time, seems highly unlikely (even impossible) without the divine hand of providence guiding the process.

The Bible also boasts a multiplicity of authors. Over forty God-called men took part in the writing process, including Moses, David, Solomon, Isaiah, Amos, Micah, Matthew, Luke, John, and Paul, who all lived at different times and in different places. These men came from different cultures and classes, possessed different educational levels, and worked in different occupations. David and Solomon were wealthy kings, Amos was a farmer, Matthew was a despised tax collector, Luke was a Gentile physician, and Paul was a well-educated and legalistic Pharisee. And on we could go.

In addition to their background and occupational differences, the biblical authors were also motivated by vastly different reasons in the writing of their respective books. For example, Moses had certain reasons for writing Deuteronomy that are different reasons than John had for writing I John. Matthew's account of the life of Christ was designed for a Jewish audience while Mark's was originally intended for Gentiles.

But in spite of all these differences between the authors and the times in which they lived, the singular theme and striking unity of the Bible still comes shining through. And there are no internal inconsistencies or contradictions in the Bible. All of this is amazing! If you put ten people in a room and told them to discuss a topic (let's say global warming) the chances of them agreeing on every point is virtually zero. This is true because people see things differently, especially people in different time periods, from different cultures, working in different vocations, and with different educational backgrounds. But the Bible was written by more than forty authors of great diversity, yet their ideas and themes all remain unified and centered on the person and work of Jesus Christ.

In order for you to really understand this incredible unity, you have to read the Bible for yourself, keeping in mind the time period in which each book was written, and who was writing it. The more you read the more you'll see it. This organic unity, which is impossible from a human standpoint, magnifies the divine atmosphere of the Bible and is a strong defense of its trustworthiness. What is impossible with man is possible with God (Matthew 19:26)!

THE BIBLE CONTAINS MANY FULFILLED PROPHECIES

Fulfilled prophecy is another indicator of the divine edge of the Bible and provides another line of support for its authenticity. As indicated in the previous chapter, a prophecy is a prediction that a certain event will come true in the future. It is fulfilled when it actually comes true.

There are hundreds of prophecies and their fulfillments recorded in the Bible, and only a deep and thoughtful study of them will do justice to their enormous value. Here, we will cover only a few of them, hopefully to whet your appetite to study more on your own.

Perhaps the most important prophecy given in the Bible is this one: "I will put enmity between you and the woman, and between your offspring and her offspring; he shall bruise your head, and you shall bruise his heel" (Genesis 3:15).

Here God is speaking to the serpent, the devil. He basically foretells, in one simple statement, what the rest of history is all about. The devil would successfully bruise the heel of the offspring of the woman. Who is this offspring?

> But when the fullness of time had come, God sent forth his Son, *born of woman*, born under the law, to redeem those who were under the law, so that we might receive adoption as sons. (Galatians 4:4-5, italics ours)

The eventual offspring of Eve is Jesus Christ himself. He was "born of a woman." The bruising of the heel of Christ is a prediction of the suffering of the Son of God. Indeed, the devil did bruise his heel, literally, on the cross.

But that is not the end of the prophecy. God also informs the serpent that the Son would bruise his head. This is a prediction of the defeat and doom of Satan and all of his minions and power. The book of Revelation records those events for us, set in the future.

> The devil who had deceived them was thrown into the lake of fire and sulfur where the beast and the false prophet were, and they will be tormented day and night forever and ever. (Revelation 20:10)

103

So the prophecy of Genesis 3:15 has been fulfilled – at the cross and resurrection of Christ – and is continuing to be fulfilled right before our very eyes. Amazing! Every single person is living in this story of conflict between the seed of a woman, Jesus Christ, and Satan, the serpent. Our lives will truly make sense if we begin to see what part we play in this ultimate story, summarized in this incredible prophecy.

But this is not the only prophecy in the Bible. The book of Daniel also records some astounding predictions, many of which are already fulfilled. "You saw, O king, and behold, a great image. This image, mighty and of exceeding brightness, stood before you, and its appearance was frightening" (Daniel 2:31).

In this story the great king of Babylon, Nebuchadnezzar, had a dream that really messed him up. It was a confusing dream and he desperately wanted to know the meaning of it.

Daniel was summoned into the king's presence to inform him concerning the content of the dream and its interpretation. But this was no average nightmare. Nebuchadnezzar's dream is actually a mammoth prophecy of the future, as you will see. In the dream, Nebuchadnezzar saw a great and frightening statue.

> The head of this image was of fine gold, its chest and arms of silver, its middle and thighs of bronze, its legs of iron, its feet partly of iron and partly of clay. As you looked, a stone was cut out by no human hand, and it struck the image on its feet of iron and clay, and broke them in pieces. Then the iron, the clay, the bronze, the silver, and the gold, all together were broken in pieces, and became like the chaff of the summer threshing floors; and the wind carried them away, so that not a trace of them could be found. But the stone that struck the image became a great mountain and filled the whole earth. (Daniel 2:32-35)

So this colossal image in the king's dream is composed of four differ-ent metals. The head is gold, the chest and arms are silver, the middle and thighs are bronze and the legs and feet are iron. The feet also have clay mixed in with the iron.

Next Daniel speaks of a massive stone that crashes this image to smithereens. The statue is crushed and the wind blows the bits away. But what does all of this mean?

> This was the dream. Now we will tell the king its interpreta-tion. You, O king, the king of kings, to whom the God of heaven has given the kingdom, the power, and the might, and the glory, and into whose hand he has given, wherever they dwell, the children of man, the beasts of the field, and the birds of the heavens, making you rule over them all- you are the head of gold. (Daniel 2:36-38)

Now we are getting somewhere. The head of gold is Nebuchadnezzar. He was the king of the Babylonian empire at that time (605-562 B.C.), which means that he was the most powerful man in the world, as far as political clout is concerned. But, the next verse tells a different story. "Another kingdom inferior to you shall arise after you, and yet a third kingdom of bronze, which shall rule over all the earth" (Daniel 2:39).

These words were bad news for King Nebuchadnezzar. Here Daniel tells him that Babylon will eventually come to an end. They will be defeated by an inferior kingdom that is represented by the sil-ver on the image. As we study the book of Daniel, we find out which kingdom conquers Babylon – it is the Medio-Persian Empire (see Daniel 5:31).

Next another kingdom will eventually defeat the Persians. Our study of history shows us that the Greeks match this kingdom of bronze. Alexander the Great, ruler of the Greeks, would grow in such power that he would conquer Persia and become the ruler of most of the world.

Daniel was writing about this bronze empire some 200 years or more before it ever ascended the world's throne! This is a prophecy that we know for certain was fulfilled in history concerning the rise of the Greek empire. Later in the book of Daniel, this empire is described in greater detail and the descriptions match Greece perfectly (Daniel 7:6; 8:5-8).[52] Plus, there is more:

> And there shall be a fourth kingdom, strong as iron, because iron breaks to pieces and shatters all things. And like iron that crushes, it shall break and crush all these. And as you saw the feet and toes, partly of potter's clay and partly of iron, it shall be a divided kingdom, but some of the firmness of iron shall be in it, just as you saw iron mixed with the soft clay. And as the toes of the feet were partly iron and partly clay, so the kingdom shall be partly strong and partly brittle. As you saw the iron mixed with soft clay, so they will mix with one another in marriage, but they will not hold together, just as iron does not mix with clay. (Daniel 2:40-43)

This "iron" kingdom is Rome, which took over the world after the Greeks. The clay mixed in the feet shows that all of these kingdoms do not have a very solid foundation (represented by the feet of the statue). The clay compromises the strength of the iron.

From history we know that the Roman Empire was filled with bitterness and infighting, just as this prophecy states, "They will not hold together." During this iron/clay reign, something else happens, as Daniel's prophecy foretells:

> And in the days of those kings the God of heaven will set up a kingdom that shall never be destroyed, nor shall the kingdom be left to another people. It shall break in pieces all these kingdoms and bring them to an end, and it shall stand forever, just as you saw that a stone was cut from a mountain by no

human hand, and that it broke in pieces the iron, the bronze, the clay, the silver, and the gold. A great God has made known to the king what shall be after this. The dream is certain, and its interpretation sure. (Daniel 2:44-45)

Our study of history shows that Jesus Christ was born during a time when the Roman Empire (iron) exerted tremendous control across the world. But wherever Jesus Christ is, there is the Kingdom of God. Christ is the King of kings who conquers, and eventually smashes, all earthly kingdoms represented by the image in Nebuchadnezzar's dream. These prophecies in Daniel are astounding! They reach beyond Daniel's time period and give an overview of the future of the entire world. But this is just the kind of book the Bible is!

PROPHECIES OF CHRIST

As we see from Daniel, fulfilled prophecies are incredible, but especially the ones that relate to the specifics of the life of Jesus Christ.[53] Let us show you a few more prophecies, written hundreds of years before Jesus was ever born that foretell his birth, teachings, and sufferings.

But you, O Bethlehem Ephrathah, who are too little to be among the clans of Judah, from you shall come forth for me one who is to be ruler in Israel, whose origin is from of old, from ancient days. (Micah 5:2)

Here, the prophet Micah names the town where the Messiah would be born. Luke 2 confirms that Bethlehem was indeed the birthplace of the Savior. There is no way a normal man could have controlled where he was born! But God has arranged historical circumstances in just such a way that a couple living in Nazareth had to journey to Bethlehem in order to be counted for a census. There Jesus was born to Mary, just as Micah predicted.

Here is another major prophecy of Christ, this time from the great prophet Isaiah.

> For to us a child is born, to us a son is given; and the government shall be upon his shoulder, and his name shall be called Wonderful Counselor, Mighty God, Everlasting Father, Prince of Peace. Of the increase of his government and of peace there will be no end, on the throne of David and over his kingdom, to establish it and to uphold it with justice and with righteousness from this time forth and forevermore. The zeal of the LORD of hosts will do this. (Isaiah 9:6-7)

Isaiah looks ahead into the future under the inspiration of the Holy Spirit and sees the birth and power of Jesus Christ. The language he uses is much too exalted to refer merely to an earthly king. There can be only one who is "Everlasting Father." Isaiah also informs us that this Messiah King would come in the lineage of King David, which both Matthew and Luke both confirm is true of Jesus Christ (Matthew 1 and Luke 2). Keep in mind, Isaiah wrote these words about seven hundred years before Jesus was born!

Here is another tremendous prophecy of the coming King. This time Isaiah speaks of the Messiah suffering for his people:

> For he grew up before him like a young plant, and like a root out of dry ground; he had no form or majesty that we should look at him, and no beauty that we should desire him. He was despised and rejected by men; a man of sorrows, and acquainted with grief; and as one from whom men hide their faces he was despised, and we esteemed him not. Surely he has borne our griefs and carried our sorrows; yet we esteemed him stricken, smitten by God, and afflicted. But he was wounded

for our transgressions; he was crushed for our iniquities; upon him was the chastisement that brought us peace, and with his stripes we are healed. All we like sheep have gone astray; we have turned every one to his own way; and the LORD has laid on him the iniquity of us all. He was oppressed, and he was afflicted, yet he opened not his mouth; like a lamb that is led to the slaughter, and like a sheep that before its shearers is silent, so he opened not his mouth. (Isaiah 53:2-7)

Only willful blindness could hide the obvious – this is a prediction of the sufferings of Jesus. "He has borne our griefs and carried our sorrows." He was led "like a lamb...to the slaughter." These are direct and specific prophecies that came true when Jesus was crucified.

These fulfilled prophecies are momentous in showing that we can trust the Bible. These are just a few examples, but there are literally hundreds of these kinds of prophecies recorded in the pages of Scripture!

It would be one thing if the Bible had one or two prophecies that coincidentally came true. But the sheer number and the specific fulfillment of these prophecies should lead us to believe that the Bible is no ordinary book. It speaks of things beyond the work of mere human hands.[54]

NOSTRADAMUS, FORTUNE COOKIES, AND HOROSCOPES

You might have heard of Nostradamus. He lived from 1503-1566 and was a popular astrologer who supposedly predicted many world events. To this day, Nostadamus is still a prominent figure in popular culture. Tabloids, usually displayed prominently in grocery store checkout lines, frequently declare that Nostradamus predicted some major disaster or sometimes even the end of the world.

But can we trust Nostradamus? No way! His predictions of the future were so vague and general that they could be construed and applied to almost anything. Consider the following prophecy that some say refers to the terrorist attacks of September 11, 2001:

> The year 1999, seventh month,
> From the sky will come a great King of Terror:
> To bring back to life the great King of the Mongols,
> Before and after Mars to reign by good luck.[55]

Well, if this prophecy is of 9/11, the first thing you notice is the wrong year, and the wrong month! Sure it is close but it is wrong. Prophecies in the Bible do not just get close; they get it exactly right.[56]

Nostradamus does say that "a great King of Terror" would come out of the sky, but we know that there were actually four different hijacked airplanes on 9/11. So is it one king of terror or multiple kings of terror? Maybe it is referring to Osama Bin laden as one king of terror, but then Bin Laden never came out of the sky. Though he planned the attacks, he did not execute them.

Another problem with applying this text to 9/11 is the part about the "King of the Mongols." The Mongols originated from China and today continue to live there, though they have also spread out into other places including Russia. The majority of them are Buddhists. It is certainly unclear who the "King" of them would be and how or why 9/11 would bring him back to life.

There is obviously no connection between this "prophecy" and 9/11. Nostradamus purposely wrote vague, unconnected sayings that could be interpreted to fit many different situations. But he never gave precise and detailed predictions that actually came true.

His prophecies are much like fortune cookies. They are so universal that they could be applied to any number of circumstances. One fortune cookie says, "Embrace change; don't battle it." But is that a

110

fortune or just advice? It could apply to anyone at anytime so it could be anybody's "fortune."

Horoscopes are exactly the same – vague and general. Anybody could read any horoscope and say, "That is my horoscope." Here is a random horoscope found online:

> Travel is very favorably aspected today, but make sure you don't overlook a friend if you do decide to take off some-where. Be inclusive; invite your friends to join you; chances are you'll be glad that you did. For that extra bit of clarity keep a piece of amber with you today.[57]

This was the September 27, 2007 horoscope for those who have the sign *cancer*. But really, anybody born on any date of the year could read this and think, "This applies to me."

Think about it – most of us travel all the time. It does not say a short trip or long trip, but just the general idea of "travel." Notice it uses the word *if*: "If you decide to take off somewhere." It does not say you *will* decide to take off somewhere, but only *if* you decide to take off somewhere. Most everybody has friends, so it also talks vaguely about inviting friends.

This horoscope does not give direct, specific information. It does not say, "You will travel to Oakland, California next Tuesday with four friends." But this is precisely where the Bible is different from Nostradamus, fortune cookies, and horoscopes. The Bible gives direct, specific predictions that come true exactly as predicted. Here is one more example to make the point clear:

> Rejoice greatly, O daughter of Zion! Shout aloud, O daughter of Jerusalem! behold, your king is coming to you; righteous and having salvation is he, humble and mounted on a donkey, on a colt, the foal of a donkey. (Zechariah 9:9)

111

Compare this prophecy with its fulfillment in the Gospel of Matthew:

> They brought the donkey and the colt and put on them their cloaks, and he [Jesus] sat on them. Most of the crowd spread their cloaks on the road, and others cut branches from the trees and spread them on the road. And the crowds that went before him and that followed him were shouting, "Hosanna to the Son of David! Blessed is he who comes in the name of the Lord! Hosanna in the highest!" And when he entered Jerusalem, the whole city was stirred up, saying, "Who is this?" And the crowds said, "This is the prophet Jesus, from Nazareth of Galilee." (Matthew 21:7-11)

THE BIBLE IS CONNECTED TO HISTORY

Unlike many religious texts, the Bible is not some mystical text of devotional instruction. Of course it does teach us how to honor, love, and worship God, but that is not all. The Bible is also vitally connected to history. It recounts the actual stories of people's lives and the life of an entire nation – Israel. Since this is the case, there are many historical evidences that we can point to that verify the teaching of the Bible.

For example, we see the existence of people today called *Jews*. They are still around after all this time! God made a covenant with these people and he showered them with his mercy in delivering them from Egyptian bondage (Exodus 14:30-31), yet they forsook the covenant of God and turned their back on him (Isaiah 1:4). As we study history we find this nation existing just as the Bible tells us it did.

Archeological digs have uncovered thousands of artifacts in the land and region of Israel. These findings support the idea that the Bible is telling the truth and is historically accurate. Chapter 6 will show you several of these findings to further demonstrate how closely connected the Bible is to history.

But what does this connection to history prove? It proves that the Bible is not just some made up collection of stories. Instead, the Bible is the account of an actual God working in actual history. If it were just a fake document you would not expect this close connection with real-life history.

The Bible Has Strong Manuscript Support

It may surprise some people to know that the Bible was not originally written in English. The Old Testament was written primarily in Hebrew and the New Testament in Greek. Our English versions – all of them – are mere translations from these original languages.

The Old Testament was finished about 2,400 years ago. The New Testament was finished about 1,900 years ago. Do we have any of those original copies of the letters and books that make up the Bible? The answer is no. No original copies can be located today.

But even though no original copies are around (that we know of), there are plenty of *very old* manuscripts or copies of those originals. Some of the oldest manuscripts of the Old Testament date back to before 200 B.C. The Dead Sea Scrolls are a collection of ancient manuscripts, many of which date back to these very early years.[58]

Some of the oldest New Testament manuscripts date back to 130 A.D. or so (some perhaps earlier than that). These copies were made only 40-60 years after the New Testament was completed – not a very long time at all for determining literary accuracy. Take for example Homer's *Iliad*. Although probably written between 900 B.C. and 800 B.C., the earliest manuscript in our possession was copied around 400 B.C., nearly five hundred years later. Yet the majority of literary scholars agree that when we read the *Iliad* today, we are, for the most part, actually reading the text as originally penned.

These facts count as strong evidence that the Bibles Christians read 1,900 years ago are the exact same Bibles we are reading today. The Bible was not corrupted or changed throughout the years. When we read Romans, we are reading what Paul actually wrote to the church in Rome (translated into English from Greek, of course).

If you have a good working knowledge of ancient biblical manuscripts and the science behind textual reconstruction, then you will not be fooled by people who say the Bible has been tarnished through the years. All you have to do is research the ancient manuscripts and see that they match today's Bibles.[59]

THE BIBLE HAS NO CONTRADICTIONS

Many skeptics and unbelievers say that the Bible cannot be trusted because it contains errors and contradictions. We have never personally seen one, but the opponents of the Bible say those contradictions are there.

What leads people to see these supposed contradictions? First, many times people do not have all of the facts about a particular passage. Take these two passages for example:

"Again you have heard that it was said to those of old, 'You shall not swear falsely, but shall perform to the Lord what you have sworn.' But I say to you, Do not take an oath at all, either by heaven, for it is the throne of God, or by the earth, for it is his footstool, or by Jerusalem, for it is the city of the great King. And do not take an oath by your head, for you cannot make one hair white or black. Let what you say be simply 'Yes' or 'No'; anything more than this comes from evil." (Matthew 5:33-37)

For when God made a promise to Abraham, since he had no one greater by whom to swear, he swore by himself, saying, "Surely I will bless you and multiply you." (Hebrews 6:13-14)

Okay, this is confusing! In Matthew Jesus instructs his followers not to swear and take oaths. But in Hebrews 6 God himself is swearing and taking an oath. Is this not a glaring contradiction? Certainly not.

In Matthew Jesus is giving his famous Sermon on the Mount. In that message, he was confronting the hypocrisy and legalism of the Pharisees, the Jewish leaders of the time (see 5:20). One of the things the Pharisees did was set up a system of oath taking. You could swear by Jerusalem, or by heaven, or oddly enough, you could even swear by your own head. Some of these things were greater to swear by than others.

Suppose I promise you that I am going to come over and wash your car tomorrow. You say, "Okay, I really need you to wash my car. You will be there, right?" I say, "I swear by a double cheeseburger, I will be there!"

Tomorrow comes and uh-oh, I slept late and did not come over to wash your car. So you come looking for me. Waking me up you say, "You swore you would come and wash my car!"

I reply: "Wait a minute! I only swore by a double cheeseburger. I did not swear by a quarter-pound cheeseburger! If I had sworn by the greater burger, I would have been more obligated to be there, but as it is, I only swore by the lesser burger and so too bad!"

Believe it or not, this was what those people were doing (less the burgers). They had set up an elaborate system of oath-taking that actually allowed them to *get out of keeping their promises*. It was just part of the super messed-up system by which the Pharisees were living.[60]

Jesus came along and essentially said, "Enough of the oath-taking garbage already! Quit playing those silly games with each other and be people of honesty and integrity. When you say 'yes,' let that be good enough. When you say 'no,' let that be good enough."

He does not condemn *all* promises or oaths for all time. He speaks to those people in their cultural situation and makes a strong point about the importance of integrity and character.

115

So when God makes an oath as recorded in Hebrews 6, he is not contradicting Jesus' words in Matthew 5. He is taking an oath in the right way, not on the basis of a system designed to promoted lies and dishonesty.

A little more information about the historical background of the passages shows that there is no contradiction between them. Many passages in the Bible that seem to contradict on the surface, actually do not contradict at all when a bit more research is done.

INTERPRET THE BIBLE IN CONTEXT

Another reason that skeptics see contradictions in the Bible that are not really there is because they very often take verses out of their contexts. Read these two verses out of their contexts to see what we mean:

> You see that a person is justified by works and not by faith alone. (James 2:24)

> Yet we know that a person is not justified by works of the law but through faith in Jesus Christ, so we also have believed in Christ Jesus, in order to be justified by faith in Christ and not by works of the law, because by works of the law no one will be justified. (Galatians 2:16)

If you pulled these two verses out of the Bible and placed them side-by-side, it would appear clearly that they contradict each other. If they do contradict each other, then logically one of them must be wrong, or both of them are wrong, but they can't both be right. If they are not both right, than the Bible has a glaring error. If it has an error in one part of it, then how can we trust any part of it? This is very serious to us who believe the Bible as our source of knowledge for all faith and practice.

116

So how do we deal with this? We begin by analyzing the contexts in which these passages appear. You will find that Paul in Galatians is speaking of the **root** or the initiation of salvation. We are saved (in this sense) by faith alone. Our works *cannot* bring us into that initial entrance of a relationship with Christ. This becomes clear in reading chapters 2 and 3 of Galatians.

> Is the law then contrary to the promises of God? Certainly not! For if a law had been given that could give life, then righteousness would indeed be by the law. But the Scripture imprisoned everything under sin, so that the promise by faith in Jesus Christ might be given to those who believe. (Galatians 3:21-22)

James, on the other hand, is speaking of the **fruit** or the sanctification element which is also a part of the salvation process. We are saved by faith alone, but faith is not alone. Real faith produces real works. If Christians do not have real works then they do not have real faith. Again, reading the context of the passage shows this:

> So also faith by itself, if it does not have works, is dead. But someone will say, "You have faith and I have works." Show me your faith apart from your works, and I will show you my faith by my works. You believe that God is one; you do well. Even the demons believe- and shudder! Do you want to be shown, you foolish person, that faith apart from works is useless? (James 2:17-20)

James wants to be sure that we understand that faith *is seen by works.* That is why he states that people are justified by works as well as faith. Our works are a *necessary outworking* of our salvation. But Paul wants us to understand that we do not *enter* into this salvation by our works, but by faith alone.

In context, these two passages are speaking of two distinct parts of the salvation process. Paul and James are not disagreeing with each other nor do they contradict each other. Both of them are right and there is no error here.

In fact, it seems clear that God very often teaches truth by creating tension. In the case with James and Paul, the tension is between free grace and obedient sanctification. We see other passages where Paul says we are free and slaves at the same time; free from sin and slaves to Christ (Romans 6:7; 18). We also see that in order to gain our lives we must loose them (Mark 8:35).

This type of tension is found throughout the Bible. These are not contradictions, but brilliant ways of teaching truth. But one must interpret passages in their contexts in order to see this. People who read the text in a shallow way will come away convinced that there are contradictions.

ALLOW THE BIBLE TO USE ORDINARY LANGUAGE

There is yet another reason that skeptics see contradictions in the Bible when there are none there. They often forbid the Bible to speak in ordinary language even though the Bible was not written in the technical language of scholars, but rather in the common language of the day. This means different authors might be telling the exact same story from different points of view. This does not mean they contradict each other, but just that they are telling stories the normal way people tell stories.

Read these two passages and let's see if they contradict each other as some skeptics say they do:

When he [Jesus] came to the other side, to the country of the Gadarenes, two demon-possessed men met him, coming out of the tombs, so fierce that no one could pass that way. (Matthew 8:28)

When Jesus had stepped out of the boat, immediately there met him out of the tombs a man with an unclean spirit. He lived among the tombs. And no one could bind him anymore, not even with a chain. (Mark 5:2-3)

So how many demon-possessed men were there? Matthew says there were two and Mark records only one. Surely this is a glaring contradiction in the Bible if ever there was one! Not if we let the Bible speak in the ordinary language it was written in.

Obviously, there were at least two demon-possessed men, as Matthew says.[61] So why does Mark only mention one of them? Because Mark is telling his version of the story. Therefore, he only includes the parts that are important to his telling of the story.

As you examine Mark's report of these events you will discover that one of the men developed a very close bond with Jesus, and even wanted to go back with him across the Sea of Galilee.[62] Jesus did not allow the man to go, but instructed him to stay and tell his friends and family about the power of God.

Here is the point: Mark was interested in the one demon-possessed man and his relationship to Jesus. The other man was not a concern to Mark and his telling of this story. *That does not mean that the other man was not there.* It just means Mark saw no need to mention him.

Suppose you go whitewater rafting with your youth group. Mary, Mike, Melvin, Marty, and you are all in one boat. After the trip you and Melvin both write entries into your journals about the trip.

You write these words: We just finished rafting and it was awesome! Our boat was full of people: Mary, Mike, Melvin, Marty, and me. It was one of the coolest experiences of my life and I will never forget it.

119

Melvin writes these words: Mike and I just wasted 5 hours of our lives. Neither one of us wanted to come on this silly trip. It was horrible. I will never go whitewater rafting again.

Now suppose I found Melvin's journal and your journal and I compared these two entries side-by-side. It would be clear to me that two different people were writing about the *same* event from two *different* viewpoints. I would not think Melvin was lying or contradicting you just because he did not mention every single person who was on the boat. In fact, if I only read Melvin's entry, I might be led to think that only he and Mike were on the boat. But Melvin's point really has nothing to do with whom or how many were on the boat. His point has to do with his emotional state while on the boat.

Do you see the point? The Bible uses ordinary language and tells stories in common ways from the points of view of real people. Many of these so-called contradictions are really nothing more than a misunderstanding of this fact.

CONCLUSION

We have covered a lot of ground in this chapter – even though we have only scratched the surface – and we hope it is clear that the Bible can be trusted. It is a book from God, free from error. Our prayer for you is that you would bank your life both here and forever on the vital information contained in this living book! It tells us all that we need to know about God, ourselves, and eternity.

For the word of God is living and active, sharper than any two-edged sword, piercing to the division of soul and of spirit, of joints and of marrow, and discerning the thoughts and intentions of the heart. (Hebrews 4:12)

Chapter 5 Review Exercise

1. The Bible claims to be from God. Is this circular reasoning? Explain.
2. The Bible displays incredible unity. Give a detailed explanation of what is meant by this statement.
3. What are some ways to verify whether or not a certain biblical prophecy was fulfilled?
4. How are the prophecies in the Bible different from other prophecies, like those of Nostradamus?
5. How do we know that the Bibles we read today have not been corrupted through the years since they were originally written?
6. What does it mean that the Bible was written in ordinary language? How does this affect your understanding of whether there are contradictions in the Bible?
7. What does it mean to study the Bible in context? Give an example.

Key Terms

Bible
Circular reasoning
Biblical unity
Nostradamus
Biblical manuscripts
Dead Sea Scrolls
Biblical contradiction
Context

Scripture Memory

We also thank God constantly for this, that when you received the word of God, which you heard from us, you accepted it not as the word of men but as what it really is, the word of God, which is at work in you believers. (1 Thessalonians 2:13)

CHAPTER 6:
Digging for Gold

I (Jason) remember seventh grade history because I was bored to tears. I had no clue who the Russian Czars were and I did not care. I didn't even care much about my own American history. Okay, so Abe Lincoln gave the Gettysburg Address – big deal. The Japanese bombed Pearl Harbor – what does that have to do with me? Martin Luther King Jr. marched in Selma – when is lunch?

Many, if not most, high school students feel the same way. There are some folks who have a deep interest in history, but let's be honest, most don't. For most of us, it is terribly hard to learn people's names, what they did, where they lived, and then there are all the dates: March 5, 1770, April 19, 1775, February 4, 1789, May 2, 1803, and June 18, 1812, just to name a few.

Very significant things happened on these dates,[63] but when you have to memorize what these events were, and be able to write them on a test, it can be more than a little troubling. It makes tired and weary students cry out to their teachers, "How will any of this every matter in my life?!"

LEARNING FROM THE PAST

But now it has been a few years since I was in high school, and I have changed my tune quite a bit about history. I've had great teachers who taught me an extremely wise truth: history repeats itself.

These days I am not so quick to dismiss the study of history. Rather I should learn as much about it as possible, because what happened in the past is probably going to happen again in the future! When that became clear to me, I started reading and loving history. I wanted to examine what happened in the past so that I could faithfully understand the present and be a part of making the future better.

As I studied, I noticed how closely history and the Bible match. The things that the Bible say are true, are proven *actually* true by an examination of history. This is an amazing fact and shows just how awesome and trustworthy the Bible (and the Christian faith as a whole) really is.

DIGGING UP EVIDENCE

There are people in the world who love to dig stuff up out of the ground. They visit sites where ancient cities used to be and sit out in the hot sun with little shovels and brushes and spend hours and hours picking through dirt, finding lots of cool things.

It must be difficult to be an archeologist (the official title of these dirt-diggers). It doesn't seem to be a very desirable job, especially on the days when they don't find anything at all. It can't be very exciting to find a bucket of dirt!

Archeologists however tend to have a great passion for their job and they seem to do it well. They understand how important their task is and they work hard to perform their duties carefully and correctly. Why is their job such a big deal?

Because the things they dig up out of the dirt tell stories. A piece of pottery, a wall of a city, an inscription on a stone, weapons, tombs, and a host of other artifacts tell the story of ancient peoples.

BATTERIES AND BONE

Even though I (Jason) have no yearning to be an archeologist, once I did get a brief taste of archeology life. I was living in Reese City, Alabama, a small community that is the suburb of a small town (Attalla) that is the suburb of a small city (Gadsden). In other words, I lived in the sticks. In those days, I loved exploring the woods, definitely a good thing because woods make up the majority of Reece City. I walked many miles of trails and followed long, winding mountain streams. Even the ticks and flies did not bother me!

One day, while being adventurous, I found a cave. Well, it was actually more like a big hole in the ground. We called it a cave because a cave is much cooler than a hole in the ground. My brother Chris and another friend of ours were with me. All three of us wanted to know what was in this cave/hole.

They gave me a flashlight. After all, I was the smallest – and the least likely to be remembered if tragedy struck. They held firmly to my feet and not-so-gently lowered me into the hole. Head first. I flashed the light around and found a couple of interesting things: bones and batteries!

These two artifacts told me a story and gave me a warning. The story they told was this: somebody else had been in this hole (obvious because of the old batteries) and something had died in this hole (obvious because of the bones)! The warning these artifacts gave me was loud and clear. Get out of the hole! Which I did.

When archeologists find things in the dirt, those things tell stories about the past. Let's turn our attention now to some findings of real archeologists.

THE REAL LIFE OF PONTIUS PILATE

One clear cut example of how artifacts tell stories is a piece of lime-stone found in 1961 at the excavation of an amphitheatre near Caesarea-on-the-sea. On this stone is an inscription that reads: "Pontius Pilate, Prefect of Judea." If you know anything about the life and death of Jesus Christ, then the name Pontius Pilate is familiar to you. He was the Roman authority who ordered the crucifixion of Christ.

But in recent days, prior to the finding of this stone, many scholars actually contended that Pilate never existed. There is very little written about him outside of the Bible. Thus skeptics who do not believe the Bible began to question whether he was a true historical figure or just a fictional legend. When the inscription was found it proved the skeptics wrong. Pilate was a real man, a real Roman governor, who really lived during the time of Jesus.

If you would like (and you have the money) you can go to the Israel Museum in Jerusalem and see this inscription for yourself.[64]

THE POOL OF SILOAM

Some scholars and historians who were biased against the historical trustworthiness of the Bible have doubted seriously that there was any such place as the Pool of Siloam. Here is what the Bible says:

> Having said these things, [Jesus] spat on the ground and made mud with the saliva. Then he anointed the [blind] man's eyes with the mud and said to him, "Go, wash in the pool of Siloam" (which means Sent). So he went and washed and came back seeing. (John 9:6-7)

In 2005, this pool was found. Here is an excerpt from an article published in the L.A. Times detailing this incredible find:

Workers repairing a sewage pipe in the Old City of Jerusalem have discovered the biblical Pool of Siloam, a fresh-water reservoir that was a major gathering place for ancient Jews making religious pilgrimages to the city and the reputed site where Jesus cured a man blind from birth, according to the Gospel of John.

The pool was fed by the now famous Hezekiah's Tunnel and is "a much grander affair" than archeologists previously believed, with three tiers of stone stairs allowing easy access to the water, said Hershel Shanks, editor of the Biblical Archaeology Review, which reported the find Monday.

"Scholars have said that there wasn't a Pool of Siloam and that John was using a religious conceit" to illustrate a point, said New Testament scholar James H. Charlesworth of the Princeton Theological Seminary. "Now we have found the Pool of Siloam."

A gospel that was thought to be "pure theology is now shown to be grounded in history," he said.[65]

These are the kinds of artifacts that help us see the organic connections between what we read in the Bible and what we observe in the world around us. The stories of the Bible do not take place in fictional fairytale lands, but rather in real earthly locations, in actual space and time.

THE WALLS CAME TUMBLING DOWN

Archeologists have also found another powerful artifact that supports biblical truth – the walls of Jericho. When these walls were uncovered they actually showed signs of destruction, and not normal destruction. It appears as though at some point, these walls came tumbling down!

Experts will of course disagree over what caused these walls to fall and when exactly they fell, but the point here is clear – the uncovering of these destroyed walls confirms and supports the biblical account.

> So the people shouted, and the trumpets were blown. As soon as the people heard the sound of the trumpet, the people shouted a great shout, and the wall fell down flat, so that the people went up into the city, every man straight before him, and they captured the city. (Joshua 6:20)

We encourage you to explore the topic of biblical archeological further. Many other artifacts can be shown as evidence in favor of the authenticity of the Bible.[66] The word of God is not merely a loose collection of religious sayings, but is intertwined with history. That means it can be verified by the stories told by objects found in the dirt. But there is more.

ISRAELITE REALITIES

When defending the authenticity of the Bible, we can take the idea of its connection with history even further than archeology.

In the Old Testament, the primary focus is on the God-elected nation of Israel. Essentially, the story of the Old Testament is God's relationship to these people, their responses to him, and his gracious future promises to save them.[67]

Details of Israelite history are given to us. The Bible is not just a mix of mystical ideals or an ethical code of conduct, but rather it is the story of real people and their lives – not just individuals, like Moses or David, but an entire nation of individuals collectively called Israel.

So what? Let's suppose for the sake of argument that some mean-spirited liars just made up the Jewish and Christian faiths and they are not true at all. Let's pretend that the Bible is just a collection of documents that these manipulative people wrote in order to support their claims.

If that were true, what kind of document would that "Bible" be? Would it tell the story of God's relationship to an entire nation of people whose existence and history can be easily verified? Could the Egyptian bondage and exodus be just a "story?" Could the kingdoms of David and Solomon be mere fiction?

Absolutely not! There is too much documented history linked with these stories and too many people involved for them to be manufactured.

An amazing fact about the Jewish people being a central part of the focus of the Bible is that *they're still here!* In the land of Israel itself and scattered all around the world are people who have Abraham's blood flowing through their veins. They are actual descendants of the people we read about in our Old Testament!

Plus, many people in the world still hate the Jewish populace, and this is a biblical pattern. A glance back a few years to the reign of Adolph Hitler reminds us that this tiny nation of people still provokes world leaders to desire their extermination.

Queen Esther faced this problem in her day (Esther 3:13) and the Jewish people in our day continue to be confronted with the reality that much of the world could do without them. And yet this nation has never been fully wiped off the face of the earth. The Bible tells us why in the epistle to the Romans.

> I want you to understand this mystery, brothers: a partial hardening has come upon Israel, until the fullness of the Gentiles has come in. And in this way *all Israel will be saved*, as it is written, "The Deliverer will come from Zion, he will banish ungodliness from Jacob and this will be my covenant with them when I take away their sins." As regards the gospel, they are enemies of God for your sake. But as regards election,

they are beloved for the sake of their forefathers. For the gifts and the calling of God are irrevocable. Just as you were at one time disobedient to God but now have received mercy because of their disobedience, so they too have now been disobedient in order that by the mercy shown to you they also may now receive mercy. (Romans 11:25-31, italics ours)

God has plans to save these people. The best interpretation of Romans 11 is that God will in the future bring into the Church of Jesus Christ a great number of ethnic Israelites. Jews will be saved through the blood of Christ in mass numbers. Of course for that to happen there must be Israelites alive (which there are)!

It is clear that the story of God's nation (Israel) and the even bigger story of the multinational Church that begins to grow in the New Testament are both stories that could not be faked! They are too closely connected to long periods of history for that. The fact that the Bible recounts history goes a long way in supporting that the Bible is true and actually from God. Let's look at this principle from another perspective.

FAMILY LINES

As you read the Bible, you will notice the emphasis placed on various families, the family of Jesus Christ in particular. This emphasis on family lines shows a connection to history that can be used to verify the truthfulness of the Bible. It is a book about real people who lived in various family groups in certain places at certain times. We see this throughout the Bible with passages like this one:

These are the generations of the sons of Noah, Shem, Ham, and Japheth. Sons were born to them after the flood. The sons of Japheth: Gomer, Magog, Madai, Javan, Tubal, Meshech, and Tiras. The sons of Gomer: Ashkenaz, Riphath, and Togarmah. The sons of Javan: Elishah, Tarshish, Kittim, and Dodanim. From these the coastland peoples spread in their lands, each with his own language, by their clans, in their nations. The sons of Ham: Cush, Egypt, Put, and Canaan. The sons of Cush: Seba, Havilah, Sabtah, Raamah, and Sabteca. The sons of Raamah: Sheba and Dedan. (Genesis 10:1-7)

You get the point. Some people consider these lists of names boring, but if you understand the important connections these lists make with actual historical figures and events, they become intriguing; and they lend a great deal of credibility to the Bible.

In Matthew 1, the apostle traces the family line of Jesus from Abraham to David, then from David to Christ. This genealogy, along with a similar list in Luke 3 that traces Mary's line all the way back to Adam, demonstrate that the life of Jesus was a real life. He was a real man who had a real family.

The Bible does not read like a book of myths, legends, or fables. It is a story of families. It portrays the conflict of brothers: Abel and Cain, Jacob and Esau, Isaac and Ishmael, just to name a few. It portrays the love and conflict of husbands and wives: Adam and Eve, Abraham and Sarah, David and Bathsheba, Joseph and Mary, among others.

And these family connections are seen throughout the Bible, not just in certain places. The family line of Jesus forms a golden strand that runs visibly and clearly from Genesis to Revelation.

One very clear place to see this is in the book of Ruth. Many people approach the book of Ruth thinking it is just a romantic story of love and acceptance. Ruth, the beggar, is taken in and loved by Boaz the wealthy landowner. What could be sweeter than that? Others think the book of Ruth is the place to go if you want relationship advice. And that is not wrong! But the book of Ruth is *so much bigger* than a book on relationships.

Look at this passage from the last chapter: "The women of the neighborhood gave him a name, saying, 'A son has been born to Naomi.' They named him Obed. He was the father of Jesse, the father of David" (Ruth 4:17). Naomi was bitter because her husband and two sons had died. But this is not just the story of a sad woman. The deeper problem was there was no *son to carry on the family line*. Why is that a big deal?

If the family line is cut off here, then there will be no King David. If there is no King David, then there is no King Jesus! That is why the book of Ruth ends this way:

> Now these are the generations of Perez: Perez fathered Hezron, Hezron fathered Ram, Ram fathered Amminadab, Amminadab fathered Nahshon, Nahshon fathered Salmon, Salmon fathered Boaz, Boaz fathered Obed, Obed fathered Jesse, and Jesse fathered David. (Ruth 4:18-22)

Ruth is not about cultivating good relationships, but rather the preservation of the family line through which Christ would be born! This golden strand of family connections goes a long way in showing that the Bible could not have been a manufactured book designed with deceitful motives. It is simply too big, and stretches through too much time, and involves too many families for that.

THE ENDURING CHURCH

Speaking of the Church and history, let's focus a moment on the years between Pentecost (roughly 30 A.D.) and today. About 2,000 years have passed in between these times. During this period there have been many attempts to silence and exterminate the Church.

We read of horrendous times of persecution, when Roman emperors or Muslim state officials commanded the torture and death of

Christians. Often beaten and often thrown to the lions, Christians in many parts of the world have suffered greatly for their faith in Jesus Christ.

And yet people still convert to Christ every single day! Ironically, the Church thrives during those times of the most intense persecution. How is it that the Church continues to endure and continues to believe in the same orthodoxy as the earliest Christians?

The most realistic answer to that question is that God preserves his Church. In spite of internal conflicts and impurities, external persecutions and attacks, God has kept the Church alive. If the visible Church were to completely disappear, we would have reason to doubt that it was really from God. But in spite of its many weaknesses the Church is alive and growing today, as it has been for two millennia.

Of course this argument alone cannot prove that the Church is God's institution. After all, many religions can claim longevity. Muslims and Hindus have both been around for hundreds of years, just like Christianity. But still, one would expect a true religion to be one that does not die. This fact counts in favor of Christianity, even though other groups can use the same argument.

TRUE CHRISTIANITY AND ITS EFFECTS UPON SOCIETY

One last point about history and Christianity – it changes societies for the good. That is, wherever true Christianity goes, it brings about good in that particular place.

We must be careful here because history has revealed that there are false forms of Christianity that have actually changed societies for the bad. When the Crusades of the 11th Century were commanded, this was just such a false form of Christianity. It believed that conversion could come through force, a notion that Jesus never preaches.

So when we say that Christianity affects a society in a good way, making positive changes, we need to be sure to specify which type of Christianity we are talking about. That is why we should say "true Christianity" and distinguish it from false Christianity.

True Christianity takes Jesus' teaching literally: to be peacemakers, to feed the hungry, clothe the naked, heal the wounds of the injured, and generally be good Samaritans.

False Christianity does not care much at all about what Jesus says in regard to these matters. False Christianity is often nothing but a front for the power of the state. Or it takes Jesus ethical teachings seriously as listed above, but guts the true gospel of salvation out of it. "Feed the poor, but do not preach to the soul," they say.

But Christianity is not a cover for the power of the state and it does not choose between preaching the gospel and feeding the poor. It preaches the gospel *and* feeds the poor. This is true Christianity. And wherever true Christianity goes, *that* society improves.

When the majority of people in an area are living for the glory of Christ, faithfully following his commands, intentionally loving one another, then that will be a fair and civilized area. The kind of place you would want to raise your family. It will be a place where the best medical care is provided and a place where education is treasured.

History shows us that Christians have been responsible for building thousands of churches, schools, hospitals, orphanages, and shelters for the homeless. These social institutions have drastically enhanced the overall ethical and economic condition of various societies around the world.

Compare these positive influences with the societies built in areas that are predominately Muslim. One look at Iraq as it was found under the regime of Saddam Hussein makes this point clear. The people were oppressed, the poor were downtrodden, hate was bred from father to son, women were mistreated, and murder was a way of life.[68]

Now the fact that true Christianity benefits societies does not prove conclusively that Christianity is true, any more than archeological finds that support the Bible. Nor did we take into account the obvious fact that there is no such thing as a totally pure and true Christian society (yet). There will be many Judas's who are wolves wearing sheep's clothing (Matthew 26:25).

But the fact that true Christianity (even though it appears in greater and lesser degrees) does improve society shows us that it works. And *if it is true*, we should expect it to *work in practice*.

We must also bear in mind that all of the apologetic arguments in this book, and a host of others, must be taken together as a package. When viewed in this way, as a cumulative whole, they show that Christianity is certainly true beyond all reasonable doubt.

In this chapter we have seen that Christianity is a historical religion. Its obvious connection to the past, and its powerful ability to improve the present, provide strong evidence that biblical Christianity is trustworthy and true.

Chapter 6 Review Exercise

1. Give a real life example of how history has repeated itself.
2. What role does archeology play in defending the Christian faith?
3. Name the three well known artifacts mentioned in this chapter that support the authenticity of the Bible. Can you think of any others?
4. The nation of Israel is still around today. How does this fact support the teachings of the Bible?
5. Do you agree that true Christianity has had a positive impact on societies? Why or why not?

Key Terms

Archeology
Pilate Stone
Pool of Siloam

Israel
True Christianity

Scripture Memory

Having said these things, [Jesus] spat on the ground and made mud with the saliva. Then he anointed the [blind] man's eyes with the mud and said to him, "Go, wash in the pool of Siloam" (which means Sent). So he went and washed and came back seeing. (John 9:6-7)

CHAPTER 7:
All for the Glory of God

This chapter takes a different but very important approach to defending the Christian faith. Essentially we want to show that Christianity – as a worldview system – makes life make sense. It provides order and removes chaos from our lives. It is able to do this because of its amazing ability to answer questions.

Christianity answers the toughest questions that people have about God, life, and eternity. The reason Christianity answers these questions so well is because of the foundational teaching found throughout the Bible that **God does all things for his own glory**. "I am the LORD; that is my name; my glory I give to no other, nor my praise to carved idols" (Isaiah 42:8).

Through his prophet Jeremiah, God plainly states that he delights greatly in what he does. He makes himself very happy:

> But let him who boasts boast in this, that he understands and knows me, that I am the LORD who practices steadfast love, justice, and righteousness in the earth. For in these things I delight, declares the LORD. (Jeremiah 9:24)

And when Moses asked if he could see the glory of God, God hid him in the cleft of a rock and passed by, allowing Moses to see the fading brilliance of his glory. As he moved past Moses, God worshipped himself and Moses was motivated to join God in the worship:

> The LORD passed before him and proclaimed, "The LORD, the LORD, a God merciful and gracious, slow to anger, and abounding in steadfast love and faithfulness, keeping steadfast love for thousands, forgiving iniquity and transgression and sin, but who will by no means clear the guilty, visiting the iniquity of the fathers on the children and the children's children, to the third and the fourth generation." And Moses quickly bowed his head toward the earth and worshiped. (Exodus 34:6-8)

As you can see God very much loves and honors himself. As you read the Scriptures it should become clear that the point of God creating all things is to bring maximized glory to himself. Let's not make this word *glory* too complicated. It sounds like a churchy word, but it actually has a very simple definition: to make known or to make famous.

If I (Bradley) glorify Alabama football, then that means I love the team so much that I tell other people how good they are. I would attend all the games I could, buy all the paraphernalia I could afford, probably even make up some statistic to make them look better (or just talk about Bear Bryant for awhile). *We glorify whatever we enjoy.* And if I really want to glorify Alabama football, I not only inform others how good they are as a team, but I also attempt to persuade them to join me in the fan club.

To glorify God means to make him famous. It means to enjoy him, honor him and spread the knowledge of him to others. This is exactly what God wants us to do, since he loves himself and his own glory supremely. "Be still, and know that I am God. I will be exalted among the nations, I will be exalted in the earth" (Psalm 46:10)!

Too often, Christians believe that God loves people *more than anything*. That is a false belief and should be discarded. The Bible does teach that God loves people *a great deal*. He sent Jesus in order to die on the cross for us so that we might be rescued and saved from sin. It is true that "Jesus loves me, this I know, for the Bible tells me so." But he does not love me, or anyone else, or all of humanity put together, *more* than he loves himself. God is extremely and perfectly God-centered. In fact, it is because he loves himself that he loves us as humanity. His ultimate commitment to make much of himself provides the foundation for his love for humanity. He loves himself; therefore, he also loves us.[69]

This is displayed in the reality that he would allow us to suffer if that might bring him more glory and honor (consider the stories of Joseph and Job for example)! Paul came to realize this as he suffered with a "thorn in the flesh." We are not sure what this thorn was (some speculate blindness), but we do know that Paul asked God three times to take it away. But he did not. God allowed Paul to suffer so that God could glorify himself by saying, "My grace is sufficient for you, for my power is made perfect in weakness" (2 Corinthians 12:7-9).

WHY GOD IS JUSTIFIED IN SEEKING HIS OWN GLORY

But this raises a big problem for a God that is supposed to be perfect in every way. How does his desire to honor himself not make God into an arrogant and conceited being? Since when has seeking your own glory been morally permissible behavior? This idea seems to equate God with a haughty, stuck-up person that no one wants to be around.

Certainly, for humanity, this is absolutely true. But when Deity becomes involved, the picture is entirely different. The absolute justice and righteousness of God demands that he seek the glory of the highest being in existence – himself – lest he engage in the idolatry that is so disgusting in his eyes. God will not break his own first commandment: "Have no other gods before me" (Exodus 20:3). There is no higher being than God and he knows this, so he freely loves and worships himself, without arrogance or conceit, but in the reality of his perfections.

The problem with mere humans seeking their own glory is that they don't deserve any. We are a people formed from dust, radically and utterly depraved, and hopelessly enslaved to sin apart from the grace of Christ. Our worth is found in *his image.*

But God reigns forever and ever. Righteousness and justice are the foundation of his throne, and steadfast love and faithfulness go before him. He is the Alpha and Omega, the bright morning star, a deity whose worth cannot be described, the hope of the nations, the faithful Redeemer of his people, the glorious foundation of the salvation of the saints, the One to whom every knee will bow and of whom every tongue confess, the longing of every human heart, and the object of every created thing. From everlasting to everlasting he is God, the Crafter of the planets and the Transformer of hearts, who holds the stars in his hand and yet numbers the hair on our heads. His splendor outlasts that of the noonday sun. He upholds the universe by the word of his power, his eyes are like a flame of fire, and in his mouth are words that are spirit and life. He will get glory from every human action and from every human mouth because of his perfect work. And he deserves every bit of it.

MAXIMIZED GLORY

Since God is perfectly holy and just, he will not be satisfied with only a minimal amount of glory for himself. It is absolutely necessary that his entire creation glorifies him. If his glory meter were to only register 5 out of 10, he would cease to be God. He has made it clear that he will be supremely or maximally glorified. This means he does whatever needs to be done so that he receives the most glory. A percentage of glory will simply not do.

So God does all things for his own maximized glory. In what follows you will see how this truth works to make sense of our lives. God's desire to glorify God gives our lives meaning, purpose, and direction. But how? First of all it answers really tough questions like this one:

WHY DIDN'T GOD CREATE PEOPLE PERFECT TO BEGIN WITH?

Really, why do we have to go through this whole plan of redemption where Jesus saves us from our sins? Why didn't God just make us into perfected saints in Heaven already? Why on earth does he leave us in the world to endure the difficulties of life? If he had created us perfect, it seems like it would have really saved him and us a lot of time and effort!

Think about it. If God had created us perfect then we would not have had to go through the Fall. We would not be "sinners." We would not have to suffer in a world of evil and violence. Nobody would ever make fun of us. We would never be the last one picked for the team. We could just be God's people, created to honor him. We could be like the faithful angels in Heaven who never fell into sin, who simply worship and honor God constantly. Why didn't God make us like them?

Why does he allow us to go through horrible situations in our lives? Why do we have to go through the dreaded experience of having a crush on another person knowing that he or she would rather we fall off a cliff? Why do we have to suffer the tragedy of divorced parents? Why do we have to endure the deaths of people we love? Why is each of us obligated to face death personally? "It is appointed for man to die once" (Hebrews 9:27). Sometimes it would be so nice not to be here at all, but rather to be there with him, perfected and holy like Christ (Philippians 1:21-24).

But for some reason God did not create us pre-fit for Heaven. Oh, sure, Adam and Eve were created *innocent*, and in that sense they were morally pure. But God created them with the *capacity* to mess up and fall into sin. He created them with the ability to disobey his commands.

Why did He do that?

Answer: God created humans with the capacity to sin because, by setting up things this way, *he is bringing **more** glory to himself.* Remember, life is not ultimately about you and it is not ultimately about me. It is ultimately about God maximizing his glory. So there is something about us living through life as sinners and experiencing the good and the bad and the ugly day-by-day that glorifies God more than if he had just created us perfect. There is something about our rejoicing and suffering that brings God great honor, more honor than if we never actually experienced these things.

SAYING AND SHOWING

God loves to demonstrate things. He loves to show off his power. It is not enough for him to simply say, "I am strong, just, and holy" (Psalm 9:7-8). He wants to say *and* show it. So he does things in order to display the splendor and majesty of who he is.

He crafts nations like Israel and her foe Egypt, so that he can bring them into great conflict and then, ultimately, deliver Israel from Egypt. In leading them out of bondage, he reveals to Pharaoh that he is the only God. It is one thing to say it. It is quite another thing to prove it.

> Lift up your staff, and stretch out your hand over the sea and divide it, that the people of Israel may go through the sea on dry ground. And I will harden the hearts of the Egyptians

so that they shall go in after them, and *I will get glory* over Pharaoh and all his host, his chariots, and his horsemen. And the Egyptians shall *know that I am the LORD*, when I have gotten glory over Pharaoh, his chariots, and his horsemen. (Exodus 14:16-18, italics ours)

Did you catch that? God says, "I am the Lord," and then he proves it. He wanted the Egyptians to know personally **from experience** that he alone is the Lord of the ages. He will get "glory over Pharaoh, his chariots, and his horsemen."

When it comes to our salvation, God doesn't desire to simply snap his fingers and say, "*Poof* – now you are perfect.*" Rather God wants us to *experience his grace* by living life day-by-day in his presence. He wants us to depend upon him each moment of our lives.

Trust in the LORD, and do good; dwell in the land and befriend faithfulness. Delight yourself in the LORD, and he will give you the desires of your heart. Commit your way to the LORD; trust in him, and he will act. (Psalm 37:3-5)

Why? It's because our trust and dependence upon God glorifies him in a maximized way. Our solid confidence makes him look really good and shows forth his power to others as he demonstrates it through real life events.

But you are a chosen race, a royal priesthood, a holy nation, a people for his own possession, that you may proclaim the excellencies of him who called you out of darkness into his marvelous light. (1 Peter 2:9)

His love and mercy upon us leads to our proclaiming "the excellencies" of God. But if there were no difficult situations in our lives, there would be no reason for us to trust him. If we were created perfect, there would be no reason for him to save us, and thus no maximized glory for him in saving us.

THE GLORY OF THE JOURNEY

Rick Ankiel plays professional baseball with the St. Louis Cardinals. On August 9, 2007, Ankiel was called up from the minors and started in right field. During his first at-bat the home crowd gave him a long, standing ovation. Later in the game he hit a three-run home run to lead the Cardinals to victory.

This story is significant if you know Ankiel's past. He came to the big leagues as a starting pitcher – not an outfielder. He wasn't just an average pitcher either, he was exceptional. *USA Today* named him High School Player of the Year in 1997. He was a highly scouted pitcher and the Cardinals paid him well to be one of their starting aces.

But something terrible happened. In a 2000 postseason game against the Atlanta Braves he suddenly and literally lost his ability to pitch. This was like Shakespeare loosing his ability to read. Ankiel could not manage to get the ball across the plate. He walked batter after batter and threw a laughable number of wild pitches. He was cast down to the minor leagues in 2001 but he struggled there as well.

In 2002 he could not play at all because of injury. When he came back the following season his numbers were still not impressive. It looked like it was all over for Ankiel. It was time to hang the cleats up, get a (real) job, and quit dreaming.

No, actually that is when Ankiel really started dreaming big! In 2005 he announced that he was switching to the outfield. Only a few players, including the great Babe Ruth, have ever successfully switched from pitching to playing another position. Ankiel began to work hard on both his fielding and batting skills. In the minors he began posting impressive numbers and in August of 2007 he was called back up to the Cardinals.

When he came to the plate, the crowd in St. Louis remembered him. They knew about his horrendous struggles and debilitating difficulties. That is why they gave him such a loud and vocal welcome. This is the stuff of legends! A pitcher turned outfielder! When he hit his first homerun that night, the crowd went wild! And it wasn't because they had never seen a homerun before. They see homeruns in St. Louis all the time. But this one was different. Very different.

It was his *experience* that made the difference. It was his personal history that made this homerun so historical. It was the pain, disappointment, and failure that he personally endured for several years that made that moment so powerful. He could have given up. Most players *would* have given up. But Ankiel fought his way back to the majors and is now thriving in his new position.

There is glory in the journey!

Cardinals manager Tony La Russa had tears in his eyes after the game. He could hardly speak because he was so moved emotionally by Ankiel's comeback. This was a *glorified* homerun and it was Ankiel's ability to face difficulty head on that glorified it.[70]

It is the same in our relationship with the Lord. God is highly glorified because of our enduring the lows and enjoying the highs of our lives. He is also glorified when we personally experience his love and deliverance. The life, death, and resurrection of Christ are powerful, historical demonstrations of the love of God! He does not want us just to love him because he *says* he is great. He wants us to love him because through Christ he has *shown* us that he is great. When we think of the things he has done to redeem us, our hearts are moved by those actions.

So God did not create us as already-perfected saints. Instead he gives us the wonderful privilege of depending upon him and personally seeing his grace in action. These experiences bring him tremendous glory, which is the reason why he does everything.

This is the same reason, by the way, that we are not (usually) allowed to see God. Oh, he has shown himself in the past: through a burning bush, in the Person of Jesus Christ, and in other times and ways. But for right now, we don't normally see him. Why not? Because trusting him while not seeing him, brings more glory to him than if we saw him. We are to live by faith and not by sight (2 Corinthians 5:7). For more on this, see chapter 14.

THE NARROW ROAD FOR THE GLORY OF GOD

The truth that God loves God more than anything and does all things for his own maximized glory explains everything in life! It answers every question I might have and makes life make sense.

Have you ever wondered why God doesn't save *everybody*? That seems like a good idea. Plus, God obviously has the power to open every single person's eyes to see the truth of the gospel of Christ and be saved. But for some reason God does not save everybody. There are people who are lost and who refuse to bow their knee to Jesus Christ. They are headed toward destruction and everlasting death in Hell, and God seemingly does nothing to stop them from plummeting into destruction.

Even more surprising, God seems to save only a comparatively few people. Most of the people ever born are on the "broad road that leads to destruction." Jesus informs us that the pathway to salvation is "narrow" and only a few enter onto it (Matthew 7:13-14).

But why? Why doesn't he save *all people?* Answer: God does all things for his own maximized glory. That means there is something about saving a remnant that glorifies God more than saving a majority (Romans 9:27).

Now, this is a hard teaching because it is easy to think God ought to do only what is best *for us* (as we define what is best for us). But God does not work that way. He first does what honors himself the most, and this involves saving only a portion of the world's inhabitants.

This leads to another perplexing question: how does saving only a remnant of people glorify God more than saving the majority? This is a question that human beings will always struggle to adequately answer. We cannot presume to know the heights and depths of the mind of God. As Paul pondered the wonder of the divine mind and plan, he confessed: "Oh, the depth of the riches and wisdom and knowledge of God! How unsearchable are his judgments and how inscrutable his ways!" (Romans 11:33).

But we can envision a possible answer. Imagine a room full of fifty people. They all are in rebellion against God, sinners who fall short of the glory of God (Romans 3:23). All of them deserve eternal punishment for offending an eternal and infinitely righteous being.

However, God in his mercy pours out his grace on ten of them. He opens their eyes to the death and resurrection of Christ as a means of forgiveness and redemption. They believe and are saved (John 3:16)! But the other forty people persist in their unbelief.

Now jump ahead to eternity. The ten believers are enjoying the presence of God. They are with Christ and the other saints of God, praising the King forever (Revelation 5:9-10). But then they take a fieldtrip. Isaiah the prophet tells us about this important fieldtrip at the very end of his book:

> "For as the new heavens and the new earth that I make shall remain before me," says the LORD, "so shall your offspring and your name remain. From new moon to new moon, and from Sabbath to Sabbath, all flesh shall come to worship before me, declares the LORD. *And they shall go out and look on the dead bodies of the men who have rebelled against me.* For their worm shall not die, their fire shall not be quenched, and they shall be an abhorrence to all flesh." (Isaiah 66:22-24, italics ours)

The fieldtrip is out to the pit. You see, Hell belongs to God, *not* to the Devil, or the demons, or anyone else. So the ten redeemed individuals leave their heavenly homes for awhile and go out to the prison that God has created for those in wicked rebellion against him. There, the ten saved see the other forty who are damned. They look into the flames of Hell itself, and see the anguish and torture of those who refused to trust in Christ.

By the way, we know that this passage in Isaiah is referring to the eternal state because Jesus himself picks up on the language of this passage when he speaks of Hell:

> If your eye causes you to sin, tear it out. It is better for you to enter the kingdom of God with one eye than with two eyes to be thrown into hell, "where their worm does not die and the fire is not quenched." (Mark 9:47-48)

The "worm" is probably a reference to maggots. These horrible little creatures love to consume dead bodies, but in Hell they never die. The imagery is one of eternal death, but the bodies of those who are eternally dying are somehow kept alive so that they can personally and physically experience their punishment.

According to the Isaiah passage above, the saved people go and look out at the pit where this eternal death is being demonstrated. I have often heard people say unbiblical things like: "There will be no memory in heaven," or "We will not remember those people who are in Hell." People who say these things have either never read or do not believe Isaiah 66:22-24!

So when the ten saved people come and see this place of everlasting punishment, what will be their reaction? How will they respond when they see so many people who are facing the wrath of God?

Surely, they will be struck to the heart! Oh, the justice of God is awful and perfect! They will *see* the righteous punishment being poured out upon God's enemies. They will *see* that this place GLORIFIES

148

God, because it demonstrates his holiness and justice. Perfect and eternal justice requires perfect and eternal punishment for sin.

But then God's redeemed will remember their own condition. They will remember that they deserved to be in that same place because they were just as rebellious as all the rest. They will remember the wondrous grace of Jesus in saving them from their sins. Perhaps they will remember the words of Paul:

> But God, being rich in mercy, because of the great love with which he loved us, even when we were dead in our trespasses, made us alive together with Christ – by grace you have been saved – and raised us up with him and seated us with him in the heavenly places in Christ Jesus, so that in the coming ages he might show the immeasurable riches of his grace in kindness toward us in Christ Jesus. For by grace you have been saved through faith. And this is not your own doing; it is the gift of God, not a result of works, so that no one may boast. (Ephesians 2:4-9)

After the fieldtrip to the pit, they run back to the throne. "Oh, Lord Christ, we thank you for your grace!" It is maximized grace and it provides God with maximized glory.

They fall before Jesus and praise him with a renewed sense of desire. Their worship is not mediocre, but an overflow of intense thanksgiving for salvation and mercy. They have *seen* what they have been delivered from! God is praised and honored and celebrated in a maximized way by this remnant, precisely because they see what might have been apart from God's grace. They see the suffering of the wicked and they are overjoyed at the satisfaction of being covered in the righteousness of Christ.

God does all things for *his own* maximized glory. As hard as it is to understand, this might mean that more people suffer eternally for their sins. It might mean that the path of salvation is narrow and only a few enter onto it.[71]

But in the end, the good of all this is greater than it could be otherwise, because God's justice is glorified in a maximized way through Hell, and God's grace is glorified in a maximized way through Heaven.

EVERY QUESTION ANSWERED AND EVERY PROBLEM SOLVED

So if we know that God does all things for his most maximized glory, then we have an answer for every problem and dilemma that occurs in life. We may not grasp all the "whys," but we do know the ultimate answer – it is for the glory of God!

We can even understand what the ultimate purpose of our lives is. That is no longer a question for us. This truth explains why we exist and why everything that happens, happens.

I (Jason) love taking this message that it is all for God's glory to funerals. It makes even death make sense. For nearly six years I was the pastor of a small, mostly senior-adult church. Over that course of time I preached this truth at twelve funerals. It was amazing to watch the people respond. We were able to turn these overwhelmingly sad occasions into times of intense worship. Even death makes sense in the light of God's glory.

I love to meditate on this teaching when all the money runs out. I understand why I must be content without money (so that I trust in him and not in money).

I love knowing these truths when relationship problems come up. It helps me to calm down and try to make peace with people. It helps me to take a slap in the face and turn the other cheek.

God does all things for his own maximized glory! This is the central truth that governs the operation of the entire vast expanse of creation for all of eternity. And it is the single, central truth that makes life make sense.

The Center Holds

Philosophers and artists alike have searched for hundreds of years for some central, unifying truth that holds all things together and makes everything else make sense; something that is linked to everything else and chains it all together. They have been searching, metaphorically speaking, for the foundation of the skyscraper.

You have no doubt seen these giant buildings that comprise the skylines of major cities. They are enormous. Most of the building is thrust up into the air. But it could not stand there without the bottom being firmly intact. Every square inch of a skyscraper is closely connected to the foundation, because the foundation is the power structure that makes the rest of the building sound.

But what about truth? Is there some foundational truth that holds up every other truth? Is there some central idea that makes every other idea make sense?

Eastern religions have come up with the notion of Brahman. This is like "god" for them: a central idea that connects everything together. A concept like this is seen clearly in the *Star Wars* movies with the mysterious "force." When Yoda died he was "absorbed" into the force because all living things are connected by it.

In the West in recent days, many people have given up the search for a central and unifying truth altogether. With the rise of relativism, people just simply say there is no central, absolute truth. Instead, something can be true for you but not for me.

"Are you a Christian?" you ask a person.

"No, I am not," they reply.

You continue, "May I tell you the truth about Jesus Christ and how you can be reconciled to God through his work?"

"Well, sure, but I have already heard about that. It is a really good story. And it might be true for you, but it is not true for me."

This basic conversation characterizes the way many people in our culture view truth today. They believe that there is no central, all-encompassing truth upon which all other truth is based. But this type of thinking ends up making life very confusing! People don't know what to believe, and often conclude that it doesn't really matter anyway because it is all relative.

Before iPods, all music came on CDs, and even before that, cassettes. Music came as a package, and the collection contained every song that the artist intended to include on the album. But with current music technology, everyone simply picks and chooses what songs they want to download and leave the rest behind.

And it is all relative. If you like the song you buy it. If you don't like the song, you don't. Your music library is custom fit to whatever it is you want it to be. People do that with truth now. There is no "album" as far as this relativistic view is concerned, that holds all the "songs" of reality together.

But what about the truth that God does all things for his own maximized glory? If that is the central, unifying truth that holds everything else together, then we do have an album! Trees make sense when we consider that they exist for the glory of God. Hurricanes and tornadoes make sense when placed next to the truth that God does all things for his own glory. The existence of a planet called Earth, history, science, occupations, humans, animals, suffering, all make sense – that is, they serve a purpose and are all part of the same "album." *Everything* makes sense when we realize this central truth: God does all things for his own maximized glory!

GOD'S LOVE MAXIMIZED THROUGH HIS GLORY

This concept gets even better. Not only is the glory of God the philosophical center that holds all things together, but – and this is a beautiful thing about our involvement in God's passion for his own glory – we get to experience the incredible love that he pours out *on us* as a result of his love for himself.

The pursuit of his own glory is the greatest gift that God could ever grant to man, for it is the deepest desire of man's heart to bring glory to his Creator. Giving God glory through our lives *does not* confine us to a dungeon of joyless and miserable work to be dreaded. Rather, we find that "in [God's] presence there is fullness of joy; at your right hand are pleasures forevermore" (Psalm 16:11). God "delivered us from the domain of darkness and transferred us to the Kingdom of his beloved son" (Colossians 1:13).

Paul writes this concerning his interaction with the world: "I count everything as loss because of the surpassing worth of knowing Christ Jesus my Lord. For his sake I have suffered the loss of all things and count them as rubbish, in order that I may gain Christ and be found in him" (Philippians 3:8-9). In other words, the love of God streaming through Christ made Paul very happy and satisfied. God's holy and joyful love for himself spills over into the lives of the redeemed.

Jesus describes himself as the very "bread of life" (John 6:35) and claims, "whoever drinks of the water I will give him will never be thirsty forever" (John 4:14). Christ offers a freedom from the bondage of sin and decay in order that we may take hold of that which is truly life.

The gospel is fundamentally the offer of God as the gift of himself. It is the promise that we ourselves can be "partakers of the divine nature" (2 Peter 1:4). Only this will bring humanity the fullness of joy, peace, and satisfaction. It was this that Jesus purchased with an unfathomable amount of humility:

Though he was in the form of God, [Christ Jesus] did not count equality with God a thing to be grasped, but made himself nothing, taking the form of a servant, being born in the likeness of men. And being found in human form, he humbled himself by becoming obedient to the point of death, even death on a cross. Therefore God has highly bestowed on him the name that is above every name, so that at the name of Jesus

153

every knee should bow...and every tongue confess that Jesus Christ is Lord, to the glory of God the Father. (Philippians 2:6-7)

God's pursuit of an eternal, unfading, all-encompassing glory was accomplished through redeeming man with the disgraceful and wretched cross, a beautiful glory perfected through captivating humility, and achieving "glory as of the only Son from the Father, full of grace and truth" (John 1:14). What great love has been poured out on us, that we may be a part of this glory so far beyond ourselves! "To him be the glory forever and ever. Amen" (Romans 11:36).

Chapter 7 Review Exercise

1. What kinds of problems might people have with the teaching that God does all things for his own glory? Are there any solutions to those problems?
2. Can you think of at least one Bible passage not mentioned in this chapter, where God is most interested in his own glory?
3. How does a person's journey glorify God in a maximized way?
4. According to the Bible, how does the existence of Hell glorify God?
5. According to the Bible, how does the existence of Heaven glorify God?
6. How does having a life that makes sense, change our behavior?
7. Describe how God's ultimate love for himself is the most loving thing he can do for us.

Key Terms

Glory
Hell

Scripture Memory

Be still, and know that I am God. I will be exalted among the nations, I will be exalted in the earth! (Psalm 46:10)

CHAPTER 8:
Something and Not Nothing

So far we have seen many reasons to believe that Christianity is *actually* true and the *only* truth.

We believe what has been discussed so far is extremely convincing and ought to be extremely convicting. The first argument given in chapter 2, that Jesus saves and forgives people of their sins, and that the Holy Spirit testifies to this in the heart of a believer, is all the evidence a person needs to be a Christian, and to be one rationally.[72] But this knowledge, although it can never be replaced by external evidence, can certainly be supported and defended by it, as seen in chapters 3-7.

Now, we change gears again in order to usher in even more evidence for the truthfulness of the Christian worldview. What follows in the next three chapters are the most popular and effective arguments for the existence of God. You might pause and ask, "We've already seen that the Bible is true, and since it is, this automatically means God exists, so why would we now move to mere logical arguments that demonstrate the same thing?"

There is a reason. These arguments have been a major part of apologetics for many years and God has used them to open the minds of many skeptics. Here is a question for you to consider: if God does exist, can we see evidence of his existence *from the things that he made?* Can we dust creation for his fingerprints? If so, then creation itself serves to *confirm* what Jesus and the biblical authors have taught us. There are organic connections between the teachings of Scripture and the external creation that serve as a verification factor.

Paul understood this reality when he wrote in Romans 1 that all of creation points to the existence of God:

> For what can be known about God is plain to them, because God has shown it to them. For his invisible attributes, namely, his eternal power and divine nature, have been clearly perceived, ever since the creation of the world, *in the things that have been made.* So they are without excuse. (Romans 1:19-20, italics ours)

But how does this work? How do we go about deducing from the things God made to the fact that God exists? We will now explore how the Cosmological Argument for the existence of God answers this question.[73]

Why Does Anything Exist At All?

Look around you. What do you see? Of course, no matter where you are while reading this, you can name a thousand things: a wall, a tree, a butterfly, the sun, the moon, a house, a computer, a book, etc. But you do see *something*, right? There are "things" of all kinds all around you.

But why is there something and not nothing? Please forgive the double negative, it may not be good grammar, but it is on purpose. It helps us think carefully about this question. Why do things exist instead of nothing? How does something come out of nothing? How do things come into existence at all? Where did they come from? Did things just pop into being from nothing like popcorn? But that cannot be right because popcorn does not pop into being from nothing. Popcorn pops into being from something else, namely, raw kernels. And the raw kernels come from cobs of corn, which come from corn stalks, which come from seeds planted in the earth. But where did the earth come from?

The logic is clear – things don't come into being by themselves. Someone or something must have caused those things to be there or else they would not be there. This truth gives rise to the Cosmological Argument for the existence of God. It states that God is the *first cause* that *causes* everything else to exist. Here is the formal argument:

1. Every contingent thing has a cause.
2. There cannot be an infinite regress of causes.
3. Therefore, there must be a first cause.
4. This first cause is either matter and energy or God.
5. The first cause is not matter and energy.
6. Therefore, the first cause is God.

Okay, if you are not familiar with this, you are probably rolling your eyes and trying to figure out why you are wasting your time reading this book. If this is you, press on! You can get this! If you have studied apologetics or philosophy before, you are familiar with this argument and hopefully want to understand it better. Either way, let's work through each step carefully.

EVERY CONTINGENT THING HAS A CAUSE

Without going into a great amount of detail as to how it happened, you know that your parents caused you to exist, right? But did someone cause them to exist as well? Yep, their parents caused them to exist.

But guess what? Your grandparents also had parents. And their parents had parents who also had parents who also had parents. Every person who has every lived was caused to live by someone else. This is called a *causal chain*. One person caused another who caused another and so on.

It might help to think about a train. Suppose you drive up to a railroad crossing and you see all the train cars going by one-by-one. They are all attached to each other and they are all causing each other to move, so they make up a causal chain.

Now, notice the word *contingent* in the premise above. A contingent thing is something that *requires* something else for its existence. It is a dependent thing, a thing that *must have a cause*. A beautiful painting is contingent upon a skillful painter. A flying airplane is contingent on air, fuel and pilot (assuming it is not remote-controlled).

As you will see momentarily, not everything is contingent. But if something *is* contingent, then *it has a cause* which brings it into being. But these causes can't go back forever.

THERE CANNOT BE AN INFINITE REGRESS OF CAUSES

Causes and effects can go back for a long time. Remember your parents and their parents and their parents and so on. Well, we could just keep on going with that. Your great, great, great, great, great, great, great, great, great grandparents had parents. And your great, great, great, great, great, great, great, great, great, great grandparents had parents. And on and on we could go.

Or could we? Can this causal chain just keep going back forever? Or does this regress of causes ever stop? Is there a point where you get to your very first parents who themselves had *no* human parents?

Think about the train again. You see five cars, then ten cars, then thirty cars, then fifty cars, then seventy-five cars, then ninety cars go

160

by – and you are frustrated because you are late for work! Can this train be a never-ending train?

Is it possible for you to sit in your car at the railroad crossing and watch the train go by every day, week after week, month after month, year after year, without ever coming to an end (or beginning)? Of course not! An infinite, never-ending regress of causes is impossible.

The same is true with the existence of the universe. The earth was caused to exist, since it is a contingent thing, but what caused it to exist? Galaxies were caused to exist, but what caused them to exist? In other words, what was the very first thing that ever existed that caused everything else to exist? This leads us to the first major conclusion of the Cosmological Argument:

Therefore, There Must Be a First Cause

To most people, this seems to make a lot of sense and is the natural conclusion of the first two premises. At some point you have to have parents who are your *first* parents who have **no prior** human parents (Adam and Eve we'll say). The train at some point must end. There must be a cause (the engine) that is making all the other cars move.

The universe has to have a first cause too. There has to be some type of "engine" that is driving and causing everything else to exist. It is important to note that whatever this first cause is, it must be both *uncaused* and *eternal*.

What does it mean to be uncaused? It means that the first cause could not have been caused by anything or anyone else (including itself). Logically, it must have no cause at all. This first cause just *is*. It would necessarily be an ever present eternal being or substance. Something like this would appropriately be called *It Is*, or perhaps more appropriately *I Am*.

Why? Well, if the first cause has a cause, then it is not the first cause. If something created *it*, then it is not the *first* cause. This means that the first cause, whatever it is, must by necessity be uncaused and thus eternal. Eternal because if it is uncaused, then there was never a time when it did not exist and never a time when it will not exist. If there was a time when it did not exist, but it does exist now, then it was caused. In fact, that is what it means to be caused – to not exist and then to exist. But the first cause was not and could not have been caused at all. So if it is uncaused, it is also eternal.

This means the first cause must have no beginning and no ending. It must be what philosophers call a *necessary being*. Without it, nothing else exists. You might call it the First and Last or maybe even the Alpha and the Omega (Revelation 1:8).

Remember above when we were talking about the word contingent? A contingent thing is a thing that depends on something else for its existence. We stated that not everything is a contingent thing. Actually, the first cause is the only thing that is *not contingent*. It stands alone as the only thing in the universe that does not depend on something else for its existence since it is uncaused and eternal. It cannot be born and it cannot die. It cannot be created and it cannot be destroyed.

Now, this is where our illustrations about parents and trains break down and quit working. Your parents can go back a long way and you can have first parents, but Adam and Eve are not eternal beings because they too *had a beginning*. Something brought them into being, even if it wasn't "human" parents. They cannot be the first cause, even though they are the first human parents.

On the train, of course, the source of the movement of all the cars is the engine. The engine might be called the first car, since it propels the other cars, but the engine is a contingent thing too. It requires fuel in order to operate and an architect and builder to put it together, so it is a caused thing as well. It might be the first car, but it cannot fulfill the role of first cause. But what, or who, can fulfill the role of first cause? The answer can basically be reduced to two options.

This First Cause Is Either Matter and Energy or God

This premise is given in a dilemma form. This means it presents only *two options* for the first cause. But to be fair, there is another possibility that people have considered, but it is filled with problems. Let's take a brief look at this view.

The Matrix Briefly Considered

Some say that all of reality is nothing but an illusion. These people fight the logic of the first cause argument with the simple denial that there is a first cause at all. They do this by holding to the belief that in reality there is *nothing at all*.

A modern illustration of this belief was presented in the movie *The Matrix*. A little kid dressed in Hindu garb gazes at a spoon that bends in his hand like melting wax. He informs the lead character, Neo, that he could bend the spoon with his mind because the spoon wasn't really there. Some folks actually believe that! But this option – officially called pantheism – is filled with logical and philosophical problems and will be refuted in chapter 11.

Sure, it is possible that we are all living in the matrix. It could be that we all are not really here, but rather we are actually in a cold, dark room somewhere, unconscious, with our brains hooked into a master computer that is feeding our minds mere images of the world. This scenario is logically possible and it does make for a good story, but we have no real reason at all to believe that it is true. In fact, everything we sense and see tells us just the opposite. The word is a real, material place.

BACK TO REALITY

So this brings us back to the idea that the first cause is *either* matter and energy or God.

What if we say that it is matter and energy? There are many, many people who hold to this option or some form of it. They are called Naturalists. Some believe that matter and energy, which is essentially viewed as different forms of the thing substance, caused itself to exist, while others assert that it simply always has existed (that it is eternal). Still others hold that humanity just cannot know how it got here. Yet regardless of their viewpoint, the unifying belief is that matter and energy is ultimately all that there is.

Now when we say *matter* what are we talking about? The most basic known form of matter is the atom and the particles and energy that make it up. Atoms, of course, form into molecules, which form into bigger substances such as water, dust, rocks, and ultimately planets, stars and galaxies. The naturalist believes that the universe is only made up of these material things. This stuff, understood as a complete whole and described as matter and energy, is the first cause. Famous naturalist Carl Sagan once said, "The universe is all that is or ever was or ever will be."[74]

THE FIRST CAUSE IS NOT MATTER AND ENERGY

But there are many problems with naturalism. Those who hold that matter is *self-caused* have a really big problem. Self-causation is utterly illogical and impossible. In order for something to cause anything, it must first exist. But if it does not exist, it cannot cause anything at all to happen. If it cannot cause anything at all to happen, then it certainly cannot cause itself to exist. This option simply cannot work. But the idea that matter and energy is *eternal* is also highly problematic. It is difficult to conceive of atoms and other material entities as never having a beginning. It takes a great deal of blind faith to believe such a thing, especially since there isn't any evidence for it.

Another obvious problem with naturalism is that it cannot explain the presence of life. Life does not come from non-life. Even if it were accepted that matter and energy is eternal, it is obviously not *personal*. How do dirt and dust give "birth" to the complex and living systems which make up the human body, or even the simplest cell? Life only comes from life. The naturalist is reduced to believing that the entire universe is the product of unguided and unintelligent non-life. Somehow, he believes, life sprung into being from this non-life and non-intelligence gave rise to intelligence.

They also have to admit that ultimately there is no real purpose or meaning at all in the universe! After all, if human beings are mere accidents who will soon be extinct, nevermore to be remembered, then nothing we do in life really matters in any kind of significant way.

Even if a person goes on a murderous rampage and kills fifty people, it doesn't really matter *ultimately.* Even though these horrible actions might affect the people he kills and the families of his victims for a long time, it still will not be significant ultimately. And even though these actions might affect the killer himself (say he is put to death for his deeds), it still will not matter ultimately.

Think about it. Will anybody care about the killer or his victims when the human race ceases to exist? In 700 billion years, long after the sun and solar system have run their courses and are gone forever, who will care about this murderer and his horrible deeds? If the naturalist is correct, then nobody will care. Because there will be *nobody at all* in 700 billion years *to* care. But people know that what we do matters. We know that love is right and unjustified killing is wrong and that all of our actions have real and ultimate meaning.

Naturalism is a position that is not acceptable to billions of people. Even if mainstream science is dominated by people who believe that matter is the first cause, it cannot be accepted and must be declared false. This of course leaves us only one viable option:

THEREFORE, THE FIRST CAUSE IS GOD

The first cause must be uncaused and eternal. God is uncaused and eternal. He has no beginning and no ending. Most children wonder about this. "Who made God?" is the question. The answer is *nobody*. He did not even make himself. He is not self-caused (again, that is impossible), but rather he is uncaused.

How can this be? If everything has to have a cause, what was it that caused God? But let's be clear here: the naturalist must assert that matter and energy is uncaused just like the Christian must assert that God is uncaused. Just because we cannot explain *how* God is eternal does not negate the fact that there must be something that *is* eternal. We may not be able to explain the eternality of God, but without it we can explain nothing else. The crux of the Cosmological Argument is the necessity of a self-existent entity to justify the existence of the universe.

The first cause must also be alive and intelligent, since it brings into existence things that are alive and intelligent (look in the mirror). God is alive and intelligent and we could see why he might desire to create other life and other intelligence. On every account, God is a much better explanation of the first cause than matter and energy.

LIMITS OF THE COSMOLOGICAL ARGUMENT

We must stress the limits of the Cosmological Argument. It really is powerful and effective in showing the extreme high probability of God's existence, but it does not distinguish between false gods and the real God. A Muslim or a Mormon could also use this same argument, but neither the Muslim god nor the Mormon god is actually God. They have constructed false gods and worship them instead of the one true God.

166

This is why the Bible is vital to the apologetic process! The trustworthy word of God is used by the Spirit of God to show us that the first cause is not just any old god, but rather the one and only true God of the Old and New Testaments. Jesus Christ came to verify this fact by dying on the cross to reconcile sinners and rising from the dead.

Just remember, we cannot use only one defense of our faith, but we must have an arsenal of reasons for the hope that is in us (1 Peter 3:15). The Cosmological Argument for the existence of God is one arrow in our quiver, but it is not the only one.

Chapter 8 Review Exercise

1. For practice write out the major points of the Cosmological Argument for the existence of God.
2. The first premise of the Cosmological Argument states that every contingent thing has a cause. Do you agree or disagree? Explain.
3. Why can't there be an infinite regress of causes?
4. Why, if something is uncaused, must it also be eternal?
5. What are some of the problems with saying that matter and energy is the first cause?

Key Terms

Cosmological Argument
Contingent
Cause
Infinite regress
First cause
Eternal

Scripture Memory

In the beginning, God created the heavens and the earth. (Genesis 1:1)

CHAPTER 9:
Design versus Chaos

High school students are growing up in a terrific scientific age. It was only a century ago or so, when if you wanted to go to town, you had to hook the horse up to the buggy, or really enjoy walking. A century ago there were no TV's, no laser surgeries, no computers, and no iPods.

But all of this has changed now and continues to change at a rapid pace. The scientific enterprise has opened new doors in every field of knowledge and has brought tremendous benefit to humanity, along with some very serious ethical concerns – nuclear bombs and human cloning are two huge examples.

Christians have taken different stances in regard to all of this change. The Amish are famous for attempting to live the old life and ignore most of the technological advances that have been made. Other Christians fully embrace this new age and attempt to implement these technological advances in every way possible to further the truth of the gospel.

As for the authors, we believe that the scientific enterprise is extremely valuable on a practical level, but also that its findings strongly support and confirm belief in God. In this chapter we hope to show that the best science available to modern man reveals incredible signs of design and points to the existence of God.

THE SCIENCE OF DESIGN

You have probably heard at least a little bit about Intelligent Design (ID).[75] Headed by insightful scientists like Michael Behe and William Dembski, this movement is very different from Creation Science, although the court systems and the news media place them in the same category.[76] But how are they different?

Creation Science is a method of scientific inquiry that *begins with the Bible*. The creation scientist takes Genesis 1-2 as truth first and then engages in asking and answering scientific questions. He assumes God exists and that God is the Creator *before* he ever looks at a butterfly, for example, for scientific purposes. Then when he goes to observe, dissect, and describe the butterfly scientifically, he does so through the lens of Genesis, his prior assumption.

Intelligent Design does not approach science in the same way. In fact, a scientist might be part of the ID movement but not even be a Christian. A person might buy into ID theory and simply say that there is a god, but people do not know or cannot know who he is or what he is like. This approach is much different than Creation Science.

Rather than starting with the Bible (or any other religious / philosophical assumption), an ID scientist attempts to begin the scientific process from a totally unbiased perspective. He wants to be careful not to bring any assumptions at all to the scientific endeavor.[77]

If he is a Christian he does not want his Christian beliefs to sway his scientific results. If he is Jewish he does not want his Judaism to sway his scientific results. He just wants to look at the butterfly and let the butterfly "speak," rather than come to the butterfly already persuaded about what the butterfly is from prior assumptions.

Of course, most mainstream naturalistic scientists also say that they come to their work unbiased, but this is false. They are openly committed to *methodological naturalism*, or the belief that only natural explanations can be given for natural phenomenon. So for them it is off limits to evoke the supernatural when doing science. This is a prior assumption they make *before* they begin the scientific process.

In other words the naturalist assumes that the butterfly is purely a result of naturalistic processes and that supernatural processes (like Creation) are either impossible or unknowable, and therefore will not be admitted in the scientific results. If the naturalistic scientist finds serious evidences of design in the butterfly, this evidence is ignored or reinterpreted because it does not fit into his prior assumptions. ID scientists, on the other hand, make every effort to remove *all* biases before they begin the scientific process.[78]

CAN ANYONE TRULY BE UNBIASED?

We must offer a bit of critique here of the ID movement and any other group that claims to be totally unbiased. Although what they are doing is commendable (attempting to do science without prior assumptions), we think that it is essentially impossible. Even if they say they are interpreting scientific data without bias, it is not clear at all that they are.

Why not? People cannot be truly unbiased because they have assumptions about reality that are hard to ignore. A person who is engaged in science will interpret scientific findings in a way consistent with their established worldview commitments.[79]

If I believe that there is a Creator, no matter how hard I try to look at a butterfly without bias, alas, I cannot. I cannot genuinely say, "This butterfly might have a Creator, but it might not." I *know* that it does, and my scientific results will always *show* that it does.

ID advocates also have prior beliefs. Try as they may to be neutral about things, as many naturalistic scientists also do, they cannot. People are driven by their philosophical and theological convictions and will find it virtually impossible to do science apart from these convictions.

Having made these points, however, we do want to emphasize the great amount of scientific data that is available that points to the existence of God, or at the very least a grand designer. ID scientists are doing a fantastic job showing off this evidence. Though scientific findings cannot be judged in a purely neutral way, yet the overwhelming amount of material in the universe that exhibits signs of order and design is incredible, and is certainly consistent with a theistic view of the world.[80]

HOW DO WE KNOW WHEN SOMETHING IS DESIGNED?

Many naturalists have attacked ID theory by saying that the universe only *appears* to be designed. Richard Dawkins, a preeminent naturalist and aggressive atheist once wrote, "All appearances to the contrary, the only watchmaker in nature is the blind forces of physics."[81]

They hasten to add, however, that even though the universe may have "appearances" of design, believers in God are reading too much into these signs. They say that theists are only seeing what they want to see – finding God under every rock, so to speak. But is this the case?

In recent years, there have been strong attempts to show that certain features of design can be identified and verified by using various scientific formulas.[82] If an object exhibits certain degrees of artistic arrangement and complexity, for example, we can say it was designed.

Archeologists use similar formulas as they dig through the ground and find various artifacts. If an arrowhead is found, for example, it will be accepted as something that has been designed by an intelligent being. Why? An arrowhead has been obviously manipulated to serve a certain function. There is a meaningful shape to it and it is symmetrical, things which set it apart from other ordinary rocks. There is a complexity about it that does not appear when we examine common rocks. There might be interesting figures artistically carved on it, whose origin cannot be explained by purely natural processes, and attempting to do so would be absurd. Thus there is no question among archeologists – the arrowhead was intelligently designed!

The same method can be used when we observe Mount Rushmore. Most mountains we see do not contain the familiar faces of four U.S. presidents. It would take a person of very low intelligence or one who simply denies reality to say that Mount Rushmore was not designed.

THE WATCH AND THE WATCHMAKER

Certain patterns and arrangements of matter indicate design. In his 1802 publication *Natural Theology*, well known Christian apologist William Paley proposed the issue along the following lines. Suppose you are walking along a road and find a watch. As you observe it, you see the intricate details and the small gears functioning together causing the watch to work. The tiny hands move in complex precision in a seemingly meaningful way.

Obviously, you do not assume that it is a "natural" product of the wind, rain, and other elements. These things do not "design" objects of such specified complexity. Where there is a watch there must be a *watchmaker*, who must be living, skilled, and intelligent.[83]

The universe itself bears similar artistic arrangement and complexity. There is an order, for example, to the heavenly bodies and their movements. This is why we use the word "system" when we describe what is going on in the sky above us. We speak of galactic systems and solar systems. The implication is that these things have been systematically arranged to operate as they do.

But the signs of design are even clearer when we observe things on the earth. We find weather systems, ecological systems, all types of biological systems, such as visual systems, respiratory systems, circulatory systems, skeletal systems, digestive systems, reproductive systems, and nervous systems and others. There is an obvious arrangement of matter that one would not expect to happen accidentally or by unguided natural processes.

What's more, we see intelligence, especially within the human family. That is, people are capable of learning new things and adapting to new situations and environments based on what was learned. We are even able to communicate what we have learned to others. As amazing as this phenomenon is, the naturalist is committed to saying that intelligence is a mere by-product of natural processes and really means nothing at all. But does intelligence come from non-intelligence? Even more fundamental, does life come from non-life?

It seems inconceivable that complex biological, emotional, spiritual, and personal beings (such as humans are) could come about by unintelligent, non-living, accidental processes. In fact, it seems more logical to believe that Mount Rushmore just so happened to form because of years of rain, wind, and erosion, than to believe that the vast ordered universe and the complex human creature came about by mere coincidence – a quirk of nature.

WHEN CEREAL TALKS

Consider an often used illustration to help shed light on this issue of design. Suppose that on your kitchen counter, there is a box of Alphabits, an old-school cereal meant to help children learn their letters. One day you walk into the kitchen and the box has fallen over, spilling the cereal all over the counter. As you look at the scattered letters you see the following:

174

GJ OK LJCA R H BVW STPK KL Q PA G F   H
IK   L   B N   V   JPOI FE   U
X   DW I Y FSE D ZB   I OP WLK HRA

In addition, these letters are not all straight as they are pictured. Some are turned sideways, others diagonal, and a few are upside down.

Nobody would assume upon seeing this arrangement that these letters were placed in this position by an intelligent agent. Of course, we can't rule that out, but neither can we just assume it, since the letters are lying in such a random fashion. There seems to be no order to it, even though on the first line we see the letters C, A, and R, which spell the word *car*, lying side-by-side. Because of the context of randomness, however, we would not assume that someone put those three letters in that order, but we would rather assume that these letters fell into this order coincidentally.

On the other hand, suppose the box of Alpha-bits had fallen over and you walked into your kitchen and saw the following arrangement in two straight lines:

BILL CLINTON WAS THE FORTY SECOND PRESIDENT
OF THE UNITED STATES OF AMERICA

You wouldn't need to think twice about whether this arrangement of letters was designed or not. You would see the meaningful order and detailed complexity and you would know that *someone* had arranged these letters in this fashion, furthermore, someone with a high degree of intelligence. The person would have to understand something about communication, grammar, and history. Chance, of course, knows nothing of these things.

THE LANGUAGE OF GOD

Dr. Francis Collins, a brilliant geneticist and former director of the National Human Genome Research Institute, has written a powerful book called *The Language of God*. Collins was appointed by President Clinton to head a team whose goal was the mapping and sequencing of all human DNA, a goal they incredibly accomplished. For his leadership, Collins received the Presidential Medal of Freedom in 2007.

Having examined DNA structures perhaps more closely than any previous scientist, Collins and his team revealed the incredible amount of genetic information and instruction contained within each strand of DNA. These encoded recipes for life, in effect, store the blueprints containing the necessary data for building cells. But vast amounts of carefully crafted information, such as is contained in these genetic blueprints, do not happen by mere chance. You wouldn't, for example, point at a computer with a hard drive full of data and say, "This machine and the information contained on it have no intelligent cause."

The undeniable complexity and organization of DNA is an obvious sign of design, like the second Alpha-bits example. Because of this, it is extremely rational to believe that an intelligent being designed DNA, and placed the information into the strands that allows for the existence of life. Dr. Collins indicates this with a powerful thought in *The Language of God:*

Many will be puzzled by these sentiments, assuming that a rigorous scientist could not also be a serious believer in a transcendent God. This book aims to dispel that notion, by arguing that belief in God can be an entirely rational choice, and that the principles of faith are, in fact, complementary with the principles of science. [84]

IRREDUCIBLE COMPLEXITY

Scientific findings of design are further supported by a phenomenon called irreducible complexity. An object is considered irreducibly complex if it is a system that only functions properly *if every part of the system is present.*

A simple mousetrap can demonstrate irreducible complexity. This contraption of death is made up of five parts, each of which *must be present* in order for the mousetrap to work: the base, spring, latch, flapper, and holder. If any one of these parts is removed, you do not have a functioning mousetrap. Of course, this means that each of those parts must be placed into the system *at the same time* in order for it to work. But this strongly implies that some intelligent being must be present to place those parts together at the same time! Mousetraps do not occur by the interactions of unintelligent, unguided natural forces. [85]

As we observe organisms around us, we find that many of them are irreducibly complex or contain irreducibly complex systems. The human eye is one solid example of this, since each part of it must be present at the same time in order for it to work properly. Evolution of each part over a long period of time is highly unlikely considering the complexity of each part, and the dependency that each part has on the other parts in order for the eye to function properly. Alvin Plantinga explains:

> Consider the mammalian eye: a marvelous and highly complex instrument, resembling a telescope of the highest quality, with a lens, an adjustable focus, a variable diaphragm for controlling the amount of and optical corrections for spherical and chromatic aberration. And here is the problem: how does the lens, for example, get developed by the proposed means: random, genetic variation, and natural selection, when at the same time there has to be development of the optic nerve, the

177

relevant muscles, the retina, the rods and cones, and many other delicate and complicated structures, all of which have to be adjusted to each other in such a way that they can work together? Indeed, what is involved isn't, of course, just the eye; it is the whole visual system, including the relevant parts of the brain. Many different organs and suborgans have to be developed together, and it is hard to envisage a series of mutations which is such that each member of the series has adaptive value, is also a step on the way to the eye, and is such that the last member is an animal with such an eye.[86]

Scientists also point to the bacterial flagellum as an example of irreducible complexity. This common organism, considered to the most basic type of life in existence, works almost like a mini submarine, many parts working together to produce motion. It contains a motor, propeller, universal joint, stator, bushing, and many other necessary parts that work together to allow the creature to be mobile. The DNA inside the nucleus contains the information to build the motor and propeller system while other parts of the cell actually carry out the building process, using proteins as the building blocks.

This "simple" organism is incredibly complex. In fact, it is irreducibly complex. Again, this means that if any of its parts were removed, it would cease to be able to function properly. This strongly implies that each part was carefully *placed* in order to achieve proper function. But if the parts were placed, of course this means *someone* had to place them.

Charles Darwin himself confessed that if an example could be found of an organism that was irreducibly complex, then his theory would crumble: "If it could be demonstrated that any complex organ existed which could not possibly have been formed by numerous, successive, slight modifications, my theory would absolutely break down."[87]

178

Darwin's prophecy has proven true by the discovery of many bio-logical systems that exhibit irreducible complexity.

The Fine Tuning of the Universe

Another example of a design argument that points to the existence of an eternal creator is called the Fine-Tuning Argument.

Physicists tell us that the universe is held together by various cosmic constants, each of which has to be precisely "set" in order to sustain life in the universe. These particular constants have the appearance of being fine tuned. That is, it seems like someone has turned the dials to the precise numbers that allow the universe to exist and life to flourish in it.

If you are familiar with the guitar, you understand how important fine tuning is. If only one string is even slightly out of tune, every chord will be disharmonious. The fine tuning of a guitar implies an intelligent tuner who sets each string to its precise position to create perfect harmony.

On a broader scale, the universe exhibits the same principle. If there were a slight deviation of the power of gravitational pull in the universe, for example, then the universe would either implode on itself, or expand too rapidly to allow life to exist on earth. So the gravitational constant appears to have been "set." Many other constants exhibit this same setting, such as how quickly matter expands, ratios of carbon to oxygen, and the ratio of protons to neutrons. If these constants, or any one of them, were anything other than exactly what they are, the universe would be in a radically different place, most likely devoid of life. Stephen Meyer, cofounder of the Discovery Institute,[88] explains:

Imagine that you are a cosmic explorer who has just stumbled into the control room of the whole universe. There you discover an elaborate "universe-creating machine," with rows and rows of dials, each with many possible settings. As you investigate, you learn that each dial represents some particular parameter that has to be calibrated with a precise value in order to create a universe in which life can exist. One dial represents the possible settings for the strong nuclear force, one for the gravitational constant, one for Planck's constant, one for the ratio of the neutron mass to the proton mass, one for the strength of the electromagnetic attraction, and so on. As you, the cosmic explorer, examine the dials, you find that they could easily have been tuned to different settings. Moreover, you determine by careful calculation that if any of the dial settings were even slightly altered, life would cease to exist. Yet for some reason each dial is set at just the exact value necessary to keep the universe running. What do you infer about the origin of these finely tuned settings?[89]

The question Dr. Meyer raises is best answered by an intelligent agent. A finely tuned machine or musical instrument is not a freak accident of nature, but rather a carefully constructed and meaningful creation by an intelligent cause. Thus, if the universe exhibits incredible degrees of fine tuning we should draw the same conclusion.

This fine tuning cannot have happened by random chance, as naturalists often believe. How can fine tuning come out of pure chaos? Naturalists however will say that given enough time, chance can bring about fine tuning. But really, that would be like taking a guitar and six unattached strings, throwing them off the top of a skyscraper hoping that, by chance, while falling, the strings will attach themselves to the guitar and tune themselves to a point of harmonious perfection with each other. It really doesn't matter how many times you try to throw the guitar and strings, this will never happen. It is impossible. Likewise, chance plus time is not a strong enough explanation for the incredible fine tuning exhibited in the universe.

A broad number of scientists have made remarks along the same lines. John O' Keefe, an astronomer at NASA has said,

> We are, by astronomical standards, a pampered, cosseted, cherished group of creatures...If the Universe had not been made with the most exacting precision we could never have come into existence. It is my view that these circumstances indicate the universe was created for man to live in.[90]

Arno Penzias, winner of the Nobel Prize in physics once remarked,

> Astronomy leads us to a unique event, a universe which was created out of nothing, one with the very delicate balance needed to provide exactly the conditions required to permit life, and one which has an underlying (one might say 'supernatural') plan.[91]

The fine tuning of the universe is powerful evidence that God designed the universe specifically for man to live in. Naturalistic explanations of fine tuning are simply insufficient and do not do justice to the evidence.

WHICH GOD?

In this chapter, we hope you have seen how creation bears the fingerprints of God. Like the Cosmological Argument, design arguments for the existence of God are very potent in showing the rationality of believing that God exists, but these arguments are limited. They do not tell us which God is the real God! We must be sure to use *all* of the apologetic arguments for Christianity, including those that show the Bible is true and that Jesus Christ rose from the dead, when defending our faith. Muslims and Jews are very content to use the exact same design arguments that Christians do, so we must offer more.

Even still, we should never shy away from using design arguments. The heavens are declaring the Glory of God (Psalm 19:1) therefore we should point to the heavens to show off the splendor of our King. It is the God of the Bible who has designed all things for his glory and for his good purposes.

Chapter 9 Review Exercise

1. Describe the difference between Creation Science and Intelligent Design.
2. Do you believe scientists can approach their studies in a purely unbiased way? Why or why not?
3. Explain how the information contained in DNA is an argument for an intelligent designer.
4. The human eye is an example of an irreducibly complex system. How might a naturalist evolutionist explain the human eye from his standpoint? How could an Intelligent Design advocate respond?
5. In your own words, explain the Fine-Tuning Argument for the existence of God.

Key Terms

Creation Science
Intelligent Design
Methodological naturalism
Paley's Watchmaker
Irreducible complexity
Fine-Tuning Argument

Scripture Memory

The heavens declare the glory of God, and the sky above proclaims his handiwork. (Psalm 19:1)

CHAPTER 10:
Right and Wrong

The ever insightful Francis Schaeffer was a Christian thinker who coined the phrase, "mannishness of man." [92] He meant that human beings have certain qualities about them that make them human and, therefore, different from animals, even animals of higher intelligence. Though he certainly tries, man cannot escape the reality that he is created in the image of God.

For example, people tend to enjoy things with aesthetic value. Dogs have never truly enjoyed the beauty of a sunset or appreciated the splendor of a work of art. This desire to enjoy beauty is unique to humanity and raises the perplexing question, what causes people to possess this unique quality?

There are many other "mannish" qualities that we could discuss, but let's think specifically about one of them – moral sensibilities. In this chapter, we will make the case that the moral sensibilities built into human beings is the result of objective moral laws; and that the existence of objective moral laws provides strong evidence that God exists. That is a mouthful, so let's unpack it a bit.

People all around the world, in every culture, have a basic understanding of morality, or the differences between right and wrong. Honesty is right and murder is wrong. Caring for children is right and torturing children is wrong. Being faithful in marriage is right and committing adultery is wrong. People just simply and intuitively know these moral facts.

This deeply imbedded understanding of morality is not simply a matter of human law, but of something much more significant. Here is a very simple, but detailed argument showing that the best explanation for these moral sensibilities is the existence of God:

1. People universally know the difference between right and wrong.
2. Therefore, there is a universal moral law.
3. A universal moral law requires a universal moral lawgiver.
4. God is the universal moral lawgiver.
5. Therefore, God exists.

Before we look at each point in this Moral Argument for the existence of God, you should know that this particular argument was very compelling to C.S. Lewis, who made the move from atheism to theism. This beloved and brilliant Oxford professor of English Literature devoted the opening chapters of his treasured book *Mere Christianity* to an examination of morality and how it points solidly toward God.[93]

Of course, we must always remember that apart from the illuminating power of the Holy Spirit, no argument will convince an unbeliever to trust in God and certainly not to yield to Christ. But this particular argument has proven very powerful and the Holy Spirit has used it on many occasions as a means of opening the eyes of the blind. Now we consider the first point.

People Universally Know the Difference between Right and Wrong

We must begin by admitting that this premise is somewhat questionable. After all, we look around the world and we see people committing incredible acts of atrocity toward one another. Murder, robbery, and adultery are as common as flies. Do the people who engage in those activities really understand the difference between right and wrong?

But wait, let's be careful here. Premise 1 does not say that people always *do* what is right. It only says that they *know* what is right. People in every culture in the world, during every period of history, have all generally agreed that killing someone without justification is a moral evil – it is wrong. Of course people do it, but when they do, they know that their actions are wrong.

Deep within the consciousness of humanity, we simply understand that there is a right and a wrong. We know that lying is wrong. When someone is dishonest with us, we say, "Why did you lie to me?!" It makes us angry because we feel violated and offended. It appears that we and the liar both understand that a law has been broken.

When someone breaks line in front of us, after we have been waiting for hours, we often loose our patience and ask, "What gives you the right to break line?" In other words, we are appealing to some moral law that says, "It is wrong to lie and it is wrong to break line." We know that the lawbreaker also understands these laws because, interestingly, if someone cuts line in front of *him*, he also will appeal to the same law.

So if every person in every land at every time period *knows* that there is a right and wrong, this leads us to a very important question. *How* does every person know this? Where did this universal sense of morality come from? The answer is clear:

187

THEREFORE, THERE IS A UNIVERSAL MORAL LAW

This means that there is an objective law that everybody knows about and that is above every human law.[94] This universal law says things like "unjustified killing of other human beings is always wrong," "adultery is wrong," and "honesty is right."

These laws are universal in that they are not confined to just one place or people. They are not just American laws. They are not just Russian laws, or Chinese laws, or Kenyan laws, or any other specific places. These laws apply to everyone and we know it.

In America, we have laws against murder. If you do it, you pay with a long prison sentence (perhaps the rest of your life) or in some states you pay with your life. But even if we did not have those laws in America, we still would know murder is bad. We would know because there is a higher law, a universal law, and it tells us murder is bad.

DARCY AND EDDIE ON THE MOON

Suppose an independent astronaut named Darcy moved up to the moon in order to escape civilization. She lands, sets up her moon-house and begins to live alone. Several miles away from Darcy's new home, Eddie, another space-traveler with loner tendencies, also lands and builds his home. Here on the moon, there are no written human laws. Darcy and Eddie are far away from earth and the laws of people who live there.

Well, one day Darcy gets angry at Eddie. He threw some trash out and it floated over to her place and caused some damage to her moon-house. So Darcy concludes that the moon is not big enough for the both of them and decides to take Eddie's life.

Question: would it be wrong for Darcy to kill Eddie? If you say "yes," then what law would you appeal to? There is no written human law on the moon. There are no peace treaties or cease fire agreements to which you might appeal.

This illustration makes it clear that even where there is no official declared human law, there is still a law in effect. Eddie has the right to live, even on the moon. This is the universal law that we are talking about. It is above and indeed is the basis of our written laws.

Many people, however, do not believe that there is such a thing as this universal moral law. They think that we believe certain actions to be right and certain actions to be wrong simply because we have been culturally conditioned to believe these things. In other words, I believe stealing is wrong because my church culture, or my American culture, has drilled it into my brain that stealing is wrong. But our moon illustration makes it clear that this is not a correct analysis.

If some person stands up in a crowd and says, "I think it is okay to torture little children for the fun of it," the rest of us in the crowd would not say, "Well, maybe it is okay, since morality is only an opinion, and this guy is of the opinion that it is okay." Instead, we would say that this man is missing a few marbles and that his elevator does not go all the way up to the top. We would not excuse his desire to torture children because his moral basis was supposedly "culturally conditioned." No, we would lock this guy up to prevent him from engaging in what every rational person knows is immoral. He would be punished for not understanding the objective difference between right and wrong.

And we know that torturing little children for the fun of it is immoral, not only because the laws of our land tell us so, but for a more important reason: there is a higher law than the laws of our land. We know that torturing little children for the fun of it would be just as wrong on the moon, where there is no written human law. This means there is an undeniable, universal moral law that is in effect for all people, everywhere they live, in all time periods.

THE FOLLY OF MORAL RELATIVISM

Moral relativists would disagree and say that each society makes its own laws and keeping the laws of *that society* is what is "right." To break the laws of *that society* are to be considered "wrong." That is what the term *relativism* means – morality is relative to each individual person or society.

This is a foolish notion, however, that often leads to horrendous atrocities. Consider Nazi Germany for example. Hitler's regime took over Germany and declared that exterminating Jews was the "right" thing to do.[95] A moral relativist would have to admit that a moral citizen of Germany, while Nazism was in charge, would have had to take part in these atrocities in order maintain his good moral status! But we intuitively know this is false! Just because a society declares a certain thing as law does not mean that society is "right," for there is a *higher law* than the laws of that society and to which that society is held responsible.

Furthermore, if the relativist is correct and societies decide what is "right" and "wrong," then that would lead to another absurdity – namely, all moral reformers would, by definition, be "wrong."

Martin Luther King Jr., for example, would be considered "wrong" when he took a stance against a particular society and the laws of that society. In the state of Alabama in the 1960's, there were laws on the books that called for racist behavior. For example, black people were not allowed to ride in the front of a bus or drink from certain water fountains. But King opposed these laws and encouraged others to oppose them as well.

If the relativist is correct, however, King's actions would be considered "wrong" for he was going against the established laws of the society. But common sense tells us that King was, in fact, doing the right thing. It was the state of Alabama that was wrong and needed reformation. We know this because there is a higher law than Alabama state law. King was appealing to the higher law that declares, "All men are created equal and deserve equal treatment."

Think about this from another perspective. Throughout different ages and cultures there is one common thread among those who claim to create their own law – an attempt to justify it. Even those who blatantly steal from others still seem to determine some reason why it is okay for them to be a thief. They may excuse their actions by saying that the person didn't need what was stolen or perhaps it is okay to steal something if it was acquired through dishonest means.

Those who murder will often appeal to some higher authority in stating that they are justified in their particular decision to take a life. The killer might claim, "I killed him because he deserved it," or "he was harming others," or "he stole my wife." But do you see what they are doing? They are also appealing to a higher law, and saying that, for some reason or another, their action is an exception to it. They are acknowledging the existence of the objective moral law ("stealing is bad" and "murder is bad"), in the very act of creating an exception to it ("it is usually bad to steal and kill, but in my case it was justified"). Even if it is not always articulated, this behavior makes the point clear. Every individual knows what is right and what is wrong.

This raises another important question. If there is a universal moral law that governs human behavior, where did it come from? This question leads us to the following conclusion:

A UNIVERSAL MORAL LAW REQUIRES A UNIVERSAL MORAL LAWGIVER

This conclusion seems to be intuitive. If there is a law, how did it come about? Surely it was given by a person who is interested in moral behavior – a lawgiver.

But naturalism teaches that the only things that exist are matter and energy (see chapters 8 and 11). But if naturalism is correct, and all things came about by unguided, unintelligent, and unmoral evolutionary processes, we would have no reason at all to believe that such a universal moral law would exist.

Matter is not moral and matter couldn't care less if people are moral or not. There is nothing at all in the naked laws of physics or biology that would demand a certain standard of morality. Only conscious and intelligent beings care about moral issues! This evidence ought to lead us to believe the following:

God Is the Universal Moral Lawgiver

That is, an intelligent being who is concerned with the behavior of his creatures, is the being who provided this universal moral law that is true for all people, in all places, at all times. This is the best explanation of all the evidence and it is the explanation that led C.S. Lewis to abandon his atheism. Of course, if God is the universal lawgiver, then the conclusion of the argument follows:

Therefore, God Exists

Interestingly, we read in the Bible that God is extremely concerned about moral behavior. He tells His people: "Be holy, for I am holy" (Leviticus 11:44; 1 Peter 1:15-16). He provides a list of Ten Commandments that we are to follow in order to exhibit what he means by holiness (Exodus 20). We are to love our neighbors as ourselves (Leviticus 19:18; Romans 13:9-10) and so on. So the God revealed in the Bible is the kind of God that we see necessitated by the Moral Argument.

However, as with the Cosmological Argument we must be careful not to expect too much from the Moral Argument. It does not point us directly to the God of the Bible, even though it is powerful in showing

192

us that some god – a god interested in human morality – exists.

Here we need to go back to the previous sections of this book and remember the trustworthiness of the Bible, the testimony of Christ in showing that he is God, the explanatory power of the axiom "God does all things for his own glory," and the testimony of the Spirit with our spirits that we are the children of God. For the Christian, it is obvious that the moral law-giver is the God of the Bible. For the unbeliever he needs help to make this connection.

This point leads us to consider how we might use this argument when we are sharing Christ with others.

USING THE MORAL ARGUMENT IN EVANGELISM

Apologetic arguments are not only designed to defend the Christian faith, but also to help people come to faith. The Moral Argument has a strong evangelistic quality about it that is very effective in moving people to think about their relationship to the Lord. How so?

Christ once asked, "Why do you call me good? No one is good except God alone" (Mark 10:18). This is the core of the teaching of Jesus while he was on earth. A rich young ruler, who seemed to have everything going for him, came to Jesus asking how he could obtain the only thing he lacked – "eternal life." Yet Jesus tells the man that God *alone* is good. How this must have broken every moral notion that this young man had built up for himself! If God alone is good, then that means he isn't! He honestly thought he could save himself by keeping all of God's commandments. He believed he could achieve perfection by his own power and be pleasing to God as a result. He bragged to Jesus about the commandments, "Teacher, all these I have kept from my youth" (Mark 10:20).

We do exactly the same thing today. We fabricate our own moral law for ourselves, and try our best to keep it for our own purposes. The words of Jesus to the rich young ruler were radical; the very essence

193

of morality is in none other than God himself. Any standard less than his holy character is insufficient. We may be able to measure up to our weak substitutions of morality, but when at the feet of Jesus we can see how the Final Standard of morality is one that we have all fallen short of. And here is the key problem that people have. We are sinners. We are morally evil.

> What then? Are we Jews any better off? No, not at all. For we have already charged that all, both Jews and Greeks, are under sin, as it is written: "None is righteous, no, not one; no one understands; no one seeks for God. All have turned aside; together they have become worthless; no one does good, not even one. Their throat is an open grave; they use their tongues to deceive. The venom of asps is under their lips. Their mouth is full of curses and bitterness. Their feet are swift to shed blood; in their paths are ruin and misery, and the way of peace they have not known. There is no fear of God before their eyes. (Romans 3:9-18)

This passage and the Moral Argument point out to us that we are guilty lawbreakers. We *know* that we are evil and not good. It seems that people lie, steal, cheat, and generally engage in evil acts without much training or persuasion. These things simply flow out of our hearts and most people feel a serious sense of culpability about doing these things.

If you are talking to an unbeliever and you walk them through the Moral Argument, they may begin to sense this guilt in their own hearts. Sometimes people revolt defensively, and are deeply offended by the thought that they are morally evil. But could there possibly be a better time to tell them the good news of Christ? The best time to show people God's grace and mercy is when they are feeling hopeless and lost. "God shows his love for us in that while we were still sinners, Christ died for us" (Romans 5:8).

As we defend our faith and demonstrate that it is rational with the Moral Argument, we must be ready to immediately jump to a solid and accurate presentation of the gospel for those who desire to have their guilty stains washed away.

Chapter 10 Review Exercise

1. This chapter identifies a famous author who analyzed the Moral Argument for the existence of God; name the author and his book on the same topic.
2. List the points of the Moral Argument for the existence of God.
3. Recount some of the reasons given for believing that moral laws are objective and not mere opinion.
4. What are some of the problems with moral relativism?
5. Why does it make sense to say that a universal moral law requires a universal moral lawgiver?
6. Why does it not make sense to claim that moral laws could somehow arise in a purely naturalistic fashion?

Key Terms

Objective moral law
Moral Argument
Moral relativism

Scripture Memory

As obedient children, do not be conformed to the passions of your former ignorance, but as he who called you is holy, you also be holy in all your conduct, since it is written, "You shall be holy, for I am holy." (1 Peter 1:14-16)

CHAPTER 11:
The Superiority of the
Christian Worldview

The past several chapters brought to light some of the amazing arguments for the deity of Christ, the trustworthiness of the Bible, and the existence of God. These arguments, especially taken together as a set, are powerful and persuasive to the rational mind who considers them. In the next two chapters we will take a different, but also convincing approach to Christian apologetics – a worldview approach. How does this work?

Imagine a person examining a buffet holding several different "foods," each one in a large container. One of them is full of cement casserole. Another has dirt pudding. Still another has macaroni and cheese, but it is old, stale and has green cotton-like mold growing on it. Finally, there is a container with hot and fresh lasagna. If the observer of the buffet had to make a choice about which food to eat for dinner, and must choose only from the options on the buffet, then his choice would be obvious. A comparison of the "foods" would make it apparent that the hot and fresh lasagna is the only real alternative, far superior to the other selections.

The same thing happens when we compare and contrast various religious and philosophical systems. It will become clear as we put them side by side that Christian theism stands alone as far superior.

Way back in Chapter 1 we introduced the idea that every person has a worldview. All people are wearing "sunglasses" that tint the way we interpret the world around us. Though many people are oblivious that they even have one, it is possible to be keenly aware of our worldview. In fact, we can apply certain tests to it in order to see if it is true. We can even change it, if the evidence leads us to do so.

But there is a problem. In attempting to choose a worldview, people have a tendency to grow frustrated, because there seems to be so many worldview possibilities. A person can choose from atheism, agnosticism, Christianity, Islam, Judaism, Buddhism, Hinduism, Scientology, Mormonism, deism, or hundreds of others. How do ordinary folks weed through all these options and make a decision, especially about a matter as important as this? How does a person choose his religion, or choose not to have one at all?

It is not as difficult as it may seem. It might surprise you that there are essentially only three broad worldviews categories on the buffet. All available religious and philosophical options can be listed underneath one of them. This really simplifies the process. So let's move into an examination of these three categories.

THE BIG THREE WORLDVIEW CATEGORIES

First, there is naturalism. We have discussed naturalism in previous chapters and you probably already know that naturalists contend that the only things that exist are natural things; there is nothing other than the physical. They do not believe that there is a spiritual realm: no angels, no spirits, no souls, no god(s), or anything else that is not composed of matter and energy.

The second major category is called pantheism. There are many religions and philosophies that are defined as pantheistic, the largest of which is Hinduism. Pure pantheists are the opposite of pure naturalists, stating that only spirit exists.[96] They combine the concept of "god" with creation itself. So they look at trees and say trees are god, or at least an extension of god. They look at rocks and rivers and say these too, are a divine spark of god. They look in the mirror and say that ultimately they themselves are god, exhibiting the essence of the divine. Hence the name pantheism; "Pan" means *all* and "theism" means *god.*

It is important to note that pantheists do not believe that "god" is what Christians say God is. The pantheist maintains that god is just a word to describe the indescribable. To them, "god" is an impersonal thing, more of a force than a personality.

We see a clear picture of their views in the *Star Wars* movies, where the Jedi hope the "force" is with them. What is this force? It is not a person, but just a movement – a connection of life forms. Pantheists believe that all things are connected to this god-like force.

The third major worldview category is called theism, which is the belief system that says there is a creator God who *is separate* from his creation. He is not a tree, rock, or planet, but he made trees, rocks, and planets, and he is above and separate from those things.[97]

DIFFERENT TYPES UNDER THE BIG THREE

Every belief system can be classified underneath one of these big three worldview categories, or some combination of them. However, it must be repeated for the sake of fairness and clarity, there are many different types of worldviews under each category, some of which have considerable overlap. Just as there are many different types of dogs (i.e., dachshunds, cocker spaniels, and border collies) and yet all of them are essentially dogs, so there are many different types of naturalists, and yet all of them are essentially naturalists. The same is true for pantheists and theists.

For example, many Buddhists are pantheistic and so are many Hindus. But they would describe their pantheistic beliefs in different ways, sometimes extremely different ways. Yet at the core, they are both pantheistic religions.

Likewise, there are many different types of theists. Christians are theists, believing in a creator God, separate from creation, but so are Muslims and Jews. These religions are all different expressions of the theistic worldview category.[98]

When we examine worldviews, we certainly want to be fair to each type, and respect the differences between them. But since we can group every type under one of the big three categories, it does simplify the process of testing worldviews to see which of the big three is superior. To this testing process we now turn.

TESTING THE BIG THREE

Those of you who are currently students are probably very familiar with what is involved in taking tests. Questions! When you take a test in your science class, you have to be able to answer the questions your teacher asks. This is easier for some people than others. Some people study hard and can provide the right answers, or at least better ones. But other folks, particularly those who watched TV until two o'clock in the morning, rather than reviewing their study guide, supply wrong or inferior answers.

In the same way, some worldview categories can answer questions better than others. So let's ask five of the most important test questions we can think of, and see which worldview category – naturalism, pantheism, or theism – answers the questions best.[99]

QUESTION 1: WHAT IS REALLY REAL?

This question is perhaps the most basic question of all, and it takes us back to the Cosmological Argument discussed in a previous chapter. It is basically the same question as, "What is the first cause?" James Sire tells the story of an eternal Elephant to help us understand the question better:

> One day a little boy came to his father and asked, "You know, Dad, our teacher just showed us that the world is really round and that it is just out there alone. Gee, Dad, what holds it up?"
>
> His father, thinking his son would be satisfied with a child's answer, said, "Well, son, a camel holds the world up." His son, always trusting his father, looked puzzled but walked away satisfied – for a while.
>
> The next day after he thought this over, he came back to his dad and asked the obvious question. "Dad, you know, you said yesterday the world rests on a camel. But what holds the camel up?"
>
> His father, a bit perplexed, quickly thought, "You know, this kid's got a good question. I don't know the answer to it, but I'd better make up one – and fast." Like most fathers he knew instinctively that a quick answer turneth away further questions. So he said with confidence, "Son, a kangaroo holds the camel up."
>
> So his son went away but returned a short time later and said, "Hey, Dad. I've still got a problem. What holds up the kangaroo?"

His father was now desperate, so he thought quickly and figured he would make one last try. So he searched his mind for the largest animal he could think of, and he put a capital on it and said loudly (if you shout, people believe you): "An Elephant holds the world up."

"Come on, Dad," his son said, having now caught on that his father was not getting to the bottom of things, "what holds up the Elephant?"

So his father came back in an exasperated stroke of pure genius, "Son, it's Elephant all the way down."[100]

The little boy in this story wanted his dad to get to the bottom of things. For the dad, the Elephant is uncaused and is the foundation for everything else that exists! So the *really real* is that which is eternal and upon which everything else rests. It is ultimate reality, or the first thing. And as Sire's story helps us see, there *must* logically be something that holds everything else up. Different worldviews disagree on what this first cause is. Let's see how each of the big three categories defines the really real.

The Answer of Naturalism

Naturalists hold that the really real is matter and energy – stuff like atoms, molecules, dirt, dust, and the like, which forms into bigger things like stars, planets, and people. Lifeless matter and energy is ultimate reality, the cause of everything else that exists.[101]

But there are many major problems with believing this. First, matter and energy are not eternal. It seems totally illogical to hold that dirt has no beginning and no ending, and there is certainly no proof of this. But whatever is really real has to be eternal, because it cannot be caused (or else whatever caused it is really real).

Secondly, this view is insufficient as an explanation for life and intelligence. It is inconceivable that matter and energy, without any help from a designer at all, designed living and intelligent things. But we know that there are living things, some which possess high degrees of intelligence. John Piper articulates the position of naturalism well:

> Here is the great division between the atheistic worldview and the Christian worldview: For the atheists, everything begins with inanimate matter and energy. It's just there. Since there was nothing there before to make it what it is, it could have been anything. It could have been Life. But atheists choose to believe that in the beginning was matter and energy. They don't know this. They guess. They say that impersonal matter and impersonal energy are original. They are absolute. They are ultimate.
>
> Then for billions of years, with no creator, no intelligence, no design, no purpose, no plan, there emerges from mindless, lifeless, random matter and energy not only the irreducible complexities of interdependent biological structures, but also this glorious thing called living personhood. That's their account of life.[102]

The verdict is in: the answer of naturalism to the question "What is really real?" does not seem to be a very good answer at all. However, if a person artificially removes God (or at least spirit) from the picture as a possible explanation for the existence of things, this is the only alternative with which he is left.

The Answer of Pantheism

Pantheists believe that what is really real is the divine universe itself. Everything is divine, therefore everything is ultimate reality. A pantheist should feel comfortable saying, "You and I are the cause of all things."

But there are many problems with pantheism. First of all, it totally contradicts itself. Many forms of pantheism, for example, state that all things are an illusion. But if all things are a mere illusion, then the statement, "All things are an illusion" is just an illusion also. Why should we trust a statement that is only an illusion? This is self-defeating, like shooting oneself right in the foot.

This leads to a second and greater problem for pantheism. On what authority should a person believe any pantheistic teaching? Who says the universe is divine, that reincarnation is reality, and that we are all waiting to be absorbed into nirvana or Brahman? Why should people believe the gurus and teachers of these doctrines?

Pantheists say that their gurus are enlightened and that is why we should trust them. But how do we know this? As Christians, you see, we can look to Jesus, who *proved* that he was enlightened by his miracles, fulfilled prophecies, perfectly consistent teaching, and ultimately by his resurrection from the dead. What have these pantheistic gurus done to prove their position is true? Especially when they hold many contradictory beliefs and pretend that it is okay to do so. A person should not feel comfortable trusting their eternal destiny into the hands of someone who holds a self-defeating belief!

The Answer of Theism

Of course, theists believe that God is the really real – the Elephant that goes all the way down. God is the Maker and Designer of all things. He is the source from which all other things flow, who is himself eternal and uncaused. His existence explains and upholds our existence. This is one of the facts God taught Moses at the burning bush: "God said to Moses, 'I AM WHO I AM.' And he said, 'Say this to the people of Israel, "I AM has sent me to you."'" (Genesis 3:14)

It seems strange that God declares that his name is a verb of being. But the point is clear. God has no beginning and no ending, no past or future. He simply *is*. He is the existing one, the Alpha and Omega, from which all other things derive their existence.

Theism is not free from its own problems, however, and many of these will be dealt with in Chapter 14, but theism does make the most sense in answering this question of the really real. A personal, conscious, and intelligent being is the best explanation for a planet full of personal, conscious, and intelligent beings.

QUESTION 2: HOW DO WE COME TO KNOW ANYTHING AT ALL?

This is the next question we ask of the big three worldviews. How do human beings acquire knowledge? How is it that we come to know things? How does information get inside our heads so that we can say things like, "I know grass is green," or "I know that I live on a planet called earth," or "I know that roses are red and violets are blue?"[103]

This may seem like a tough thing to consider, but we encourage you to trudge through these next paragraphs. You can get this!

The Answer of Naturalism

Naturalists say people acquire knowledge through either their senses (eyes, ears, nose, taste buds, nerve endings, etc.) or through logical deduction (figuring things out in our minds) or some combination of both of these.

Some naturalists say *seeing is believing*. If you can sense it, then you can know it. Other naturalists say *figure it out*. If you can deduce it logically, then you can know it, like 2 + 2 = 4. Again, other naturalists combine these two approaches.

What is important to note is that these are the *only two ways* that pure naturalists allow for knowledge to be acquired. If information does not come through the senses or through deduction, then it will not usually be allowed as true knowledge.

This means that if a Christian says, "I read in the Bible that I am a sinner," then the naturalist would probably reply: "The Bible claims supernatural origin, but the Bible cannot be verified as supernatural by either the senses or deduction, therefore the information it contains cannot count as knowledge." So in a word, naturalism limits the scope of what can be included in the category human knowledge, and generally, information supposedly presented by God doesn't make the cut.

The Answer of Pantheism

Pantheism also has an answer to how humans come to knowledge. It all begins with a clearing of the mind. Clear your mind of all the things you think you know, and search deep within yourself to come to an understanding of the divine essence. As one pantheistic source puts is:

> The Transcendental Meditation technique allows your mind to settle inward beyond thought to experience the source of thought — pure awareness, also known as transcendental consciousness. This is the most silent and peaceful level of consciousness — your innermost Self. In this state of restful alertness, your brain functions with significantly greater coherence and your body gains deep rest.[104]

So as the pantheist meditates, he believes he is coming to knowledge essentially by forgetting everything he knows. He must "settle inward beyond thought." As Yoda informed Luke, "You must unlearn what you have learned."[105] All knowledge lies within your own essence, since you are a spark of the divine.

Interestingly, the naturalist says you can only use sense perception or deduction to obtain knowledge. The pantheist, on the other hand, says you must forget them both! Surely, there is a better answer than either of these two alternatives.

The Answer of Theism

The naturalistic and pantheistic answers are both terribly insufficient. The naturalist limits the scope of how knowledge might be obtained, and the pantheist moves against all logic to "know" something that is not even real.

But theists think much differently. They believe that God created us in his image, with the capacity to find knowledge. They agree with the naturalist, that our senses are one way of coming to know things. If you see a tree, and you have good reasons for believing your senses are functioning properly (that is, you are not hallucinating), then you can rationally know the tree is there. They also agree with the naturalist that if you can properly deduce something in your mind, you can also know it is true. If a person can deduce that Mercury is the closest planet to the sun, then he can know it is true, even though he has never personally seen it.

But theists add one more thing that the naturalist leaves out – revelation. If God exists, and the theist knows that he does, then he has every reason to hold that God might communicate to humanity. Theism is not closed to the possibility that someone outside of the natural realm may be interested in us. The Bible is the definitive and permanent word of God, given to humanity as a revelation of himself to us. Thus, it counts for true knowledge.

Theism again provides the better answer. It does not deny possible revelation from God as a means of knowledge, like naturalism. And it does not deny that knowledge comes through the senses and logical deduction, like pantheism.

QUESTION 3: WHAT IS A HUMAN BEING?

This question is major because your answer to it will determine how you treat other people and how you expect to be treated. Your answer will reveal whether you think of humanity as just another animal or something else – something special. Which of the big three worldview categories gives the right answer?

The Answer of Naturalism

No doubt, naturalism falls short of providing a sufficient answer. Naturalists believe that human beings are merely the highest evolved animal on planet earth. They believe that there is nothing special about people. Homo sapiens were not designed or created. Rather they are cosmic accidents that so happened to develop into introspective high primates, but who will cease to exist very soon, never to be remembered again.

This sounds terrible! Naturalists agree. Some of them simply ignore the horrors of this belief and pretend that it isn't so bad. Other naturalists are more honest, and say that we must bite the bullet and accept this horrible future for the human race, because we can do nothing to change it.

Of course, if the naturalist is correct about what a human is, then ultimately nothing we do matters! You might save a person's life who is about to be hit by a truck, but so what? Who cares? That person and you will soon die and never be remembered again. Your bodies will both return to dust and fly in the wind, so it doesn't matter if you save another person's life or not!

In fact, if naturalism is true, it would be totally idiotic to save another person's life, if your life were risked in the process. If you truly believed that once you died it was all over, then you would be out of your mind to do anything at all for the benefit of others, if that action was risky to your own well-being.

Naturalism, as a worldview, offers no sufficient and objective basis for treating people with dignity and respect. It is a worldview that, if truly believed and followed consistently, leads a person to pure selfishness.

The Answer of Pantheism

Pantheists believe that human beings are extensions of the divine essence and are not true selves. In other words, if you think you are an individual person, then you are wrong. For Mel Gibson to say, "I am Mel Gibson," is a serious error. Personal identity, according to a pure pantheist, is nothing more than an illusion.

One day, when "Mel Gibson" is absorbed into the eternal and infinite divine essence, which is Brahman, he will not be called "Mel Gibson" anymore. In fact, he will be one with the absolute and will cease to exist as an individual person.

But this view has many problems. Essentially, it makes people out to not be people at all. Rather than being human, and living as such, pantheists declare that through the process of Karma and reincarnation, people must cease to be people. What a mess! A person should not give up the reality of their personal identity without good reason.

So since naturalism offers such a horrific answer to the question, "What is a human being?" and since pantheism denies that humanity existences in any real way at all, then surely there is a better answer!

The Answer of Theism

All theists believe that God created humanity as a special type of being. Christian theists in particular believe that people share much in common with the animals, especially on a biological level, but human beings are not mere animals.

Genesis 1:26-27 declares that God created man "in his image." Whatever else this might mean it certainly indicates that we share some important things in common with God, like the ability to reason through complex issues and communicate on a detailed level with one another. It also means that humans are created with built-in dignity. That means all people have value and should be treated as such. The bum on the street is valuable, not because of what he does or does not do, but just because he is human. He must, therefore, be treated with dignity.

QUESTION 4: HOW DO WE KNOW WHAT IS GOOD AND BAD?

From the answers given to the other questions above, you should have a good idea about what answers will be given to this one. What makes something moral? Other connected questions include: What is a right action? What is a wrong action? How do we determine when someone did a "bad" thing or a "good" thing? What is the standard of morality by which we measure actions?

The Answer of Naturalism

Naturalism offers very little here. Because they lack belief in God or any other transcendent being who holds people accountable, they believe that people are ultimately accountable only to themselves. That means each individual person determines what is right and wrong as they see it. After all, there is no God who will judge us. After we die, there is no everlasting soul and no reward in Heaven and no punishment in Hell.

This means if a nation passes a law that says, "Do not kill others," a naturalist might feel free to reply, "Mind your own business. You have no ultimate right to tell me what to do!" Each person simply does what is right in his own eyes.

210

It gets worse. If naturalism is true then we cannot even reasonably use words like "right" and "wrong." Why not? Because there is no standard definition to those words. If everybody defines "right" and "wrong" as they see fit, and there is no moral lawgiver to explain to us what these words mean, then my "right" is just as right as your "right."

Hitler, who was a naturalist, believed that it was right to exterminate Jews, because he thought of them as an inferior race. If naturalism is true, nobody can legitimately say that what Hitler did was "wrong." We might say, "I *think* that he was wrong based on my own definition of wrong." But if there is no higher authority, who is above us all, then we cannot say, "Hitler *was* wrong." We cannot say, "Hitler will be punished and pay for what he did."

But surely Hitler was wrong! Even Naturalists inconsistently and hypocritically say that Hitler was an immoral person. Common sense tells us that killing six million people for no good reason is wrong. But if it is wrong, then somebody bigger than us is enforcing the rule, "Do not murder." And this rule is much bigger than opinion.[106]

The Answer of Pantheism

Pantheism maintains that good and evil do not actually exist, but they are only illusions. You have probably seen the Yin-Yang symbol. It shows black and white, intertwined and balanced. This means, according to many forms of pantheism, that good and evil balance each other out in the end, so that ultimately neither of them exists.

But if this is true, then we run into the same problems we find in naturalism. How can we say that something is truly bad, if it will eventually be cancelled out and cease to exist? The murderer could just plead with the judge to let him go free, after all, evil is not actually real.

What about good deeds? If pantheism is true, they are not really good, but just an illusion of good. That was nice that you helped the little old lady across the street, but don't pretend that it was *actually* a good thing to do. It just *seemed* to be good.

But why in the world would we believe this? It doesn't make any sense at all. Pantheists say that we have to trust gurus and "enlightened teachers" who say they have spiritually progressed enough to understand these things. But they don't seem so enlightened, for to deny what is common sense – the existence of good and evil – is not enlightenment but rather irrationality.

The Answer of Theism

Again, theism wins the day. If there is a God who has made clear to us what is right and what is wrong, then we have an objective ethical standard. He has spoken and said, "Do not murder." That means unjustified killing is wrong. We know it because he said it. Plus, he tells us that he will personally hold each of us accountable for obeying his commands.

This means Hitler was wrong and must pay for his crimes in an ultimate sense, unless he received Christ's forgiveness at some point before he died – an unlikely possibility. Theism sees "wrong" not just as an opinion. It is *really* wrong.

Theism also sees "right" as *really* right. If you obey God and do what he has required, then you have done something objectively right. If you love your neighbor as yourself, then you have been truly moral. Given theism, our moral choices actually count for something. Now we come to the last worldview test question:

QUESTION 5: WHAT IS THE MEANING OF HISTORY?

Why are we on this planet? What do all of our daily activities ultimately mean? Would it make a difference if I were not born? Is human activity actually going somewhere or are we just spinning around on our little planet for a few years until we die?

The Answer of Naturalism

The naturalistic worldview again falls flat upon its face. It is reduced to teaching that there is no ultimate meaning in anything at all. Humans are worthless and history is meaningless. After all, says the naturalist, within a few million years, the sun will burn out and the solar system will dissolve. At that point humans will cease to exist. There will be nobody around to remember history. Nobody will say, "Let's study the Civil War." The Civil War will mean nothing, nor will anything else.

This is why naturalists tend to focus heavily on the here and now. "Eat, drink, and be merry for tomorrow we die" is a fitting motto for naturalism.

Of course, if naturalism is true and there is no ultimate meaning, it follows that motivation to change society for the good disintegrates. Why should a person sacrifice his time, energy, money, or anything else to improve a society that will soon be destroyed and forgotten? Instead, he should use all of his resources to bring about the greatest amount of worldly pleasure for himself while he still has a little bit of time. Once it's over, it's over.

The Answer of Pantheism

As unusual, pantheism fares no better. Pantheism says the goal of history is to be absorbed into the divine essence and everything becomes one. At that point, there will be no individual identity, no memory, nothing at all.

So this means pantheists see history as essentially meaningless too. This is why they teach their followers yoga and transcendental meditation techniques, to enable them to elevate above all the stuff down here and tap into the divine essence.

The Answer of Theism

People should not be happy at all with living meaningless lives. Thankfully, we do not have to. Theism offers a far superior answer than the other alternatives. God created the heavens and the earth *for a reason.* So that he himself might be glorified in it. The goal of human history, therefore, is the glory of God.

This means that our lives not only have meaning for the here and now, but everything we do – everything! – is infused with deep and eternal meaning. For example, if we love our neighbor by sharing our money when he is in need, we are doing something that has eternal value to it.

Likewise, if we neglect the things that matter, this too has eternal effects. If we refuse to love our neighbor or share the gospel or worship God, then there is an eternal price to pay. These things have objective and real meaning.

THEISM – THE SUPERIOR CHOICE

This concludes our comparison of worldview-buffet options. What has our quiz shown? When the big three worldview categories are put to the test, it is obvious which worldview is superior. Theism answers more questions, and is more livable than either of its competitors. Naturalism and pantheism are incredibly weak options.

So theism is the hot and fresh lasagna! It makes good sense and makes the alternatives look very undesirable (like cement casserole and dirt pudding). But that leads us to a major problem. Which form of theism is correct? Christians, Jews, Muslims, Mormons, and Jehovah's Witnesses are all theists, and yet they teach totally contrary things about God, the world, people, and salvation. How do I know what is the one true theism? To this question we turn in the next chapter.

Chapter 11 Review Exercise

1. Summarize how each of the big three worldview categories answers the question "What is really real?"
2. Summarize how each of the big three worldview categories answers the question "How do we come to know anything at all?"
3. Summarize how each of the big three worldview categories answers the question "What is a human being?"
4. Summarize how each of the big three worldview categories answers the question "What is right and wrong?"
5. Summarize how each of the big three worldview categories answers the question "What is the meaning of history?"

Key Terms

Naturalism
Pantheism
Theism

Scripture Memory

God said to Moses, "I AM WHO I AM." And he said, "Say this to the people of Israel, 'I AM has sent me to you.'" (Genesis 3:14)

Chapter 12:
The One True Theism

In the previous chapter, three broad categories of worldviews were described and tested: naturalism, pantheism, and theism. The case was made that theism (the belief that there is an eternal person called God who is separate from creation) is a far superior category than the other two, because it answers more questions in more reasonable ways, and because it provides meaning to history and an objective foundation upon which to build ethics.

But what if a person is a theist yet is not sure which religion is the correct expression of belief in God? What if God exists, but has not expressed himself through a religion at all? In other words, which version of theism is right? These are important questions that will be the focus of this chapter.

It is our strong conviction that Christianity is the one true version of theism. Jesus Christ has come to communicate his word to creation (John 1:1-3; 14). He rose from the dead to prove his status as the Son of God. A good part of this book is dedicated to showcasing his life, his teaching, and his miracles (chapters 3 and 4).

Let's now place Christian theism next to some of its theistic alternatives and see how it stands up. Sometimes comparing truth with counterfeits makes the truth shine even brighter.

DEALING WITH DEISM

First, let's focus on deism. Deists believe that there is a God, but that he is currently apathetic. That is, he is not concerned with people or his creation. He simply designed the universe and then left it to operate according to natural laws. In the *Dictionary of the History of Ideas*, this view is carefully defined as follows:

Deism is the belief that by rational methods alone men can know all the true propositions of theology which it is possible, necessary, or desirable for men to know. Deists have generally subscribed to most of the following propositions:

1. One and only one God exists.
2. God has moral and intellectual virtues in perfection.
3. God's active powers are displayed in the world, created, sustained, and ordered by means of divinely sanctioned natural laws, both moral and physical.
4. The ordering of events constitutes a general providence.
5. There is no special providence; no miracles or other divine interventions violate the lawful natural order.
6. Men have been endowed with a rational nature which alone allows them to know truth and their duty when they think and choose in conformity with this nature.
7. The natural law requires the leading of a moral life, rendering to God, one's neighbor, and one's self what is due to each.

8. The purest form of worship and the chief religious obligation is to lead a moral life.

9. God had endowed men with immortal souls.

10. After death retributive justice is meted out to each man according to his acts. Those who fulfill the moral law and live according to nature are "saved" to enjoy rewards; others are punished.

11. All other religious beliefs or practices conflicting with these tenets are to be regarded critically, as at best indifferent political institutions and beliefs, or as errors to be condemned and eradicated if it should be prudent to do so.[107]

A couple of these points need to be emphasized. Note point 5 which says, "There is no special providence" of God. In other words, God does not intervene in time or history. He does not work miracles. Though he is viewed as the divine creator of all things, he does not directly interact with his creation. Also point 10 shows that deism is clearly a works-based system of salvation, in which people are only "saved" if they are able to work more good in this life than bad.

It is important to think carefully through these deistic beliefs because many people today are "closet deists." That is, they hold the deist view of God, even though they do not openly admit it. Many people attend church, for example, but they do not actually believe everything the Bible says about God and they are certainly not interested in obeying the dictates of Scripture. In their estimation, God exists, but he is not involved in the affairs of real life.

Is it possible that deism is the one true theism? Deism actually runs into some major problems. First of all, it is not based on any real authority, but rather only on man using his autonomous, rational faculties to dream up what he thinks God is like. If the God of deism is the real God, then he has not told us about how he did things – in fact, if he has revealed himself at all, then deism is false by definition because deists claim God has not revealed himself at all.

This also means that deists cannot claim that there is a "bible" somewhere that tells us God created all things and then left his creation alone. They simply deduce logically that this is what God has done. But perhaps their logic is flawed. Certainly Christians who study the Bible would say so. "The heart is deceitful above all things, and desperately sick; who can understand it?"[108] Human reasoning has its place, but it is tainted severely with sin. If we attempt to deduce the nature of God, using nothing but human reason, we are sure to end with a mere idol, a mental image that looks very little like the actual God.

Beyond the problem of lacking authority, deism also proves to be a cop-out. It attempts to maintain some of the benefits of having a God, while at the same time take advantage of not having to be fully accountable to him, since he is not really interested in people and their behavior. He just wants the good to outweigh the bad in the end.

So deists are attempting to get the best of both worlds. They get a "God," so they have an explanation for how the universe began and why it contains intelligent life. This distant God also provides history with some meaning and gives humans value and dignity, because God made them.

But at the same time, desists do not feel direct moral responsibility to God. When it comes to ethics, they might feel like some things are obviously wrong, like murder, but other things are questionable, like adultery let's say. So a deist may believe he should not murder, but justifies "lesser sins" like adultery. All that matters is that in the end his good deeds outnumber the bad. This best-of-both-worlds mentality, however, is a cop-out. It is a refusal to be either a true theist or a true naturalist.

In addition, deists seem to ignore the overwhelming evidence that the Bible is trustworthy and that Jesus said he was God and proved it. They seem to dismiss the case for the resurrection offhand, without truly considering its strengths. Essentially, they ignore this evidence so that they can create their own tame "god" who is not God at all. Though it is a far superior worldview option than any form of naturalism, nonetheless deism should be discarded. It is not the one true theism.

Judaism – the Religion of the Old Testament

Deism has typically been an unorganized "religion," more the faith of those who consider themselves to be the rational elite. But in our pursuit of the one true theism, we now consider some of the more organized versions of theism. There are two major forms to consider besides Christianity – Judaism and Islam. It would honestly take another entire book to do justice to any analysis of these two. To compound this problem, there are hundreds of Bible-based cult groups, like the Mormons, that would also be considered forms of theism that must also be examined. Here, we will only briefly consider several major options, and how they compare with Christianity.

First is Judaism, the religion of Moses, David, and Jesus himself. Christians shouldn't feel comfortable saying that Judaism is entirely wrong, after all, that might imply that Jesus himself was somehow wrong for being a Jew. But here is the major issue – in its Christ-denying form, Judaism has strayed horrifically from the original intention God had for it. It is like a car without wheels. The Old Testament without the New Testament is a stunted religion that is missing its key element. Christianity is the fulfillment of Judaism and without Jesus the Jewish Messiah, Judaism is gutted of its true meaning. Jesus himself taught this with an astonishing rebuke of the religious leaders of his day:

You hypocrites! Well did Isaiah prophesy of you, when he said: "This people honors me with their lips, but their heart

221

is far from me; in vain do they worship me, teaching as doctrines the commandments of men." (Matthew 15:7-9)

These people were the leaders of the Christ-denying Judaism so
prevalent in Jesus' time, and even though he was a Jew by blood and
by conviction, he did not stand for their false and empty version of
Abraham's faith. Judaism without Jesus at the center is unfulfilled,
and leads to futile attempts to earn one's own salvation instead of depending upon the grace of God.

The most important reason to abandon any form of Judaism that
denies Christ is the witness of Christ himself. He claimed to be the
Messiah of the Jews: "The woman said to him, 'I know that Messiah
is coming (he who is called Christ). When he comes, he will tell us
all things.' Jesus said to her, 'I who speak to you am he'" (John 4:25-
26).

Not only did he claim to be the Messiah of the Jews, but he also
proved it by fulfilling hundreds of ancient prophecies concerning his
life. Many of these have been explained in Chapter 3. And he proved
himself in an even greater way when he rose from the dead. Because
of the person and work of Jesus Christ, Christianity is to be preferred
over Christ-denying Judaism.[109]

ISLAM – THE RELIGION OF SURRENDER

Since September 11, 2001, interest in Islamic theology and practice
has been on the rise. In fact, the threat of Islam against the forces of
democracy and freedom in the world has been one of the chief reasons
for the resurgence of Christian apologetics in recent years.

Islam is the second largest religion in the world with over a billion
adherents. Roughly one in every five people in the world (20%) claims
that Muhammad is the final prophet of Allah.[110] The word *Islam* means

to surrender, thus a Muslim is one who surrenders himself completely to the will of Allah.

The majority of the Muslims in the world are not viewed as a terrorist threat. Only a minority take Islam serious enough to murder innocent people in an act of Jihad, or holy war. But it should be noted that the militant Muslims are the ones who take the Muslim holy book, called the Qur'an, most seriously. Consider some of these passages from the Qur'an.

> The punishment of those who wage war against Allah and His Messenger, and strive with might and main for mischief through the land is: execution, or crucifixion, or the cutting off of hands and feet from opposite sides, or exile from the land: that is their disgrace in this world, and a heavy punishment is theirs in the Hereafter. (Our'an 5:33)

> Remember thy Lord inspired the angels (with the message): "I am with you: give firmness to the Believers: I will instill terror into the hearts of the Unbelievers: smite ye above their necks and smite all their finger-tips off them." (Qur'an 8:12)

These passages are clear – terror is the way of true Islam. Those who take this religion seriously will seek to cleanse the earth of the infidel, or unbelievers, and remove them. Those who are called peaceful Muslims (and we are thankful that they are in the majority) do not take the Qur'an, or at least these parts of it, as a document to be strictly followed. They are moderate Muslims.

Why should Islam be rejected as the one true theism? To show that Christianity is superior to Islam, one must first look at the dates of the two religions. Christianity was well established by 35 A.D. and the New Testament was completed by 90 A.D., but Muhammad did not write the Qur'an until 633 A.D.! This means Christianity had been established for nearly six hundred years when Muhammad came to power and declared all other religions wrong. But why should we believe Muhammad? There doesn't seem to be any good reason to think he was accurate in his criticisms of the Bible. Amazingly, early in the Qur'an he seemed to have a great deal of respect for the Bible (Qur'an 2:62; 8:12), or least he said he did, but he later claimed that it had been distorted and corrupted. He claimed he was on earth as a prophet from Allah to correct the mistakes.

But, again, why should we trust him? Muhammad was a man of intolerance, violence, and debased morality. He was a man who sought riches and unjustly destroyed the lives of others.

Furthermore, he *alone* was the author of the Qur'an. Since he was the single author, it is a strong possibility that he simply made up a new religion, and simply wrote it in a book. This is clearly what he did. The Bible was written by over forty people, most did not know each other and could not have shared their stories. This means the Bible has multiple independent witnesses and provides a more than adequate measure of accountability. It has built in checks and balances.

But Muhammad wrote alone. He could have easily faked the whole thing and created a religion for the sake of personal gain. Without eyewitnesses and independent voices, we can never know. And if we have no good reason to doubt Jesus Christ, who was alive and proving his divine nature a full six hundred years before Muhammad, then we should be assured that Christianity is superior.

For these and other reasons, it is not at all likely that Islam is the true expression of God.[111]

CULT THINKING – MORMONISM

Another possible theistic expression that we will cover here is found embodied in Bible-based cults. These groups use the Bible as their "authority," but twist it beyond comprehension in order to make it fit their perspective and ultimately to control their followers. Hundreds of such groups exist including the Church of Jesus Christ of Latter Day Saints (LDS), Jehovah's Witnesses, Branch Davidians, and Christian Science. Other books provide extensive details of all these, and many other Bible-based cults, so, for the sake of space, we will only consider the LDS church, otherwise known as Mormonism. Many of the other groups follow a similar pattern as Mormonism, so showing some of the errors in the LDS church will also serve to refute some of the other groups.

Mormonism was founded by Joseph Smith who, just like Muhammad, claimed that orthodox Christianity had become corrupted and was filled with error. Smith claimed that as a fourteen-year-old boy, God the Father and Jesus appeared to him in a vision. In his testimony about this supposed event, Joseph Smith recounts:

> My object in going to inquire of the Lord was to know which of all the sects [Christian denominations] was right, that I might know which to join. No sooner, therefore, did I get possession of myself, so as to be able to speak, than I asked the Personages who stood above me in the light, which of all the sects was right (for at this time it had never entered into my heart that all were wrong)--and which I should join.
>
> I was answered that I must join none of them, for they were all wrong; and the Personage who addressed me said that all their creeds were an abomination in his sight; that those professors were all corrupt; that: "they draw near to me with their lips, but their hearts are far from me, they teach for doctrines the commandments of men, having a form of godliness, but they deny the power thereof."
>
> He again forbade me to join with any of them; and many other things did he say unto me, which I cannot write at this time. When I came to myself again, I found myself lying on my back, looking up into heaven. When the light had depart-

ed, I had no strength; but soon recovering in some degree, I went home.[112]

So Smith taught that all Christian denominations were an "abomination" in the sight of God and should all be abandoned. Smith also claimed to be the prophet sent from God to "correct" all these errors and restore God's true church on the earth. The official LDS website overtly makes this claim:

> When Joseph Smith was 14 years old, he wanted to know which church he should join, so he asked God in sincere prayer. In response to this prayer, God the Father and His Son, Jesus Christ, appeared to Joseph and told him the true Church of Jesus Christ was not on the earth and they had chosen Joseph to restore it.[113]

Smith also claims that in 1823, while calling on God in his room, an angel named Moroni appeared to him. Moroni informed him that God had given him a job involving golden plates and a long-term translation process. Smith tells the story like this:

> He said there was a book deposited, written upon gold plates, giving an account of the former inhabitants of this continent, and the source from whence they sprang. He also said that the fulness [sic] of the everlasting Gospel was contained in it, as delivered by the Savior to the ancient inhabitants. Also, that there were two stones in silver bowls—and these stones, fastened to a breastplate, constituted what is called the Urim and Thummim—deposited with the plates; and the possession and use of these stones were what constituted *Seers* in ancient or former times; and that God had prepared them for the purpose of translating the book.[114]

226

The document supposedly produced from these golden plates is called the Book of Mormon and it is the foundation of the LDS faith. Even though Mormons typically give lip service to the Bible, they elevate the Book of Mormon to a much higher status, and in the places where the two books disagree, the Book of Mormon is always right and the Bible always wrong.

One of the chief marks of a Bible-based cult is the introduction of new revelation that supersedes the Bible. Whether it is a written document like the Book of Mormon, or whether it is a "prophet" who claims to receive updated information from God, the result is the same. The cult leader uses this "new revelation" to manipulate people for his own personal gain.

But just like the Qur'an, the Book of Mormon cannot be trusted, since it was written by only one person. There is no proof that Joseph Smith ever saw God, Jesus, or an angel, since he was unaccompanied when these "visions" occurred. Mormons must take his word *alone* for these outrageous claims. And since he wrote the entire text by himself, the entire Book of Mormon is also suspect, since there are no other authors to provide checks and balances, as there are in the Bible. Smith could very well have manufactured the entire LDS religion for personal gain; and no evidence exists that proves he didn't.

The Book of Mormon also makes the fantastic claim that Jesus appeared to a group of American Indians called Lamanites, who were supposedly descendents of the Israelites. But anthropologists who specialize in tracing the DNA strands of various people groups have demonstrated with conclusive evidence that no American Indians whatsoever are from Middle Eastern descent.[115] It is clear that Smith was writing a fable, even though Mormons seem certain that the book of Mormon is historically accurate.

More problems with Mormonism could be compounded at this stage, but we hope the point is clear – Christianity stands as far superior to a religion created hundreds of years later, that borrows (or shall we say steals) the terminology of true Christianity in order to manipulate and deceive. In the search for the one true theism, Mormonism is disqualified.

Other Bible-based cult groups run into similar problems. Upon close examination it is evident that all these groups are following into the same error of twisting the words of the Bible in order to control their followers, therefore they should be discarded as well.

CONCLUSION – CHRISTIAN THEISM IS SUPERIOR

Though this chapter does not give a detailed and thorough examination of all forms of theism, it does show some of the major difficulties with Christianity's chief competitors. Judaism is shortsighted and fails to connect the faith to Jesus Christ, the Jewish Messiah. Islam came six centuries after Christianity and claims that Muhammad is the actual prophet of God, and that everyone before him got it all wrong. Bible-based cult groups twist the words of the Bible in order to manipulate people and take advantage of them.

Christianity is the only form of theism that is based in history and proves itself to be true, primarily by the resurrection of Christ from the dead. It is the only form of theism that provides a holy book that is established as authentic by many proofs. Christianity offers real life solutions and hope to people who are hurting. It answers all the toughest questions about reality and offers a coherent system for understanding it – namely, that God does all things for his own glory. Christianity is the one true theism.

Chapter 12 Review Exercise

1. List two major problems with holding to deism.
2. Why is Christian theism a superior choice over Judaism?

3. When was Islam founded? How does this reality show Christian theism to be superior?
4. How many people wrote the Qur'an? How many people wrote the Book of Mormon? Why is this significant?
5. What are some of the major problems with believing Mormon doctrine?

Key Terms

Deism
Judaism
Islam
Qur'an
Bible-based cult
Mormonism
Book of Mormon

Scripture Memory

So for the sake of your tradition you have made void the word of God. You hypocrites! Well did Isaiah prophesy of you, when he said: "This people honors me with their lips, but their heart is far from me; in vain do they worship me, teaching as doctrines the commandments of men." (Matthew 15:7-9)

CHAPTER 13:
Don't Know and Don't Care

Millions of people in the world are not happy at all with any of the labels we have discussed in the previous two chapters. They don't wish to be called "Christian," or "Muslim," or "atheist," or "religious," or "secular," or any other such marker. Consider the thoughts of "Armine" who posted the following words in an online forum:

> I have recently come to the realization that I am an agnostic in terms of my views on religion. I was raised as a Catholic but I…have some serious doubts about its teachings. Additionally I really don't like it when people try to convert me to a particular religious viewpoint; I think a lot of what is wrong with the wider world today is the constant clashing over which religious school is "right" and therefore everyone else is wrong. I think there has to be more leeway, more tolerance and more acceptance of differing points of view. I am a passionate agnostic – and I don't want to convert anyone to my camp![116]

"Armine" is agnostic when it comes to religion. The technical definition of agnostic is a person who maintains a position of uncertainty when it comes to the existence of God. They simply do not know if God exists or not, so they are unwilling to identify themselves with any particular viewpoint.

Furthermore, the agnostic is usually deeply disturbed by people who claim to know the truth and attempt to convert others. But it should be pointed out, that even though "Armine" is against attempting to convert others, the words he or she wrote and posted are an attempt to convince people to buy into the agnostic point of view. "Armine" is a passionate agnostic and believes everyone else should be too. That is the point of advising people to have "more leeway" and "more tolerance." Everybody is an evangelist for their own worldview position (even if it is I-don't-knowism) and trying to deny this is futile. But that is really beside our current point, so now let's focus on the details of agnosticism, the worldview of uncertainty.

WHY PEOPLE BECOME AGNOSTIC

As we examine this position we quickly discover that not all agnostics are created equal. They come in different stripes. There are at least four possible reasons why a person might choose this position as their worldview option.

First, some claim ignorance of God for intellectual reasons. Many people have honestly pursued the question of the existence of God and have found the evidence lacking. They see naturalistic explanations as sufficient for the origin of and design in the universe, and for the existence of life and morality. To many of them, the whole idea of God seems illogical. They often cannot understand why a good, loving, and powerful God would allow so much evil and suffering in the world (a problem we will deal with in the next chapter). These are people who believe they have done the difficult research and have sought for answers, but the evidence for God's existence has been insufficient to convince them.

On the other hand, these same people are not convinced that atheism is true. They are not ready to say it is *impossible* for God to exist. They realize that people are finite creatures and cannot know all there is to know, so it cannot be said for sure that there is no God. Even in his famous tirade against all religions, *The God Delusion*, Richard Dawkins is not prepared to say with absolute certainty that there is no God. Instead he maintains that God *probably* does not exist. In so doing, he is being inconsistent with his self-label, since he calls himself an atheist.

This type of agnostic has done his homework, or at least he thinks he has. He has examined evidence for God and has decided that it doesn't add up. For what its worth, this is certainly the most respectable form of agnosticism.

Secondly, some become agnostic for pragmatic reasons. Life is busy after all, and it takes a great deal of time to do the research concerning the existence of God. Some folks feel their life is far too hectic, filled with ordinary, real-life activities, and thus they cannot commit any time toward such a consuming question like the existence of God. They may rationalize: "If God does exist, it would not make any perceptible difference to my life anyway."

Other agnostics are not too busy, but rather too lazy. It isn't time they are worried about, it is the hard work needed to research the question they want to avoid. As a teacher of apologetics, I (Jason) see this type of attitude often in my students. Some feel the Cosmological Argument, or the Moral Argument, or design arguments are just too difficult to understand. So they prefer to stay in an agnostic position in order to avoid the work.

Thirdly, some people remain agnostic for moral reasons. This reason is more common than most people care to admit. A woman is caught in a cycle of immoral behavior. Perhaps she is an alcoholic, or perhaps she is involved in an adulterous relationship. Under her current agnostic viewpoint, with its extremely loose moral code, she has no reason to halt her behavior. As long as she "doesn't know" if there is God, she feels she doesn't have to answer to him for what she is doing.

Some people in this category may even concede that evidence for God's existence is strong. But to admit fully the existence of God would mean accountability for their actions and they may have to cease the immoral behavior. Because of sinful hearts (Romans 3:23), great numbers of people are not willing to give up depraved actions, so the agnostic position is irrationally maintained, even in the face of tremendous evidence for God's existence.

Finally, some agnostics withhold judgment as to the existence of God for fear that they will be labeled as intolerant by society. "Armine" seems to fit nicely in this category. In order to avoid the controversy of being "Christian" or "religious," many people opt for the I-don't-know position.

This attitude is understandable. After all, there have been so many religious conflicts throughout history. Plus, all too often in many circles, Christianity has a bad name, frequently deserved. Unbelievers hesitate to commit to a religious point of view in order to avoid being labeled intolerant or contentious or, in some cases, down right stupid.

Whatever! The I-Don't-Care Worldview

Pragmatism is also a very popular worldview alternative that is linked with agnosticism. But pragmatists go a step further – they don't know *and they don't care*. Some agnostics care about worldview issues, but pragmatists don't at all. If you mention theism or pantheism to them, they just frown and say, "I have no idea what you are talking about and I couldn't care less!" (You might be one of these people and someone is forcing you to read this book)!

It might be tempting to say these people don't have a worldview at all, since they would not call themselves naturalists, pantheists, or theists – they just don't care. But even though, in a sense, it is a non-worldview, pragmatism actually becomes its own worldview.

For example, the word *pragmatism* essentially means to do what works. In this context, it refers to people who are interested in whatever makes life work. These people approach life as something to get through, or perhaps enjoy, but not something to think about. Many people will never think deeply about eternal issues, because they do not see how it can help them make it through another day at work or school.

Pragmatists say, "Who cares what worldview you hold to! You need to get off your rear end and make some money." Or "I do not have time to read the Bible, how can that help me get a good grade in Algebra!?" Or "If I think about my worldview I will not have time to talk three hours on the phone to my boyfriend about our favorite movies and songs."

These same people shy away very quickly from religious questions. "Do you believe in God?" is not something they even want to think about. It isn't that they want to say "Yes" or "No," they simply want to say "Who cares?" So pragmatism is the worldview of those who hold this "whatever" mentality when it comes to God.

A DANGEROUS RIDE

Agnosticism and pragmatism are both extremely precarious positions, as seen in the following story:

Ben was minding his own business while riding on a train from Cincinnati to his hometown of Pittsburgh. The man sitting in front of Ben (whose name happens to be Will) suddenly turns around, holding his cell phone in his hand. He speaks directly to Ben, but in a loud voice so that all the passengers can hear. "I have been on the phone with my wife who is watching CNN. She saw a report that our train is in danger. The bridge we are supposed to be crossing about ten miles down the track has been washed away by a flooding river. We must do something!"

Ben is naturally troubled by this report and turns his ipod off to concentrate. Just then Mary, the lady sitting behind Ben, leans over the seat and retorts to Will: "Oh, don't be such an alarmist! I've been speaking with my family too, and they say the bridge has sustained some damage, but it's only minor. They say it should hold our train just fine. We have nothing to worry about!"

Ben is officially an agnostic. He honestly *doesn't know* whether the bridge is safe to cross or not. Should he believe Will or Mary? In his gut, Ben is aware of his need to find out for sure. So he begins to research the situation in careful detail. He says to Will, "Okay, tell me exactly what your wife said she saw on CNN." Will repeats his wife's story that the bridge is totally washed out.

Ben turns to Mary, "Which network was your family watching?"

"I'm not sure," she says, "and now I can't get a cell phone signal to call them back."

Ben feels a sense of panic and decides he needs to act quickly to get more accurate information. He walks the aisle to the cabin and knocks loudly on the locked door. One of the engineers cracks the door and peeks out. "Yes?"

"Have you guys been watching the news?" asks Ben politely.

"No. Why?"

Ben recounts the information to the engineer, stressing that the train could be in serious trouble if the bridge is out. But the engineer is not interested. "We haven't heard anything. If there was a problem the station would let us know." He then adds, "We are on a schedule, mister. We cannot stop this train unless it is a real emergency."

What is Ben going to do now? He feels that his own life is at possible risk, but he isn't sure. He is still basically agnostic. But this is precisely why *remaining* agnostic is so dangerous. Many people, who say they do not know if God exists, or which religion is true, seem to pretend that they are not even on the train of life. They act as though it doesn't matter whether there is a God, or which worldview is true. But in Ben's case, it clearly matters.

Most religions have some type of judgment doctrine. Christianity, for example, holds that those who die in their sin will spend eternity in Hell as punishment. So the agnostic is on the train of life and Christians are preaching, in effect: "The bridge is out. If you remain in your current condition you will soon crash and be ruined."

Of course, other people, like Mary in the story, are saying that everything is fine. No judgment is coming for anyone. Naturalists, for example, claim that when we die, we simply cease to exist. There is no afterlife to worry about.

Who should we believe? Well, at the very least the agnostic, like Ben, should get up and do more research. Maybe the Christian is wrong, but the agnostic should at least study the position very carefully before he simply dismisses it altogether. Put another way, the agnostic had better be absolutely certain that the bridge is safe before he sits back down in his seat awaiting his fate. At that point, of course, he is no longer an agnostic – he has made his decision to disbelieve.

Now the pragmatist is the person who never gets up from his seat at all to check things out. And it isn't because he can't, it's because he doesn't want to. Why doesn't he want to? Because he is listening to a cool new song on his ipod and reading the latest men's fashion magazine, and he does not want to be interrupted by talk of coming doom. He is totally disinterested in the condition of the bridge altogether. Even if you pulled his earplugs out and screamed, "We're in serious danger!" He would say, "What does that have to do with what I'm doing right now? You are so rude to interrupt my song and reading like that!" He might add, "Let the engineers worry about that. Isn't that why they get paid?" Clearly pragmatism is not a viable option.

JUMPING

Back to Ben, who warned the engineer about the bridge, but was brushed off. Suppose, as he continues thinking about the situation, he becomes more and more convinced that Will is right. He comes to believe that the bridge is actually out and that his life is in danger. If this happens, he may decide to do something radical. Perhaps he opens the door of the train, takes a deep breath, and leaps. Would that hurt? Absolutely. He would hit the ground hard, and potentially break bones. But Ben concludes that this jump is better than remaining agnostic on the train where he is facing potential death.

The Christian is the person who is convinced that judgment is coming. This is not all there is to Christianity, but this is certainly part of it. He is convinced that he is a sinner who deserves the everlasting judgment of God, and he is willing to take a leap from the train in order to avoid that devastation. Will it hurt? Yes. Will he lose things he really wants? Yes. But in the end, his life is gained. Jesus taught this when he said:

> And if your hand causes you to sin, cut it off. It is better for you to enter life crippled than with two hands to go to hell, to the unquenchable fire. And if your foot causes you to sin, cut it off. It is better for you to enter life lame than with two feet to be thrown into hell. And if your eye causes you to sin, tear it out. It is better for you to enter the kingdom of God with one eye than with two eyes to be thrown into hell, "where their worm does not die and the fire is not quenched." (Mark 9:43-48)

Agnostics and pragmatists cannot pretend that they are not on the train of life. We are all riding. But there is horrific devastation ahead. The evidence for this is highly convincing. Christ has offered us an op-

238

portunity to jump. He even promises to catch us when we leap. You should not be content to sit in your seat and await an unknown fate.

Chapter 13 Review Exercise

1. Compare and contrast atheism, agnosticism, and pragmatism.
2. List the four reasons why people typically become agnostics.
3. Is pragmatism a non-worldview? Why or why not?
4. Why is holding long term to agnosticism or pragmatism a potentially dangerous choice?

Key Terms

Agnosticism
Pragmatism

Scripture Memory

Formerly, when you did not know God, you were enslaved to those that by nature are not gods. But now that you have come to know God, or rather to be known by God, how can you turn back again to the weak and worthless elementary principles of the world, whose slaves you want to be once more? (Galatians 4:8-9)

CHAPTER 14:
Answering Objections against Christianity

Throughout this book we have attempted to build a positive case for Christianity showing that other worldviews and religions do not match up to the superiority of the Christian worldview. The case for Christianity is very sound, and trusting Christ is not merely rational, but by far the best alternative available to people. In addition agnosticism and pragmatism are far too dangerous to maintain.

Still, many people refuse to believe God and follow Christ as their Savior and Lord. They say they have objections against Christianity that prohibit them from believing that it is true. There are many such objections, but all of them can be sufficiently answered. In this final chapter, we will walk through several of these briefly, showing that each objection is really not a deal-breaker. In other words, even though there may be a few difficult questions with which we must deal, Christianity is such a strong worldview position that none of the objections offered are enough to abandon Christ as truth.

RELIGION IS A PSYCHOLOGICAL CRUTCH

Former professional wrestler and governor of Minnesota Jessie Ventura once remarked, "Organized religion is a sham and a crutch for weak-minded people who need strength in numbers. It tells people to go out and stick their noses in other people's business."

Others have similar feelings about religion in general and Christianity in particular. We live in a macho environment where each individual takes care of himself or herself, and it is often considered weak and silly to run to a "God" to take care of you! So this is an objection from bullies, getting into religious people's faces with a pointed finger and declaring that tough people don't need God.

Imagine a seven year old girl named Cassidy playing football with a group of teenaged boys. As the ball is snapped Cassidy is pummeled by a large thirteen year old bully named Eric, and she ends up with a busted and bloody knee. She naturally begins to cry for her mom. Eric smirks and jeeringly mocks, "Ah, come on, kid, don't be a wimp. You don't need your mamma!" But she quickly runs home to her mom's embrace and a band-aid.

Later in the game, a larger boy, sixteen years old, plunges into Eric and breaks his arm. Eric quickly gets up, pretending nothing is wrong and starts to play the game again. However, he doesn't do very well, since his arm is hanging like Jell-O off his shoulder.

Cassidy has returned to the game and informs Eric that he is hurt badly and should see a doctor. But Eric refuses, claiming he is too tough to need a doctor and that doctors are for weak people.

But is Eric right? Is he right to mock Cassidy for seeking help from her mom when she knew she needed it? Is he right in refusing to see a doctor when he so obviously needs one? People who object to Christianity by saying it is for weak people are like Eric in this story.

How should Christians respond to the objection that Christianity is a crutch for weak people? First, Christians should admit that our faith in Jesus is indeed a crutch! Part of being a Christian is recognizing our own inability to get through life on our own. We are like Cassidy in the story. We are broken, hurting, bruised by sin, and we know it. We seek for help with our injuries and should not be ashamed of the reality that faith helps us with daily life. So there is no reason to deny the charge that we need a crutch.

But on the other hand, Christians should most certainly take issue with the idea that having a crutch is "weak-minded" as Ventura claims. If a person breaks his leg and the doctor gives him crutches, he is not weak-minded when he uses them! In fact, it is the weak-minded person, like Eric, who fails to see his need for help in the name of being tough.

So Christians should freely admit our brokenness, our need, and our inability. But we should not be considered weak-minded just because we recognize our need and find a solution in Christ! This objection fails.

ALL RELIGIONS ARE EQUAL

Another serious objection to Christianity comes in the form of religious pluralism, or the belief that all religions are equal. The pluralist holds that all the different religions of the world are leading to the exact same place, by different roads. They view God (or the Real as he is often called) as the top of a mountain. Christianity may choose to go up one side of the mountain, while Islam may decide to go up another. Buddhists may ascend on still another path. But, says the pluralist, we all end up at the top, in exactly the same place.

President Obama appears to hold this view. In a 2004 interview for the Chicago Sun-Times, he expressed it in these words:

I'm rooted in the Christian tradition. I believe that there are many paths to the same place, and that is a belief that there is a higher power, a belief that we are connected as a people.

That there are values that transcend race or culture, that move us forward, and there's an obligation for all of us individually as well as collectively to take responsibility to make those values lived.[117]

Notice he says he is "rooted" in the Christian tradition, meaning Jesus represents the particular path he has chosen. But there are "many paths to the same place."

Pluralists use the following analogy to illustrate their beliefs. Four blind men were all touching an elephant, but came to some very different conclusions about it. The first was feeling the trunk of the elephant and said, "It is a great snake." The second felt the elephant's leg and said, "It is a tree." The third man touched the side and said, "The elephant is a towering wall." The last man felt the tail and declared, "It is a rope."

In much the same way, declares the religious pluralist, all religions are touching the exact same divine reality, and yet they are coming to different conclusions about what this divine reality is like. It follows from this that all religions are equally valid paths and all are equally true.

For the Christian, this simply cannot be the case. Jesus famously preached, "I am the way, and the truth, and the life. No one comes to the Father except through me" (John 14:6). There are some major problems with pluralism that discredit it completely as a viable challenge to the Christian faith.

First of all, pluralism is terribly inconsistent. It declares that all religions are equal – that is, except one. Religious pluralism! Think about it. The only person in the elephant illustration who wasn't blind was the person telling the story. Who was that? The religious pluralist! In other words, the person who believes pluralism is saying that all the *rest of the people* in the world, who hold to various religions, are all blind. He *sees* this precisely because he believes himself *not to be blind!* But this is a grossly inconsistent double-standard. If he demands that all religions be treated as equal, then he should believe his views are blind views too. Instead, he pretends that he alone has absolute truth and knows the nature of all the religions of the world. This is an arrogant and unacceptable position.

In the same way, pluralists intolerantly promote tolerance. They say that since all religions are equal, every religion should be tolerated as true. But if a Christian claims that Christianity is the only true religion, the religious pluralist will not tolerate him! How intolerant!

Another problem with pluralism pertains to their teaching that sincerity of belief, and devotion to a religion, is an indicator that it is true. A pluralist looks at the Muslims, Hindus, and Jews and says these people are just as sincere about their beliefs as Christians are, if not more so. How can a Christian say that Jesus is the *only* way to God when these other people are so genuine about their faith?

But as important as sincerity is, it is not an accurate test for truth. If there is actually nitrogen in the tank, it doesn't matter how sincere your belief that oxygen is in the tank. When you breathe it you must deal with reality. If it is actually rat poison in the bottle, it doesn't matter how devoted you are to the idea that it is Tylenol when you swallow it. Truth is truth no matter how sincerely one believes it. And false is false no matter how sincerely one believes it.

For these, and many other reasons, religious pluralism cannot be considered a serious challenge to Christian theism and should not be accepted. Let's move on to the next objection someone might raise against Christianity.[118]

WHY SHOULD I BELIEVE IN A GOD I CANNOT SEE?

Most Christians have struggled with the issue of God's invisibility, whether they will admit it or not. It is difficult, to say the least, to devote our lives to a being that we cannot see, or audibly hear. And many atheists scoff at the idea that Christians worship an invisible God. As one famous atheist quipped, "I do not believe in God because I do not believe in Mother Goose."[119]

Some place belief in an invisible God in the same category as believing in Santa Claus or in the Flying Spaghetti Monster. They maintain that there is no evidence for either of these beings, and therefore neither of them should be considered real.

As a Christian, I (Jason) have often wished that I could see God. Why can't I just meet Jesus down at Mcdonald's and have a cup of coffee with him? If he is real, surely he could pull that off! Plus, that would make witnessing much easier! I could bring folks to Jesus and say, "There he is!"

Seriously, I remember asking God at one point to appear to me, so that all doubt would be removed as to his existence. So far, God has not granted that request. And all of the other Christians I know also admit that God has not appeared to them either. So how do we deal with this? How can we maintain rational integrity if we are devoting our lives to an invisible, eternal being?

First, belief in God is nothing like belief in Santa Claus. This is a false analogy, much like this example:

> Harper's new car is bright blue, has leather upholstery, and gets excellent gas mileage. Crowley's new car is also bright blue and has leather upholstery. Therefore, it probably gets excellent gas mileage, too.[120]

Just because there are a couple of things in common between Harper's and Crowley's car, does not mean they have everything in common. Color and upholstery type do not say anything about the engine.

Likewise, Santa Claus and God *do* have one thing in common – they are both invisible.[121] But this is where the commonalities end. And just because they are alike in that one way does not mean they are alike in every way.

In previous chapters much clear evidence has been shown that God actually exists, but there is no such evidence for the jolly old elf. If we have good reasons to conclude that God is an actual being, then even if we cannot see him, we are still rational in believing in him. You have probably never personally seen President Obama but you are perfectly rational in believing he exists. Seeing is not always believing, especially since we can come to knowledge in ways other than visual perception.

Secondly, it is worth noting that God has not always remained invisible. He is interested in manifesting himself to people, and has done so in the past in many different ways. He appeared to Moses in the burning bush (Exodus 3:1-4), to Isaiah in the temple (Isaiah 6:1), and to many others in the Old Testament era. But most importantly, he revealed himself in the person of Jesus Christ, so much so that Jesus even said, "Whoever has seen me has seen the Father" (John 14:9).

The Bible is also clear that in the future God is going to show himself again, at the second coming of Jesus Christ, when every eye will see him: "Behold, he is coming with the clouds, and every eye will see him, even those who pierced him, and all tribes of the earth will wail on account of him" (Revelation 1:7).

So Christians worship an invisible God, but he is only invisible for the moment. Perhaps he has a good reason for not showing himself right now. Just maybe he is getting maximized glory by allowing us to wait for him to demonstrate himself to us visibly again in the future.

Jesus hinted at this when he was speaking with Thomas, just after he had risen from the dead. Thomas was skeptical that Jesus had really been resurrected, and he wanted proof, which Jesus gave him in the form of nail-scarred hands. Thomas fell down to worship Jesus, who then spoke to his friend: "Have you believed because you have seen me? Blessed are those who have not seen and yet have believed" (John 20:29).

So sure, it is difficult to believe in a God that we cannot see, but Christians do not see this as an obstacle to our faith. Rather, we wait patiently and joyfully, longing for his coming, when our faith becomes sight.

> Though you have not seen him, you love him. Though you do not now see him, you believe in him and rejoice with joy that is inexpressible and filled with glory, obtaining the outcome of your faith, the salvation of your souls. (1 Peter 1:8-9)

THE CONCEPT OF "GOD" IS ILLOGICAL

Other people object to Christianity because the very idea of God makes no sense to them. They say that God cannot exist because a being like him would have attributes that contradict each other in ways that cannot be reconciled. In order to understand this objection, consider the following question, "Can God create a stone so heavy that he himself cannot lift it?"

This appears to be a catch-22. If the Christian answers yes, then there is something that God cannot do (lift the stone) which means he is not omnipotent – that is, all powerful – and therefore, not God. But if the Christian answers no, then there is something that God cannot do (create a stone the he cannot lift) which also means he is not omnipotent and therefore, not God. So either way, God is not God!

Many unbelievers think this and other such dilemmas show clearly that there is no God, or at least, no omnipotent God. But does this objection hold any water?

Absolutely not! The Bible does not define omnipotence as God's ability to do *anything at all*, but rather omnipotence is God's ability to do anything *he wants to do*. There are plenty of things that God cannot do! For example, he cannot tell a lie (Hebrews 6:18; Titus 1:2). That would go against his perfect and holy character. Neither can he worship other gods. If he did, he would be breaking his own commandments! Neither can God cause himself to stop existing. An eternally existing being cannot stop existing.

This means the answer is a resounding *no* to the question above. God *cannot* create a stone so heavy that he cannot lift it. Why not? Because God can lift every stone without exception!

So does this mean God is limited? Yes, but it is not fair to call this a limitation, since he is limited *only by his own perfections*. The reason he cannot do certain things is because he is utterly perfect in every way. He is limited by his holiness, and therefore cannot be unholy. He is limited by his truthfulness, so he cannot tell a lie. He is limited by his eternality, so he cannot stop existing.

The limits of God are not limits at all, but rather by-products of his perfection. So even though many atheists continue to use this tired objection, it is clear that the concept of God is not at all illogical. In the face of the abundant positive evidence for the existence of God, this is a very weak protest.

THE PROBLEM OF EVIL AND SUFFERING

A much more serious objection to the existence of God, particularly the God of the Bible, is the problem of evil and suffering.

I (Jason) once preached a funeral in which the daughter of the deceased woman came to me and asked, "How can God take my mother away from me?" What she was essentially saying is that a good and loving God would not allow her to go through this horrible pain in her life.

Most people deal with this difficult issue from time to time. If God is good, and if he loves people, why does he permit evil which leads to great suffering? Why does he allow people to hate and harm each other? Here is how the formal argument unfolds:

1. God, if he exists, is omnipotent (has the ability to prevent evil), is omniscient (knows when evil will occur and how to stop it), and is all loving (would want to prevent evil).
2. But there is evil in the world.
3. Therefore, God does not exist.

If the argument above is correct, then it is fair to say that God does not exist and that Christianity is a false religion, along with every other form of theism. Even though the argument seems strong, there are several possible responses that a Christian could give to it.

The Open Theism Defense

Some have answered the problem of evil by denying either that God is omnipotent or omniscient. This view is called open theism, because it claims that God is open to change and does not know the future. His life is open, just as a human life is open.

Open theists who deny his omnipotence say that God doesn't have as much power as people have traditionally thought. He cannot be blamed for the death and devastation that comes from natural disasters, for example, since natural disasters are not within his power to control.

Open theists who deny God's absolute knowledge (his omniscience) claim that God does not know the future and, therefore, cannot be responsible when evil and suffering occur, since he doesn't *know* when and where it will happen. In fact, when bad things happen, God is just as surprised as we are. He was just as shocked as the rest of us when terrorists attacked the United States on September 11, 2001. Evil and suffering is not his fault! If he *could* stop it, he *would* stop it! Poor powerless God!

Now sure, the open theism response does solve the problem of evil and suffering. But at what price? If open theism is true, then the Bible is wrong. According to the Bible, God knows all things past, present, and future, and he is a God of absolute, sovereign power over all things. "I form light and create darkness, I make well-being and create calamity, I am the LORD, who does all these things" (Isaiah 45:7). He is never surprised or shocked by anything that happens. So for the biblical Christian, open theism just does not work in solving this problem.

The Freewill Defense

Another and much better way to solve the problem of evil and suffering is called the Freewill defense. This response says that God certainly has the power and the knowledge to prevent evil, but that he has a very good reason *not to* prevent it. Namely, he wants to maintain human freedom. That is, he wants people to make real choices and to live with the consequences of those choices.

God did not create robots. He created people, who are called to obedience. He created people who decide whether they will love God or hate God, and a world where evil is temporarily permitted, allows for this type of decision to be made. The Freewill Defense solves the problem of evil in a much more biblical way than the open theism defense. But is it sufficient? Actually, there is an even better way to solve this problem.

The Greater Goods Defense

This response to the problem of evil and suffering agrees with the Freewill defense that the world requires both good and evil in order to allow for real human freedom. But this defense adds that there are actually many very good things that God loves dearly that *could not exist without evil.*

One of these things is mercy. God is merciful. That means he grants relief to those who are suffering in misery. God is glorified in his mercy and is exalted when he shows kindness to those in need. But

251

there can be no mercy without suffering. Mercy comes to those who are suffering and suffering is caused by sin and evil. So in order for God to be exalted as a God of mercy in the actual life experiences of people, then sin and evil must be present in the world.

What about forgiveness? God tells us that he is a forgiving God. But he can't show us that, unless he actually forgives us of something. But how can he forgive us unless we do something wrong? There can be no forgiveness without disobedience. In order to arrive at the greater good of showing and experiencing forgiveness, God allows the people to commit genuine acts of evil.

We could also add the notion of trust. If there were no situations in life that were desperate, people would be much less likely to trust God. But God values trust and commands people to trust him. "Though I walk through the valley of the shadow of death I will fear no evil for you are with me" (Psalm 23:4). That verse could not have been written without a "valley of the shadow of death."

Beyond these greater goods, the most important event that ever happened in the history of the world came about through the agency of evil and wicked murderers. The crucifixion of Jesus Christ, as the sacrificed Lamb of God, is the pathway to the greater good of salvation for sinners, and brings eternally maximized glory to God.

> This Jesus, delivered up according to the definite plan and foreknowledge of God, you crucified and killed by the hands of lawless men. God raised him up, loosing the pangs of death, because it was not possible for him to be held by it. (Acts 2:23-24)

This is the gist of the Greater Goods Defense. There are many greater goods that God desires, but many of these require the experience of evil and suffering to be realized. Thus God allows the temporary presence of evil as a necessary part of bringing these greater things into existence.

This does not mean that we know specifically *why* certain horrible things happen. Though we have the general solution to the problem of evil, we must be careful about trying to figure out exactly what greater goods we believe God is bringing out of certain situations. We should not make the mistake of claiming we know exactly why God would allow Hurricane Katrina to destroy New Orleans for example. We do not and cannot see all that God sees. But what we do know is that God is bringing good things from bad things (Romans 8:28; Genesis 50:20). He has the ability and the desire to make all things new and set all things right. If you understand this, then you see there is no real problem of evil at all.

MIRACLES ARE IMPOSSIBLE

Here is another objection to Christianity that deserves much more treatment than will be given here. The answer will be short and sweet.

Some people maintain that belief in God is irrational because miracles are impossible. Miracles cannot be proven scientifically and people who believe that miracles actually occur do so in reliance upon eye-witnesses, since miracles are events that occur only once.

But if God exists, and we have every good reason to believe that he does, then it follows logically that miracles are possible.

People who object to miracles *presuppose there is no God first.* Well sure, if there is no God, then we would expect miracles to be impossible. But what if you have very good reasons to believe there is a God? In this book, many logical and rational reasons to believe that a God exists have been carefully laid out. And miracles make perfect sense in a universe where God does exist! In order to say that miracles are impossible, one has to deny the existence of God first.

Furthermore, miracles, though not scientifically provable, can be used as strong evidence for the existence of God or the deity of Christ. The resurrection of Jesus is a case in point, for there is much evidence that it actually happened, and if it did, then Jesus is God and all that he said is true (John 11:45).

CHRISTIANS ARE HYPOCRITES

Some say that Christianity can't be true, since Christians display such hypocritical behavior. Why should an unbeliever listen to someone tell them about Christ, if that same person is not living life in a way that honors Christ? Christians, often even preachers and other leaders, do not look much different from the rest of the world, engaging in many of the same sins and often falling into gross immorality. Doesn't this fact disprove Christianity?

No it doesn't. We must first admit, hypocrisy is *very real* among Christians, but it isn't *only* Christians who are hypocritical – everybody is! Hypocrisy is not simply a condition that exists among believers, but it is a global phenomenon. Everybody is a hypocrite. Every person is born with the sinful capacity to pretend they are something other than they really are. Every person has difficulty practicing what they preach. Just because someone becomes a believer in Jesus Christ does not automatically remove this sin.

Nor does the Bible teach that hypocrisy immediately disappears when someone becomes a Christian. The Bible does not say Christians are perfect, but rather forgiven and progressing, as Paul teaches here:

Not that I have already obtained this or am already perfect, but I press on to make it my own, because Christ Jesus has made me his own. Brothers, I do not consider that I have made it my own. But one thing I do: forgetting what lies behind and straining forward to what lies ahead, I press on toward the goal for the prize of the upward call of God in Christ Jesus. (Philippians 3:12-14)

But most importantly, no belief system should be judged on the basis of the conduct of its adherents, but rather on the basis of whether it is true or not. Think about it, if Isaac Newton had been arrested for burglary, would that have made his gravitational formula false? Absolutely not! If Einstein had murdered someone, would that have made $e=mc^2$ false? Of course not! It isn't a person's behavior that makes something true or false. It just simply *is* true or false, regardless of how people act. Therefore, another objection against Christianity falls by the wayside.

I'M ALREADY GOOD SO I DON'T NEED GOD

Many feel as though they are okay with God already, from a moral point of view. So they think they need not deal with him any further. These feelings, however, often arise, not out of comparing themselves with God's Law, but rather with other people. "Hey, I don't sleep around or murder, so I can't be that bad."

But deep down, we know that we are bad. When people truly consider the state of our souls, the way we think, speak, and treat others, we usually find an abundance of evil and wickedness. Perhaps it is sexual immorality, hating others, pride, stealing, unkindness, or a host of other wicked actions. When we recognize that our hearts lean in that direction, we begin to see that the Bible is correct when it says, "None is righteous, no, not one" (Romans 3:10). No human being meets God's standard of perfection. The Apostle John states, "If we say we have no sin, we deceive ourselves, and the truth is not in us" (1 John 1:8).

So we are not good enough to be able to live without the salvation and cleansing of God. But beyond this, even if we were good enough, we would still need God! After all, he is our Creator and the Sustainer of our lives. Just as clay can exist and have meaning only because of the potter, so it is with our relationship to God. No matter who you are

255

and no matter your moral condition, you need God. Don't allow this objection to stand in your way of a relationship with the King.

I'M TOO BAD SO GOD WOULD NEVER ACCEPT ME

This is the final objection we will analyze. It comes from people who, as a result of their wicked heart and actions, believe that God would never love or accept them. Unlike the people in the previous section, these folks *know* they are bad. They are aware of their own depravity and failings before the Lord. This is why they avoid him. They do not feel worthy to step into his presence. But according to the Bible, saving bad people is God's specialty: "For while we were still weak, at the right time Christ died for the ungodly" (Romans 5:6). Notice that he dies for the *ungodly.*

God receives untold amounts of glory because of his willingness and ability to take people who live in total darkness and move them into his marvelous light (1 Peter 2:9). Paul is a prime example of this, since he was a persecutor of Christians prior to his conversion (Acts 9). If anyone had a wicked past, it was Paul. But God brought him out of that state by powerful grace.

Also, the Bible teaches us that recognition of our sin is the first step in the process of redemption. We must be able to *see* our sin in order to properly repent of it, and turn to God in faith. So we shouldn't think of ourselves as *too bad* to be saved, but rather our deep sinfulness should drive us more quickly to the healer of the soul, Jesus Christ.

We must realize that our acceptance before God is not based upon our own works or merit. We have nothing positive to bring to the table. Salvation is a rescue operation, not an impress-God operation. God accepts us because we are found in Christ, who paid the penalty for our sins on the cross.

In fact, using this as an objection against become a disciple of Jesus, is actually a mock of what he did to save people. For a person to say he is too bad to be saved is to strongly imply that Jesus' atoning work is not powerful enough to wash away sin. But "if we confess our sins, he is faithful and just to forgive us our sins and to cleanse us from all unrighteousness" (1 John 1:9).

Of course, after he adopts us into his family, we should strongly desire to please him by keeping his commandments, and bearing fruit in our lives. The rest of the book of 1 John teaches us these realities. But we cannot make the mistake of thinking the fruit comes *before* the tree is planted. We enter into salvation by *his work alone*. He accepts us because of what *he has done for us*. So for the person who is focused on the power of God's grace rather than the darkness of his own wickedness, this objection fails miserably. Nobody is too bad to be rescued by God.

CONCLUSION

We hope the answers provided to these common objections against Christianity are helpful to you. There are many other objections that could be analyzed (and have been throughout this book), but we hope you see from the ones addressed here, there *are* answers when people raise protests against the truth of Jesus Christ. People should never let anything stand in between them and the redemption and love of God.

Chapter 14 Review Exercise

1. Describe why the objection against Christianity fails that says religion is merely a psychological crutch.
2. Why does God remain invisible for the time being?
3. How is belief in God different from belief in Santa Claus?
4. List the three defenses given in this chapter to the problem of evil? Which one do you think works best? Why?

5. Write out a hypothetical conversation between a Christian and an unbeliever who objects to Christianity on the basis that Christians are hypocrites.
6. Is anyone so good that they don't need God? Why or why not?
7. Is anyone so bad that God would not accept them? Why or why not?

Key Terms

Religious pluralism
False analogy
Omnipotence
Problem of evil
Miracle
Hypocrisy objection

Scripture Memory

Behold, he is coming with the clouds, and every eye will see him, even those who pierced him, and all tribes of the earth will wail on account of him. (Revelation 1:7)

EPILOGUE:
Living the Christian Worldview

At the close of this volume we present you with a challenging question. What are you going to do with what you have learned? Many people read a book like this, put it away, and then forget about it. They are confronted with powerful evidence for the existence of God and the deity of Christ, but walk away unchanged. The New Testament author James feared some of his readers would make this mistake when he wrote, "For he looks at himself and goes away and at once forgets what he was like" (James 1:24). We hope this book leads people out of self-satisfied indecision and into truth-seeking action.

Yes, some people are going to disagree with the conclusions offered in these pages and will seek to discredit the arguments. That's fair enough since they are at least *doing* something about what they have read! Others will be strengthened in their faith and will be bolder in sharing the gospel with friends and family. Still others may sense God leading them into some type of ministry. Again, these people are all doing something.

But what can you do if you are not sure what to do? Here are a few ideas. If you now see that Christianity is true, then first, you should be-

259

come a Christian, if you aren't already. Go to Jesus Christ, who is real and really hears you. Call upon his name and ask him to forgive you of your sins which deserve eternal punishment. Begin living for the glory of the only true God, and living in light of his presence and love.

Second, continue your study of reality, beginning with a detailed and devotional analysis of the entire Bible. It proves itself trustworthy and authentic, and it is the handbook for life that must be treasured and absorbed. Don't neglect your study of the Bible. Live it, breathe it, and eat it, but don't neglect it. Study other things too. Read another apologetics book, or a book on basic philosophy, or a history book, or a science book. Evaluate these other books by the absolute standard of the word of God. As a Christian, you should thirst for greater and more accurate knowledge about God, your own soul, the condition of humanity, and the world around you.

Third, since Christianity is indeed true, then love his body, the Church. The Bible tells us that God loves his people and has called them out of the world *as a group*. Christianity is not a solo project but operates as a family of Christ-followers. When Paul informs husbands that they should love their wives, he makes known God's love for his collective people, his Church:

> Husbands, love your wives, as Christ loved the church and gave himself up for her, that he might sanctify her, having cleansed her by the washing of water with the word, so that he might present the church to himself in splendor, without spot or wrinkle or any such thing, that she might be holy and without blemish. (Ephesians 5:25-27)

That does not mean every person who goes to church is perfect, but if they belong to Jesus Christ, they are eternally special to him. Therefore, we should desire to join the ranks of a local church and be deeply engrained in the lives of fellow believers. Sometimes that is not easy! Sometimes people disagree with each other and often lose their tempers. Sometimes people pull out their fighting fists, rather than showing grace and forgiveness. But Jesus said that the world would know that we are his by the way we love each other (John 13:35). If Christianity is true, we must learn to love his Church!

One final suggestion for how you can respond to what you have read in this book. Since Christianity is true, his people must reach out to those who do not believe. It might be your neighbor, your class-mate, your coworker, or someone who lives around the globe. But if we love people, we must tell them the truth and not sit idly by, allow-ing them to live in error.

Suppose you knew that a certain bottle contained deadly poison in the form of a pill. As you watched in dismay, an elderly gentleman walks up and grabs the bottle saying, "Well, I need to take my medi-cine." If you knew the bottle had poison in it, you would not keep si-lent and allow him to take a poisonous pill – unless you hated him and longed for his death! You would not simply claim a man's medicine too personal and therefore none of your business! If you loved him and cared about his welfare then you would tell him the truth.

Christian theism is the only correct worldview, and other world-views (false and therefore poisonous) lead people into ruin. We must love people enough, even if they disagree with us severely, to tell them about Jesus Christ and the availability of salvation through his blood. It might lead to persecution. People might not like you and call you names. Heck, you might even be crucified for it. But if we love people, we must tell them the truth!

So those are a few ways you can respond to what you have read. The authors have prayed for you the reader that you will not be com-placent or apathetic about the realities expressed in these pages. Having now seen that Christianity is the only truth, we hope that your life would, in every way, reflect the glory of God. And finally, that he would be your heart's full satisfaction as he heaps mercy upon you daily, and works to mold you to the image of his precious Son and our Lord Jesus Christ. This is what apologetics is ultimately all about.

Glossary of Terms

Agnosticism. The belief that knowledge of God's existence is either unknowable (hard agnosticism) or personally unknown (soft agnosticism).

Apologetics. A rational defense of the Christian faith; the protector of Christian theology.

Archeology. The scientific discipline that seeks to reconstruct the past through the findings of ancient artifacts such as pottery, tools, weapons, manuscripts, and many others.

Argument. A carefully constructed reason or set of reasons for holding a certain belief or arguing against a certain belief.

Atheism. Either the positive assertion that there is no god (hard atheism) or the withholding of belief in god (soft atheism).

Bible. The definitive set of sixty-six books written with prophetic or apostolic authority and accepted by Christianity as the written word of God.

Bible-based cult. A religious group that uses the Bible as its basic authority, but twists its meaning in order to manipulate and control its followers. The two largest Bible-based cults in the world are the Church of Jesus Christ of Latter Day Saints and Jehovah's Witnesses.

Biblical contradiction. A supposed situation where two biblical texts, when brought side-by-side, cannot be reconciled with each other.

Biblical manuscripts. Ancient copies of the Old and New Testaments.

Biblical unity. The reality that even though the Bible has enormous diversity of authorship, it tells only one overall story, with each book contributing uniquely to that story, which is the redemption of man through the work of Jesus Christ for the glory of God. This reality supports the notion that the Bible has a powerful, divine edge.

Book of Mormon. The religious text of the Church of Jesus Christ of Latter Day Saints, written by their supposed prophet Joseph Smith.

Cause. Something that brings an effect or result. Every contingent thing in existence must have a cause.

Christian. A person who believes the orthodox doctrines of the Christian faith, has received the forgiveness of sins offered by Jesus Christ, and has devoted his life to exhibiting the glory of God because of it.

Circular reasoning. An argument in which a thing argues for the validity of itself without any outside recourse. For example, "Bill is president because Bill said he is president."

Context. As it relates to the Bible, the context includes the verses that precede and come after the section being examined. The context is always critical in coming to a proper understanding of any text. The wider context of an entire book of Scripture, the corpus of writings by one particular author, and the entire Bible itself are also important in determining the meaning of any one verse.

Contingent. Something that depends upon something else for its existence. Everything except God is contingent.

Cosmological Argument. An argument that shows the high probability of God's existence by demonstrating the necessity of an eternal first cause of the universe who is alive and intelligent.

Creation Science. A method of doing science that begins with the Bible as an assumed fact. It is an admittedly biased way of doing science, claiming that neutrality in the scientific method is impossible.

Crucifixion. A form of execution in which the accused is nailed or tied to a tree, or cross, and left to die from asphyxiation or exposure to the elements. Crucifixion was popular between the 6th Century B.C. and the 4th Century A.D., when it was abolished in the Roman Empire by Constantine.

Dead Sea Scrolls. A collection of more than eight hundred documents discovered between 1947 and 1956 in eleven caves along the northwest shore of the Dead Sea. Many ancient copies of Old Testament books (some whole, some portions) were part of the scrolls, lending greater credibility to the transmission of the text of the Old Testament.

Deism. The belief in an eternal deity sometimes referred to by deists as God, who created the universe and set into play natural laws that govern it. Deists claim to formulate their view of deity purely through philosophical and scientific reasoning, and generally reject all forms of special revelation, such as the Bible claims to be.

Eternal. The state in which a thing has its existence in itself, and thus is infinite in duration. According to the Cosmological Argument, whatever the first cause is, it must be eternal.

Evangelism. Sharing the core message of the Christian faith that Jesus Christ came to save sinners.

False analogy. A logical fallacy in which two things are compared to each other and false or unsupported conclusions are drawn from the comparison. For example, many atheists compare belief in

God with belief in Santa Claus or other such mythological creatures.

Fine-Tuning Argument. The argument that examines the cosmological constants of the universe, observing the fact that they appear to be carefully set in order to allow life to exist in the universe. The best explanation for the setting of these constants is an intelligent designer.

First cause. In the Cosmological Argument for the existence of God, the first cause is the necessary explanation for the existence of all things, and therefore must be uncaused and eternal.

Glory. In Christian theology, glory is the shining of God's brilliant holiness, to be observed and enjoyed by God himself, and all his people.

Gospel. The good news that Jesus Christ is God incarnate, who has, through his life, death, and resurrection, made it possible to be reconciled to God through faith.

Grace. A gift of favor given to someone who does not deserve it and has not earned it. In Christian theology, the grace of God especially pertains to God's desire to save guilty sinners through the sacrifice of his own Son.

Guilt. The experience of realizing that a moral standard has been broken.

Hell. According to the Bible, Hell is an actual place where unforgiven sinners spend eternity, suffering the penalty of their rebellion against God.

Hypocrisy Objection. The argument against a worldview position that states since the adherents of the worldview are not living according to their own standards then the worldview itself is either false or highly suspect.

Infinite regress. A hypothetical causal series of past events that has no beginning point, or first cause. Logically, an infinite regress is impossible.

Intelligent Design. A movement of scientists attempting to be unbiased in regard to the scientific method, whose findings point to the existence of an intelligent designer.

Irreducible complexity. An object is considered irreducibly complex if it is a system that only functions properly if every part of the system is present. This phenomenon, which appears frequently in nature, strongly suggests the existence of an intelligent designer.

Islam. The religion founded by Muhammad in the 6th Century A.D., which claims that Allah is the only God and that the Qur'an is his message. Adherents to Islam are called Muslims.

Israel. A people group who trace their ancestry back to Abraham through Isaac. The Old Testament focuses on them as the chosen people of God, through which the Messiah would come. Israelites live primarily in their nation by the same name, but are also scattered throughout the earth. The reality of their existence serves to bring credibility to the Bible as an accurate historical document.

Jesus-myth hypothesis. An extreme view held by a few historians and biblical critics which postulates that the historical Jesus of Nazareth never existed, but was rather a fabrication of the early church. This view is dismissed by a huge majority of the experts who study Jesus' life and the history of the early church.

Joseph of Arimathea. A wealthy member of the Sanhedrin in the 1st Century A.D. who donated his tomb for the burial of Jesus of Nazareth.

Judaism. The religion of Israel, which through the years has involved the appointment of priests, temple rituals including animal sacrifices, prayer, fasting, and the celebration of appointed feasts throughout the year. It was the religion of Jesus of Nazareth and his family. According to Christian theology, Judaism is fulfilled in the Messianic priesthood of Jesus Christ.

Mass hallucination theory. The belief held by some historians that the disciples of Christ only thought they saw Jesus alive after his death, but that it was actually a case of multiple individuals experiencing a common hallucination.

Messiah. The title of the Anointed One, or the Christ, predicted by the Old Testament to come and deliver Israel from their sin.

Methodological naturalism. The method of scientific inquiry in which naturalism is assumed prior to investigation. If adopted, methodological naturalism will lead to naturalistic conclusions.

Miracle. An event that supersedes human understanding of scientific laws, and thus, is usually attributed to divine intervention.

Moral Argument. The argument for God's existence that sates that the existence of objective moral laws is best explained by the existence of a moral lawgiver.

Moral relativism. The belief that morality does not reflect objective and universal truths, but is rather subjective and depends upon the choice of each individual, family, or society.

Mormonism. The religion developed by Joseph Smith in the mid 19th Century in order to restore what he believed was the one true church. Smith claims that an angel named Moroni informed him of the location of golden plates, which, now translated into English, are called the Book of Mormon. The central tenants of Mormonism vary greatly from orthodox Christian beliefs. The group is often referred to as the Church of Jesus Christ of Latter Day Saints.

Naturalism. The worldview which holds that ultimate reality is composed of only matter and energy. This view strongly implies atheism.

Negative apologetics. A type of apologetic argumentation geared as a defensive mechanism against objections people raise against Christian belief.

Nostradamus. (1503-1566) A French writer of prophecies whose works continue to be examined in modern times.

Objective moral law. A universal moral law that transcends mere human law, and upon which human law is based.

Omnipotence. The ability for God to do whatever he pleases.

Paley's Watchmaker. An apologetic argument made famous by William Paley, that compares the intricacies of the universe to a watch. Paley maintained that just as the presence of a watch implies the existence of watchmaker, so the design in the universe points to a grand designer.

Pantheism. The worldview which holds that ultimate reality is essentially spirit, or Brahman. Pantheism is the broad umbrella for religions like Hinduism, many forms of Buddhism, and the New Age Movement.

Pentecost. A Jewish celebration fifty days after Passover. It is the day on which the Holy Spirit descended upon the disciples in Jerusalem, and the day that Peter preached the resurrection of Christ to thousands in Jerusalem.

Pharisees. A legalistic party of the Jews who viewed themselves as the experts in the Law of Moses and sought to impose it on people by force. They were the chief antagonists against Christ during his life.

Pilate Stone. A block of limestone found in an archeological dig around Caesarea in 1961, which identifies Pontus Pilate as a governor in Judea.

Pool of Siloam. A pool hewn out of rock excavated in Jerusalem in 2005. The pool dates back to the days of Hezekiah, and is mentioned in several places in the Bible, most notably Isaiah 8:6 and John 9:7.

Positive apologetics. An offensive type of apologetic argumentation that seeks to build the Christian faith as credible. Positive apologetic arguments supply reasons why Christianity should be believed.

Pragmatism. The worldview option held by people who are apathetic about worldview issues in general. Those who hold this view essentially desire to do whatever they perceive works best for their lives.

Problem of evil. An objection against theism that states that an all powerful, all knowing, and all good God is inconsistent with evil and suffering in the world.

Proof. Any factual evidence that helps establish something as true. Evidence that moves something beyond a reasonable doubt is usually considered adequate proof. Proof is not confined only to absolute certainty.

Prophecy. The prediction of a future event or set of events, the knowledge of which is usually said to be from a divine source.

Qur'an. The primary religious text of Islam written by Muhammad, supposedly under the direction of the angel Gabriel, in the 7th Century A.D.

Religious pluralism. The belief that all religions are different expressions of the same truth, and thus should all be accepted as valid.

Sin. According to Christian theology, sin is any condition or action that goes against the holiness of God, and thus defames his glory.

Theism. The worldview that maintains the existence of a divine being, usually referred to as God, who is the eternal and uncaused creator of the universe, and who is separate from the created order itself.

True Christianity. The version of Christianity that holds to the central and orthodox doctrines of the Christian faith, and seeks to live out that faith in love, for God and neighbor.

Worldview. A background grid of the most basic beliefs possessed by a person and by which he interprets the world around him. The three major worldviews are naturalism, pantheism, and theism.

Recommended Reading

GENERAL APOLOGETICS

Beckwith, Fancis J., William Lane Craig, and J.P. Moreland, eds. *To Everyone An Answer: A Case for the Christian Worldview: Essays Written in Honor of Norman L. Geisler.* Downers Grove: IVP, 2004.

Craig, William Lane. *Hard Questions, Real Answers.* Wheaton: Crossway, 2003.

———. *Reasonable Faith: Christian Truth and Apologetics.* 3rd ed. Wheaton: Crossway, 2008.

Frame, John. *Apologetics to the Glory of God: An Introduction.* Phillipsburg, NJ: P&R Publishing, 1994.

Hardy, Dean. *Stand Your Ground: An Introductory Text for Apologetics Students.* Eugene, OR: Wipf and Stock Publishers, 2007.

Keller, Timothy. *The Reason for God: Belief in an Age of Skepticism.* NY: Dutton, 2008.

Kreeft, Peter and Ronald K. Tacelli. *Handbook of Christian Apologetics: Hundreds of Answers to Crucial Questions.* Downers Grove: IVP, 1994.

Sproul, R.C. *Defending Your Faith: An Introduction to Apologetics.* Wheaton: Crossway, 2003.

———. *Reason to Believe: A Response to Common Objections to Christianity.* Grand Rapids: Zondervan, 1982.

Story, Dan. *The Christian Combat Manual: Helps for Defending Your Faith: a Handbook for Christian Apologetics.* Chattanooga, TN: AMG Publishers, 2007.

Zacharias, Ravi and Norman L. Geisler, eds. *Who Made God? And Answers to Over 100 Other Tough Questions of Faith.* Grand Rapids: Zondervan, 2003.

ATHEISM

Flew, Antony and Roy Abraham Varghese. *There Is a God: How the World's Most Notorious Atheist Changed His Mind.* NY: HarperOne, 2007.

Geisler, Norman L., Frank Turek, and David Limbaugh. *I Don't Have Enough Faith to Be an Atheist.* Wheaton: Crossway, 2004.

Lewis, C.S. *Mere Christianity.* NY: Harper, 2001.

McGrath, Alister E. *Dawkins' GOD: Genes, Memes, and the Meaning of Life.* Oxford: Wiley-Blackwell, 2004.

———. *The Twilight of Atheism: The Rise and Fall of Disbelief in the Modern World.* NY: Doubleday, 2006.

———. *Intellectuals Don't Need God and Other Modern Myths.* Grand Rapids: Zondervan 1993.

Schaeffer, Francis A. *The God Who Is There.* 30th anniversary ed. Downers Grove: IVP, 1998.

Story, Dan. *Engaging the Closed Minded: Presenting Your Faith to the Confirmed Unbeliever.* Grand Rapids: Kregel, 1999.

Strobel, Lee. *The Case for a Creator: A Journalist Investigates Scientific Evidence That Points Toward God.* Grand Rapids: Zondervan, 2005.

THE RESURRECTION

Craig, William Lane, Ronald Tacelli, Paul Copan, and Gerd Ludemann, eds. *Jesus' Resurrection: Fact or Figment? A Debate Between William Lane Craig and Gerd Ludemann.* Downers Grove: IVP, 2000.

Habermas, Gary R. and Michael R. Licona. *The Case for the Resurrection of Jesus.* Grand Rapids: Kregel, 2004.

Strobel, Lee. *The Case for Easter: Journalist Investigates the Evidence for the Resurrection.* Grand Rapids: Zondervan, 2004.

TRUSTWORTHINESS OF THE BIBLE

Blomberg, Craig. *The Historical Reliability of the Gospels.* 2nd ed. Downers Grove: IVP, 2008.

Bruce, F.F. *The Canon of Scripture.* IVP, 1998.

———. *The New Testament Documents: Are They Reliable?* Grand Rapids: Eerdmans, 2003.

Carson, D.A. and Douglas J. Moo. *An Introduction to the New Testament.* Grand Rapids: Zondervan, 2005.

Habermas, Gary R. *The Historical Jesus: Ancient Evidence for the Life of Christ.* Joplin, MO: College Press, 1996.

Komoszewski, J. Ed, M. James Sawyer, and Daniel B. Wallace. *Reinventing Jesus.* Grand Rapids: Kregel, 2006.

Strobel, Lee. *The Case for Christ.* Grand Rapids: Zondervan, 1998.

Wilkins, Michael J. and J.P. Moreland, eds. *Jesus Under Fire: Modern Scholarship Reinvents the Historical Jesus.* Grand Rapids: Zondervan, 1996.

INTELLIGENT DESIGN

Collins, Francis S. *The Language of God: A Scientist Presents Evidence for Belief.* NY: Free Press, 2006.

Dembski, William A. *No Free Lunch: Why Specified Complexity Cannot Be Purchased without Intelligence.* Lanham, MD: Rowman & Littlefield, 2001.

Dembski, William A. and Sean McDowell. *Understanding Intelligent Design: Everything You Need to Know in Plain Language.* Eugene, OR: Harvest House, 2008.

House, Wayne H., ed. *Intelligent Design 101: Leading Experts Explain the Key Issues.* Grand Rapids: Kregel, 2008.

Rana, Fazale. *The Cell's Design: How Chemistry Reveals the Creator's Artistry.* Grand Rapids: Baker, 2008.

ONLINE RESOURCES

Jason Dollar . Net
www.jasondollar.net

Apologetics Resource Center
www.arcapologetics.org

Stand to Reason
www.str.org

Reasonable Faith with William Lane Craig
www.reasonablefaith.org

Probe Ministries
www.probe.org

Summit Ministries
www.summit.org

Leadership University
www.leaderu.com

Ravi Zacharias International Ministries
www.rzim.org

Discovery Institute (Intelligent Design)
www.discovery.org

Endnotes

Introduction

[1] Lifeway Research and the Barna Group have both conducted surveys along these lines.

Chapter 1

[2] Richard Dawkins, *The God Delusion*, (Boston: Houghton Mifflin, 2006), 46. Dawkins is an aggressive preacher of atheism, who holds to a strict dogma: "The deist God is certainly an improvement over the monster of the Bible. Unfortunately it is scarcely more likely that he exists, or ever did. In any of its forms the God hypothesis is unnecessary."

[3] James Sire, *The Universe Next Door*, 3rd ed. (Downer's Grover, IL: Intervarsity Press, 1997).

[4] All Scripture quotations are taken from the *English Standard Version*.

[5] See chapters 3 and 4 for our answers to these questions.

[6] Beware of false prophets, who come to you in sheep's clothing but inwardly are ravenous wolves. You will recognize them by their fruits. Are grapes gathered from thornbushes, or figs from thistles? (Matthew 7:15-16)

[7] Ravi Zacharias, *Can Man Live Without God,* (Nashville: Thomas Nelson, 1996), 10-14.

[8] I am the LORD; that is my name; my glory I give to no other, nor my praise to carved idols. (Isaiah 42:8)

[9] Blaise Pascal, *Pensees*, trans. A. J. Krailsheimer, (London: Penguin Books, 1966), 173.

Chapter 2

[10] Francis Schaeffer, *The God Who Is There* in *The Complete Works of Francis A. Schaeffer*, (Wheaton, IL: Crossway, 2nd edition, 1996), 133.

[11] *Star Wars III: Revenge of the Sith.* dir. George Lucas, 20th Century Fox Lucasfilm. San Francisco, CA: Lucasfilm, 2005.

[12] *Superman Returns*. Dir. By Bryan Singer, Warner Bros. Burbank, CA: Warner Bros., 2006. Note that *El* is a Hebrew word for God. The parallels between the story of Kal-El (Clark Kent / Superman) and the life of Jesus Christ are many and not coincidental. For details see Anton Karl Kozlovic, "Superman as Christ-Figure: The American Pop Culture Movie Messiah," *Journal of Religion and Faith* 6, No. 1 (April 2002), http://www.unomaha.edu/jrf/superman.htm (accessed October 31, 2008).

[13] For while we were still weak, at the right time Christ died for the ungodly. For one will scarcely die for a righteous person—though perhaps for a good person one would dare even to die— but God shows his love for us in that while we were still sinners, Christ died for us. (Romans 5:6-8)

[14] But the serpent said to the woman, "You will not surely die. For God knows that when you eat of it your eyes will be opened, and you will be like God, knowing good and evil." (Genesis 3:4-5)

[15] I told you that you would die in your sins, for unless you believe that I am he you will die in your sins. (John 8:24)

[16] An agnostic says "I don't know," to the question of God's existence. Chapter 13 is devoted to an analysis of this view.

[17] Lorri MacGregor, *Coping with the Cults,* (Eugene, OR: Harvest House Publishers, 1992), 19-20, quoted from Ron Rhodes, *Reasoning from the Scriptures with the Jehovah's Witnesses*, (Eugene, OR: Harvest House Publishers, 1993).

[18] Spencer W. Kimball, *Miracle of Forgiveness* (SLC: Bookcraft, 1969), 325. Kimball was a former president of the Latter Day Saints who wrote, "It could be weeks, it could be years, it could be centuries before that happy day when you have the positive assurance that the Lord has forgiven you. That depends on your humility, your sincerity, your works, your attitudes."

[19] For a more detailed analysis of the pantheistic worldview, see chapter 11.

Chapter 3

[20] Harvey Frommer, "The Called Shot: October 1, 1932," Baseball Library, http://www.baseballlibrary.com/baseballlibrary/submit/Frommer_Harvey64.stm (accessed online September 13, 2008).

[21] Acts 26, for example.

[22] William Lane Craig, "Classical Apologetics," *Five Views on Apologetics*, ed. Steven B. Cowan (Grand Rapids: Zondervan, 2000). Dr. Craig details the knowing / showing distinction.

[23] Earl Doherty, *The Jesus Puzzle: Did Christianity Begin with a Mythical Christ? Challenging the Existence of an Historical Christ*, (Canadian Humanist Pubns, 1999).

[24] The Jesus Seminar is a collection of extremely liberal biblical and religion scholars well known for their radical positions on issues related to biblical criticism and the life of Jesus.

[25] For example even scholars like John Dominic Crossan, who argues vehemently against the deity of Christ and the resurrection, nonetheless agree that the existence of the man Jesus is an undeniable historical fact. See his book *The Historical Jesus: The Life of a Mediterranean Jewish Peasant*, (HarperCollins, 1991).

[26] Gary R. Habermas, *The Historical Jesus: Ancient Evidence for the Life of Jesus*, (Joplin, MO: College Press, 1996), 143-155. Habermas provides detailed analysis of these ancient creeds and in his footnotes provides many sources for further reading on this subject.

[27] An English translation of the Didache can be viewed online at the Christian Classics Ethereal Library, http://www.ccel.org/ccel/richardson/fathers.viii.i.i.html (accessed online November 9, 2008).

[28] Letters 10:96-97.

[29] History of the World 5.50.

[30] Mara Bar-Serapion.

[31] Dick J. Reavis, *The Ashes of Waco: An Investigation*, (NY: Syracuse University Press, 1998). This is a detailed account of the incident from a journalistic perspective.

[32] Luke 9:16-17

[33] Matthew 8:26

[34] Matthew 14:25

[35] John 2:1-10

[36] John 11:43-44

[37] John Templeton, *The Humble Approach: Scientists Discover God*, (Philadelphia: Templeton Foundation, 1998), 19.

[38] We will explore Islam in more detail in chapter 12, but suffice it to say Islamic beliefs do not pass the most basic tests for truth.

[39] For a classic book on this subject, see C.S. Lewis, *Miracles*, (NY: Macmillian, 1972). This topic is also covered in chapter 14 of this book.

[40] Do not think that I [Jesus] have come to abolish the Law or the Prophets; I have not come to abolish them but to fulfill them. For truly, I say to you, until heaven and earth pass away, not an iota, not a dot, will pass from the Law until all is accomplished. (Mathew 5:17-18)

[41] Then they said to him, "What must we do, to be doing the works of God?" Jesus answered them, "This is the work of God, that you believe in him whom he has sent." (John 6:28-29)

Chapter 4

[42] And at the ninth hour Jesus cried with a loud voice, "Eloi, Eloi, lema sabachthani?" which means, "My God, my God, why have you forsaken me?" (Mark 15:34)

[43] Stephen Broyles, "The Dog: Its Gradually Changing Status," The Andreas Center, http://www.andreascenter.org/Articles/Dog.htm (accessed online October 26, 2008). See also Matthew 15:26-27.

[44] Gary R. Habermas and Michael R. Licona, *The Case for the Resurrection of Jesus*, (Grand Rapids: Kregel, 2004), 38-39; 71-73.

[45] Ibid., 72.

[46] Michael Martin, *The Case Against Christianity*, (Philadelphia: Temple University Press, 1993).

Chapter 5

[47] Bible Babble, http://www.biblebabble.curbjaw.com (accessed September 19, 2008).

[48] Sam Harris, *The End of Faith*, (NY: W.W. Norton and Co.), 45. This view of the Bible commits the logical fallacy called "chronological snobbery," as defined by C.S. Lewis (see his book *Surprised by Joy*, 207-208). Just because something is old does not necessarily mean that it is bad.

[49] The Qu'ran (the holy book of the Muslims) and the Book of Mormon were both written by only one person, Muhammad and Joseph Smith respectively. This is a major difference between them and the Bible.

[50] Ronald Reagan, *Reagan: A Life in Letters*, ed. Kiron K. Skinner, Annelise Anderson, and Martin Anderson, (NY: Simon and Shuster, 2003).

[51] F.F. Bruce, "Archaeological Confirmation of the New Testament", *Revelation and the Bible*, Ed. Carl Henry, (Grand Rapids: Baker Book House, 1969), 88. An "anthology" is a collection of various writings which are not necessarily connected to each other.

[52] Many critics who do not believe in the possibility that prophecy can be fulfilled, deal with the book of Daniel by saying that Daniel, the historical figure, did not write the book. In fact, they say it was written by someone using Daniel's name several hundred years after the events it records (around 165 BC). However, internal and external evidence is consistent with an early date of the book. For a detailed defense of the early-date theory see David Conklin, "Evidences Relating to the Book of Daniel," http://www.tektonics.org/guest/danielblast.html, written 3/13/2004 (accessed online September 20, 2008).

[53] In chapter 3 the messianic prophecies of Psalm 22 are discussed.

[54] For a detailed list of prophecies fulfilled by Christ, see Robert T. Boyd, *Boyd's Handbook of Practical Apologetics,* (Grand Rapids: Kregel, 1997), 125-129.

[55] Nostradamus, Century 10, Quatrain 72.

[56] Daniel 9:24-27 is an example of a biblical prophecy fulfilled exactly. For further research on this, see Boyd, 109-111.

[57] www.horoscope.com.

[58] Will Varner, "What Is the Importance of the Dead Sea Scrolls?" Associates for Biblical Research (May 21, 2008), http://www.biblearchaeology.org/post/2008/05/What-is-the-importance-of-the-Dead-Sea-Scrolls.aspx (Accessed online September 20, 2008).

[59] For an excellent and detailed critique of the attacks against early manuscripts of the Bible, see J. Ed Komoszewski, M. James Sawyer, Daniel B. Wallace, *Reinventing Jesus: How Contemporary Skeptics Miss the Real Jesus and Mislead Popular Culture,* (Grand Rapids: Kregel, 2006).

[60] Jo-Ann A. Brant, "Jesus' Prohibition Against Swearing and his Philosophy of Language," Goshen College, http://www.goshen.edu/facultypubs/Oaths.html (accessed online February 20, 2009).

[61] Of course, there might have been even more than two. Just because no more are mentioned does not mean no more were there. But if there were more, they were not relevant to Matthew's retelling of the story.

[62] As he was getting into the boat, the man who had been possessed with demons begged him that he might be with him. (Mark 5:18)

Chapter 6

[63] Google them and see.

[64] Or get a virtual look at the stone by visiting http://www.english.imjnet.org.il/HTMLs/article_19.aspx?c0=13025&bsp=13013&bss=13025&bscp=12940.

[65] Thomas H. Maugh II, "Biblical Pool Uncovered in Jerusalem" L.A. Times (August 9, 2005), http://articles.latimes.com/2005/aug/09/science/sci-siloam9 (accessed online February 20, 2009). See also "Biblical Pool of Siloam Is Uncovered in Jerusalem,"

The Drudge Report (August 9, 2005), http://www.drudgereportarchives.com/data/2005/08/09/20050809_041200_flash1.htm (Accessed September 21, 2008).

[66] There are several online resources for those interested in a deeper study of archeology including www.bib-arch.org and www.biblicalarcheology.net.

[67] See Jeremiah 31 as a good example of this.

[68] This is not to say that some Muslims are not capable of good, but that any good produced by them is based on principles borrowed from the Christian worldview. Many societies have thrived without being Christian societies, but these were still based upon a Christian foundation.

Chapter 7

[69] For a very interesting defense of this truth see John Piper's sermon, "Is God for Us of for Himself?" Desiring God, http://www.desiringgod.org/ResourceLibrary/Sermons/ByDate/1980/242_Is_God_for_Us_or_for_Himself/ (accessed October 4, 2008).

[70] For more on Ankiel's amazing journey see www.rickankielonline.com.

[71] In this discussion we should also consider God's grace upon infants who die. We believe, as do many Christian theologians of both past and present, that babies receive a special grace from God if they die in infancy. This view is not without problems, but does make the most sense of the biblical data. Given this reality, certainly the number in Heaven will be uncountable – like the stars in the sky. For more on this, see John MacArthur, *Safe in the Arms of God: Truth from Heaven about the Death of a Child* (Nashville: Thomas Nelson, 2003).

Chapter 8

[72] Kelly James Clark, "Without Evidence or Argument: A Defense of Reformed Epistemology," Calvin College, http://www.calvin.edu/academic/philosophy/virtual_library/articles/clark_kelly_j/without_evidence_or_argument.pdf (accessed September 29, 2008).

[73] The word *cosmological* comes from the Greek word *cosmos,* meaning the totality of the universe as a harmonious whole.

[74] Carl Sagan, *Cosmos,* 1980.

Chapter 9

[75] See www.intelligentdesign.org to read more about the movement and its positions.

[76] For example Judge John E. Jones III, *Kitemiller v. Dover,* 43. Judge Jones stated that "the overwhelming evidence at trial established that ID is a religious view, a mere re-labeling of creationism, and not a scientific theory."

[77] William Dembski, "In Defense of Intelligent Design," Design Inference, http://www.designinference.com/documents/2005.06.Defense_of_ID.pdf (accessed October 4, 2008).

[78] To be fair, some naturalists also attempt to be unbiased. Some are more unbiased than others and some fields of science are more unbiased than others. For example, math can be studied in a much more neutral way than, say, psychology.

[79] Alvin Plantinga, "When Faith and Reason Clash: Evolution and the Bible," *Christian Scholar's Review* XXI:1 (September 1991): 8-33. This article can be accessed online at http://www.asa3.org/ASA/dialogues/Faith-reason/CRS9-91Plantinga1.html.

[80] A "theistic view of the world" means that a person believes that God created the world.

[81] Richard Dawkins, *The Blind Watchmaker* (London and New York: W. W. Norton and Co., 1986), 5.

[82] William Dembski, *The Design Inference: Eliminating Chance Through Small Probabilities* (NY: Cambridge University Press, 1998).

[83] William Paley, *Natural Theology,* (Whitefish, MT: Kessinger Publishing, 2003). Paley's argument has been simplified and paraphrased for explanation purposes.

[84] Francis S. Collins, *The Language of God: A Scientist Presents Evidence for Belief,* (NY: Free Press, 2006), 3.

[85] Michael Behe, *Darwin's Black Box,* (NY: The Free Press, 1996).

[86] Alvin Plantinga, 8-33.

[87] Charles Darwin, *Origin of Species*, 1859.

[88] http://www.discovery.org.

[89] Stephen C. Meyer, "Evidence for Design in Physics and Biology," *Science and Evidence for Design in the Universe*, (San Francisco: Ignatius Press), 57.

[90] F. Heeren, *Show Me God*, (Wheeling, IL: Searchlight Publications, 1995), 200.

[91] H. Margenau and R.A. Varghese, ed., *Cosmos, Bios, and Theos*, (La Salle, IL: Open Court, 1992), 83.

Chapter 10

[92] Francis A. Schaeffer, *He Is There and He Is Not Silent* in *The Complete Works of Francis A. Schaeffer*, (Wheaton, IL: Crossway, 2nd edition, 1996), 293.

[93] C.S. Lewis, *Mere Christianity*, (NY: Harper Collins, 2001). This classic was originally published in 1952 and is adapted from a series of radio interviews Lewis made between 1941 and 1944.

[94] In this context, the word *objective* is opposite of *subjective*. If a law is subjective it is reduced to a person's opinion on the matter, but if it is objective, then it is outside of humanity and much higher than mere personal opinion.

[95] Adolph Hitler, *Mein Kempf*, Hitler Historical Museum, http://www.hitler.org/writings/Mein_Kampf/ (accessed online October 4, 2008). Hitler's view of the superiority of the Arian race is spelled out clearly in Chapter XI: Nation and Race. For example he wrote, "All who are not of good race in this world are chaff [worthless]."

Chapter 11

[96] Interestingly they are like naturalists in believing that ultimately only *one* thing exists (a view called monism), but they disagree on what the one thing is. Naturalists say it is matter / energy and pantheists say it is spirit.

[97] Of the big three categories, only Theism is dualistic, meaning that it holds that the universe is made up of at least two different things: matter *and* spirit.

[98] In Chapter 12, these different forms of Theism are discussed in greater detail.

[99] The worldview questions in this section are adapted from James W. Sire, *Discipleship of the Mind*, (Downers Grove, IL: IVP, 1990).

[100] Sire, 36.

[101] Chapter 8 provides a more detailed discussion on this point.

[102] John Piper, "In Him Was Life," Desiring God, http://www.desiringgod.org/ResourceLibrary/Sermons/ByDate/2008/3279_In_Him_Was_Life/ (accessed online October 7, 2008).

[103] In philosophy, the study of this question and its many possible answers is called epistemology.

[104] Maharishi University of Management, http://www.mum.edu.tm.

[105] *The Empire Strikes Back*. dir. by Irvin Kershner, 20th Century Fox Lucasfilm. San Francisco, CA: Lucasfilm, 1980.

[106] For more on the absurdities of morality in Naturalism, see Chapter 10.

Chapter 12

[107] "Deism" in the *Dictionary of the History of Ideas*, http://etext.virginia.edu/cgi-local/DHI/dhi.cgi?id=dv1-77 (accessed online October 21, 2008).

[108] Jeremiah 17:9.

[109] For a readable account of the history and recent development of Judaism see Richard Robinson, "Judaism and the Jewish People," in *The Compact Guide to World Religions*, edited by Dean C. Halverson, (Minneapolis, MN: Bethany House, 1996), 121-143.

[110] This is the most basic belief of Islam.

[111] For a detailed comparison of Christianity and Islam see Timothy George, *Is the Father of Jesus the God of Muhammad? Understanding the Differences between Christianity and Islam*, (Grand Rapids: Zondervan, 2002). See also www.answering-islam.org.

[112] Joseph Smith, "The Testimony of Joseph Smith," http://www.lds.org/library/display/0,4945,104-1-3-4,00.html (accessed online October 24, 2008).

[113] "Joseph Smith: A Prophet of God," http://www.lds.org/library/display/0,4945,104-

1-3-2,00.html (accessed online October 24, 2008).

[114] Joseph Smith, "Testimony of the Prophet Joseph Smith," as recorded in the Book of Mormon.

[115] For example see Luigi Luca Cavalli-Sforza, *Genes, Peoples, and Languages*, (University of California Press, 2000), L.L. Cavalli-Sforza & W.F. Bodmer, *The Genetics of Human Populations*, (Dover, 1999), David B. Goldstein, *Jacob's Legacy: A Genetic View of Jewish History*, (Yale University Press, 2008), and Yaakov Kleiman, *DNA and Tradition: The Genetic Link to the Ancient Hebrews*, (Devora Publishing, 2004).

Chapter 13

[116] "I Am Passionately Agnostic," Experience Project, http://www.experienceproject.com/stories/Am-A-Hopeful-Agnostic/248020 (accessed online October 23, 2008).

Chapter 14

[117] Cathleen Falsani, "Obama: I Have Deep Faith," Chicago Sun-Times (April 5, 2004), http://www.suntimes.com/news/falsani/726619,obamafalsani040504.article (accessed online February 26, 2009).

[118] For a detailed study pluralism see Stephen Neill, *Christian Faith and Other Faiths*, 2nd Ed. (Oxford: Oxford University Press, 1970).

[119] Clarence Darrow, Scopes trial, Dayton, Tennessee, July 13, 1925.

[120] Patrick J. Hurley, *A Concise Introduction to Logic*, (Belmont, CA: Wadsworth, 2006), 137.

[121] Of course, Santa is invisible primarily because he does not exist.

Index

CPSIA information can be obtained at www.ICGtesting.com
Printed in the USA
LVOW05s0613110414

381279LV00003B/266/P